# The Political Art of Bob Dylan

## Revised and Expanded Second Edition

Edited by David Boucher and Gary Browning

imprint-academic.com

Published in the UK by
Imprint Academic, PO Box 200, Exeter EX5 5YX, UK

Published in the USA by
Imprint Academic, Philosophy Documentation Center
PO Box 7147, Charlottesville, VA 22906-7147, USA

ISBN-13: 978184540 120 7

A CIP catalogue record for this book is available from the
British Library and US Library of Congress

# Contents

# Acknowledgements

We would like to thank the following for permission to reprint Bob Dylan's lyrics: 'Jokerman' © 1983 Special Rider Music. 'Most Likely You Go Your Way (and I'll Go Mine)', © 1966, renewed 1994 Dwarf Music. 'Love Minus Zero/No Limit', © Warner Bros Inc. 1965, renewed 1993 by Special Rider Music. 'Cross the Green Mountain', © 2003 Special Rider Music. 'Hard Times in New York Town', © 1962, 1965 MCA, renewed 1990 MCA. 'It's Alright Ma I'm Only Bleeding' © 1965, Warner Bros Inc., renewed 1993 by Special Rider Music. 'The Times They Are A'-Changin' © 1963, Warner Bros Inc., © renewed 1991 by Special Rider Music. 'Things have Changed', © 1999 Special Rider Music. 'Shelter From the Storm', © 1974 Ram's Horn Music. 'Senor (Tales of Yankee Power)', © 1978 Special Rider Music. 'Shelter From the Storm', © 1974 Ram's Horn Music. 'Stuck Inside of Mobile with the Memphis Blues Again', © 1966, renewed 1994 Dwarf Music. 'Sweetheart Like You', © 1983 Special Rider Music. 'Shooting Star', © 1989 Special Rider Music. 'Caribbean Wind', 1985 Special Rider Music. 'Summer Days', © 2001 Special Rider Music. 'Union Sundown', © 1983 Special Rider Music. 'Political World' © 1989 Special Rider Music. 'Train A'Travellin', © 1968, renewed 1996 Special Rider Music. 'Slow Train', © 1979 Special Rider Music. 'Blind Willie McTell', © 1983 Special Rider Music. 'George Jackson', © 1971 Ram's Horn Music. 'Lonesome Death of Hattie Carroll' © Warner Bros Inc., © renewed 1992 by Special Rider Music. 'Hurricane', © 1975 Ram's Horn Music. 'Highway 61 Revisited', © 1965 Warner Chappell, renewed 1993 Special Rider Music. 'From a Buick 6', © 1965, renewed

1993 Special Rider Music. 'Simple Twist of Fate', © 1974 Ram's Horn Music. 'Bob Dylan's 115th Dream', © 1965; renewed 1993 Special Rider Music. 'It's Alright Ma I'm Only Bleeding', © 1965, Warner Bros Inc., renewed 1993 by Special Rider Music. 'Desolation Row' © 1965 Warner Bros Inc., renewed 1993 by Special Rider Music. 'You're a Big Girl Now' © 1974 Ram's Horn Music. 'Highlands' © 1999 Special Rider Music. 'Visions of Johanna', © 1966, Dwarf Music, renewed 1994 Dwarf Music. 'Subterranean Homesick Blues', © 1965 Warner Chappell, renewed 1993 Special Rider Music. 'Guess I'm Doin' Fine', © 1964, renewed 1992 Special Rider Music. 'Motorpsycho Nitemare', © 1964; renewed 1992 Special Rider Music. 'Like A Rolling Stone', © 1965 Warner Chappell, renewed 1993 Special Rider Music. 'Man in the Long Black Coat', © 1989 Special Rider Music. 'Lenny Bruce', © 1981 Special Rider Music. 'Love Minus Zero/No Limit', © Warner Bros Inc., renewed 1993 by Special Rider Music. 'Changing of the Guards', © 1978 Special Rider Music. 'Sweetheart Like You', © 1983 Special Rider Music. 'Mixed Up Confusion', © 1962, renewed 1990 Special Rider Music. 'Maggie's Farm', © 1965, renewed 1993 Special Rider Music. 'Love Sick' © Special Rider Music 1997. 'Trying to Get to Heaven', © 1997 Special Rider Music. 'Highlands', © 1997 Special Rider Music. Talkin' World War Three Blues', © 1963, renewed 1991 Special Rider Music. 'Hard Rain's A-Gonna Fall', © 1963, renewed 1991 Special Rider Music. 'Chimes of Freedom', © 1964, renewed 1992 Special Rider Music. 'Gates of Eden', © 1965, Warner Bros Inc., renewed 1993 by Special Rider Music. 'It's Alright Ma (I'm Only Bleeding)' © 1965, Warner Bros Inc., renewed 1993 by Special Rider Music. 'I Dreamed I Saw St. Augustine', © 1968, renewed 1996 Dwarf Music. 'Ballad of a Thin Man', © 1965, renewed 1993 Special Rider Music. 'Mixed Up Confusion', © 1962, renewed 1990 Special Rider Music. 'I and I', © 1983 Special Rider Music. 'Standing in the Doorway', © 1997 Special Rider Music. 'Where Are You Tonight? (Journey Through Dark Heat)', © 1978 Special Rider Music. 'Lenny Bruce', © 1981 Special Rider Music. 'Dirge', © 1973 Ram's Horn Music. 'Highlands', © 1999 Special Rider

David Boucher and Gary Browning

# Notes on the Contributors

**David Boucher** is Professorial Fellow and Assistant Head of School, Research, School of European Studies, Cardiff University. He is Adjunct Professor of International Relations at The University of the Sunshine Coast, and Director of the Collingwood and British Idealism Centre at Cardiff. His most recent books are *Theories of International Relations from Thucydides to the Present* (1998), *British Idealism and Political Theory* (with Andrew Vincent, 2001) and *Dylan and Cohen: Poets of Rock and Roll* (2004). His recent edited books include *Political Thinkers* (with Paul Kelly, 2003), *The Scottish Idealists* (2004) and *The Philosophy of Enchantment,* by R. G. Collingwood (with Philip Smallwood and Wendy James).

**Elizabeth Brake** is Associate Professor of Philosophy at the University of Calgary. She has been Visiting Researcher, Kennedy Institute of Ethics, Georgetown University and Visiting Researcher, Murphy Institute, Tulane University. She has published articles in the areas of Ethics, Political Philosophy, Feminist Philosophy and Philosophy and Literature. She contributed a chapter to *Dylan and Philosophy*, ed. Peter Vernezze and Carl Porter (2006).

**Chris Brown** is Professor of International Relations at the London School of Economics. He has published widely on International Political Theory/International Ethics; ethics and warfare; justice and international relations; ethics, morality and foreign policy; human rights. Among his publications are *Understanding International Relations* (with K. Ainsley, 3rd edition, 2005), *Sovereignty, Rights and Justice: International Political Theory Today* (2002), *International Relations: New Normative Approaches* (1992). He has edited, *International relations in political thought: Texts in international relations from the ancient Greeks to the first world war* (with Terry Nardin and Rengger, 2002).

**Richard Brown** is Reader in Modern Literature in the School of English at the University of Leeds. He is the author of *James Joyce: A Post-culturalist Perspective* (1992), founding co-editor of the *James Joyce Broadsheet*, and was a contributor to *Do You Mr. Jones?*, a collection of essays on Dylan edited by Neil Corcoran (2003).

**Gary Browning** is Professor of Politics at Oxford Brookes University. He is the author of *Plato and Hegel: Two Modes of Philosophising about Politics* (1991), *Hegel and the History of Political Philosophy* (1999), *Lyotard and the End of Grand Narratives* (2000), and *Rethinking R. G. Collingwood: Philosophy, Politics and the Unity of Theory and Practice* (2004). He has co-edited and co-written other works including *Understanding Contemporary Society: Theories of the Present* (2000) and *Critical and Post-Critical Political Economy* (2006). He is co-editor of the journal, *Contemporary Political Theory* (Palgrave Macmillan).

**Andrew Gamble** is Professor of Politics at the University of Cambridge. His books include *The Free Economy and the Strong State* (1988), *Politics and Fate* (2000) and *Between Europe and America: The Future of British Politics* (2003). He is currently working on a new book on the politics of the global financial crisis.

**Michael Jones** is course director for the MA in Music Industry Studies at the Institute of Popular Music, the University of Liverpool. His interest in the music industry was focused by his membership of the act Latin Quarter. Best known for their hit single 'Radio Africa' in 1986, Latin Quarter released a total of seven albums between 1985 and 1997.

**Lawrence Wilde** is Professor of Political Theory at The Nottingham Trent University. He is the author of *Marx and Contradiction* (1989), *Modern European Socialism* (1994), *Ethical Marxism and its Radical Critics* (1998), and *Erich Fromm and the Quest for Solidarity* (2004).

# *Preface*

The inspiration for the original book came from one of the contributors, Lawrence Wilde, who organised a panel at the Political Studies Association at The London School of Economics in April 2000 entitled 'The Chimes of Freedom: The Political Art of Bob Dylan' at which he and the editors gave papers, and in which Andrew Gamble participated. The same panel was given at the conference of the European Consortium for Political Research, Kent University, 2001. The success of the conferences encouraged us to develop the themes of this book further and invite further contributions. The first edition of the book was published in hardback and is now out of print. Since its publication a great deal of material by and about Bob Dylan has appeared, and the introduction and contributions have been revised to reflect this. We have added Elizabeth Brake and Chris Brown to the list of contributors to provide added dimensions to our understanding of Dylan's many and remarkable talents.

The editors would like to thank all those who attended the panels and who made perceptive and invaluable comments and suggestions. David Boucher would like to thank the AHRC (formerly AHRB) for funding research on a larger project, of which this is a part and Lisa Berni and Gemma Broadhurst for their help in preparing the text, printing various versions and for organising the scanning of images. Gary Browning would like to thank his son Conal and his daughter Eleanor for their help and inspiration. We would like to thank Keith Sutherland for his help and encouragement. We are also immensely grateful to Jeff Rosen for granting permission to quote from Dylan's lyrics, without which this book would be severely impoverished. We are also indebted to Larry Keenan for the cover photograph of Bob Dylan and Robbie Robertson of the Band at Berkeley California, 1965.

David Boucher and Gary Browning

David Boucher and Gary Browning

# Introduction
# The Political Art of
# Bob Dylan

[E]very now and then there are people ... who do have to
create the taste by which they are enjoyed (Ricks, 2008: 2).

On the Album Sleeve of *Freewheelin*, released in 1963, Bob
Dylan and Suze Rotolo, his girlfriend, strike an identical
pose to that of Dylan and Caitlin Thomas caught on camera
in New York on the same street some thirteen years before.
It was Bob Dylan's second album, and unlike the first,
almost wholly included his own compositions. Among
them are some of the anthems of the 'sixties, adopted by the
anti-nuclear and civil rights movements: 'Blowin' in the
Wind', 'Masters of War', 'A Hard Rain's A gonna Fall' and
'Oxford Town'. His astronomical rise to stardom was not
only unexpected, it was also unlikely. The Chaplinesque
figure, with a precariously perched corduroy hat, faded and
worn blue jeans, working man's check shirt and affected
Oklahoma accent, mirroring the pose of the near vagrant
Woody Guthrie, became the voice of American youth,
expressing the words and sentiments that no one else,
despite the many competing protest singers, could rival.
Although Dylan eventually abjured the responsibility of
being a spokesman for his generation, in 1962 he was certainly prepared to take up that mantle. He said, for example:
'There are so many lies that have been told, so many things
that are kept back. Kids have a feeling like me, but they ain't

hearing it no place. They're scared to step out. But I ain't scared to do it, man' (Williamson, 2004: 359).

The endurance of the appeal of Bob Dylan over five decades to an audience that spans the generations is testimony to his undeniable talent, but also to the ingenuity of his management and of Dylan himself. The five decades of Dylan's ever changing persona are projected in multiple media in a never ending present in which the many faces of Bob Dylan are simultaneously juxtaposed. The bootleg series that took control of the way Dylan was to be presented in all facets of his career; the first volume of his autobiography which carefully crafts and reinterprets his life; the films such as the re-released 'Don't Look Back' which rescued footage of a completely different Dylan from that portrayed in the original; Martin Scorsesee's 'No Direction Home', with Jeff Rosen executive producer, the architect of Dylan's career, and Dylan himself choosing the way that he is to be presented. The early Dylan endures in a perpetual stream of sound and visions. In addition to the bootlegs and numerous biographies, we are assailed with books of memorabilia (Santelli 2005) and of iconic photographs (Fenstein 2008). Add to these Dylan's own acting credits, his art exhibition, not to mention Cate Blanchett's portrayal of him in 'I'm Not There', and his idiosyncratic but engaging radio show, and you have the ineffable enigma that is Bob Dylan. Alongside this virtual Dylan represented in multiple media is the live and 'in person' Dylan and his band on the perpetual never ending tour — a constant reminder that not only is he a living legend, but that the legend lives.

Since Bob Dylan published *Tarantula* in 1966 his autobiography has been anticipated with some trepidation (Dylan, 2004). Would it be as unreadable? Would it lay to rest the misinformation spread about him and by himself. Well, it is certainly readable, and it is in fact beautifully written in a style that flows and rolls with ease. It is not a book of self-analysis, nor self reflection. It is a book of reminiscences and astute observations and characterisations of people and places, and is particularly engaging in conveying the vibrancy of Greenwich Village in the early 1960s. The style is reminiscent of a detective novel, using the typical tricks of the genre, and of film, in using flash-backs and leaps forward, as he chronicles his way through the early years of fulfilling what he believed to be his destiny. He describes listening to Ricky Nelson while waiting to be called to sing at Café Wha, and then relates how ten years later Nelson was booed off the stage for changing direction. Nelson was a man with whom he could empathise, having gone through the experience many times himself.

*Chronicles* is not a history. Bob Dylan is born on page 29, and after gliding through various episodes, including signing for John Hammond at Columbia records, he returns to describe his home town of Hibbing Minnesota on page 229. In between there is a sudden leap to 1987 when he is recuperating from a hand injury, and artistically burnt-out. He begins *Chronicles* by describing a meeting with Lou Levy, the music publisher at Leeds Music, just after arriving in Greenwich Village and ends the book by telling how Al Grossman, his manager, gave him $1000 to buy himself out of the deal shortly after.

His character sketches of the people he knew are precise and incisive, such as of Tiny Tim, later famous for his hit, sang in a falsetto voice accompanied by a ukulele, 'Tip-toe Through the Tulips'. In describing Bob Neuwirth, who became a close friend, Dylan writes, in Raymond Chandler style: 'Right from the start you could tell that Neuwirth had a taste for provocation and that nothing was going to restrict his freedom. He was in a mad revolt against something. You had to brace yourself when you talked to him'. Neuwirth appears in the Dylan Film 'Don't Look Back', and these character traits are evident in his treatment of Joan Baez.

There is a good deal of self justification in the book. Dylan tries to put the record straight on a few mythologies that have surrounded him. He treats in a cursory manner his well known predilection to fabricate stories about his own background. He explains how when confronted with Billy James the publicity man for Columbia Records, he felt intimidated by his Ivy League Harvard presence, telling him that he was from Illinois, worked on construction in Detroit, had no family, and had rode into New York on a freight train. He doesn't explain why he lied about his past to his friends, nor does he try to analyse how hurt his parents were at being disowned by him. He is quite bitter in remembering how Joan Baez criticised him for abandoning the folk movement. He vehemently denies having been a spokesman for a generation, but this is somewhat disingenuous. He didn't feel comfortable with the responsibility of being hailed as a spokesman, but there is no getting away from the fact that he consciously wrote songs, such as 'Blowin' in the Wind', 'Playboys and Playgirls', and 'The Times They are A' Changin'' in order to appeal to the social conscience of his generation. After Kennedy's assassination he felt distinctively vulnerable, and did not himself want to become a target. He has on many occasions denied that he took his name from Dylan Thomas, and once famously said that 'I have done more for Dylan Thomas than he ever did for me'. In *Chronicles* he talks about the process of choosing a stage name. He had thought of calling himself Robert Allyn, changing the e in his own name to a y. At about the same time he read some Dylan Thomas, and imagined that Dylan must have changed his name from Dillon to Dylan. Bobby Dylan, he thought, was too much like Bobby Darin, and anyway there were too many Bobbies making records. He settled on Bob Dylan, because it sounded right, not because he had any particular liking for the poetry. In fact, in an interview that is accessible in Robert Shelton's archives (Music Experience Project, Seatle), Dylan explicitly said that he disliked Dylan Thomas' flowery and affected style.

The book is not an act of self-disclosure, the mask is not taken from the face, and there is very little sense of the emotional life of the author. He says very little about intimate relations, except to express his desire to protect his wife and family from the gaze of publicity, and to complain of the constant invasion of privacy. He also says very little about his relationship with Joan Baez, or St, Joan as she was pejoratively known.

Bob Dylan's *Chronicles* were well worth the wait, and while they do not allow the reader too great an insight into the inner life of the artist, they reveal a considerable deal about his psychology, and how he is still prepared to be economical with the truth on many issues. In fact, he reveals a great deal about his manner of writing when he talks of himself and Bono, of U2. He says that they are very alike in that 'We can strengthen any argument by expanding on something either real or not real' (Dylan, 2004: 175).

Fans who were won over to Bob Dylan by the strength of his lyrics will be disappointed that he talks only of the process of writing songs, but not of their content. He makes no attempt to explain their meaning, nor to analyse their impact. This is not surprising given that when asked about the meaning of his lyrics he always got irritated and dismissed the questions with such curt answers as 'I don't know, man'.

This book takes on the challenge of developing interpretations of Dylan's art and politics in the light of his disruptive changes of identity and his inscrutability. Its chapters take Dylan as offering various forms of critique of the political world from a number of vantage points. It brings together eight authors whose expertise spans the intellectual worlds of literary criticism, popular culture and political philosophy. It demonstrates the immense possibilities of locating Dylan provocatively in different, but related discourses. The authors, as well as having a thorough grasp and enthusiasm for Dylan's work, bring their disciplinary expertise to bear on his lyrics and life in order to reveal and project new and enticing interpretations. The chapters imaginatively invoke some iconic contemporary aesthetic theories in an accessible way to illustrate how Dylan's imaginative artistry reveals compelling perspectives on the political condition. Collectively, the authors cover the whole of Dylan's career, as well as focusing on certain definitive moments in his turbulent and controversial life.

Dylan is widely acknowledged as the great pop-poet of the 1960s, transforming the popular song into a medium for questioning the personal, social and political norms of his times. Dylan's songs of the 1960s expose the futile grand illusion of the American Dream, painting disturbing and distorting images of a subterranean reality beneath the surface appearances. By the mid-1960s Dylan had created an alternative reality, one that was just as illusory: the certainty of temporal salvation through self-righteous innocence. In breaking the chains of conventionalism he and those like him became imprisoned by their own hedonism born out of a drug culture that unwittingly cultivated dependence in the name of freedom, and liberation of the mind while inadvertently enslaving the body. The Earthly Paradise of New York or Los Angeles was paradoxically more of an illusion than the great American Dream itself. The New Jerusalem was induced hallucinogenically. Far from being about self-knowledge, it was about self-delusion, fantasy and escapism. The children of the revolution, *pace* Marc Bolan, were fooled. Flower power, ostensibly an escape from the city, was nevertheless a form of escapism, the delusion of saving the world by retreating into a dream world.

The epitome of this myth was the legendary Woodstock Festival, the shrine of the 1960s, and immortalised in song by Joni Mitchell, who wasn't in fact there, and in the Summer of Love in San Francisco. Dylan, although living close by Woodstock, refused to participate. He had rejected the protest culture that he so typified and consolidated, and now rejected the sub-culture of which his poetic imagery was emblematic. Dylan derided the young who embraced flower power, believing that they had resorted to escapism in acid (LSD), disillusioned and deluded by cultural and mass overload (Jerome 1975). Recapturing the dream would come, not by exiling oneself from the culture one despised, but by rediscovering traditional roots in communing with nature: the countryside became the Promised Land, and the city, the new Sodom and Gomorrah, or the site of a new biblical Exodus from Egyptian enslavement. In Meisel's terms, the East had turned back upon itself and gone West (Meisel 1999: 8–9). Dylan's *John Wesley Harding* provides an emerging vision of the true path to salvation, self-discovery and understanding, not in dependence upon a drug culture, but in cultivating the spiritual dimension of the soul through religious redemption. Dylan himself described it as the first album of biblical rock. It was an album that confronted fear, sin and false conceptions of freedom through allegory. Andy Gill, commenting on the album and sleeve photograph, makes the interesting remark that even though Dylan seems to be wearing the same suede jacket that he wore on the cover of *Blonde on Blonde*, 'there was none of that album's air of stifling urban decadence. Instead a rural breeze whispered through its lonely margins' (Gill 1998: 126).

What Dylan offered the public was constantly in transition, and his strongest claim to being a poet is the gradual emergence of an abstract expressionist lyric, first evident on the early albums in such songs as 'Hard Rain's A-Gonna Fall' and 'The Chimes of Freedom'.[1] His musical output between 1965 and 1968 is generally taken to stake his claim to be a poet of merit much more strongly than either the earlier protest material or most of what he wrote after 1968. The poetry of his most creative period is full of social, political and psychological imagery, which explores the submerged and strange sub-cultures barely beneath the surface of a disturbing cityscape, and such images find new expression in more recent songs such as 'Mississippi' and 'Dignity'. The alternative versions of these songs that appear on *Tell Tale Signs*, volume 8 in the bootleg series, are completely different versions with which he experiments testifies to the remarkable talent he had for changing the mood, or point of songs, by different inflections. For example, one can almost weep at the tragedy that dignity is so elusive and rare in modern culture, and in an earlier alternative version one can laugh at the vain search, as in the line 'dignity' was the first to leave.

The protest songs of his early career, although exemplifications of a genre, were not, however, conventional in the 'topical' or 'finger-pointing' mode. Instead, they reveal a

---

[1] Ricks (2003), however, treats the whole of Dylan's *oeuvre* as poetic and analyses lyrics from throughout Dylan's career with the same scrupulous care.

journey of self-exploration that subsequently took him through the mellow narrative phase of *John Wesley Harding* the Country and Western air of *Nashville Skyline* and *Self-Portrait*, the religious fundamentalism of *Slow Train Coming*, and the return to his blues roots in the early 1990s on *Good as I Been to You* and *World Gone Wrong*. Interspersed in what many fans regard as these relatively low points in his career are the albums that at least temporarily signalled a return to form, such as *Blood on the Tracks, Street Legal* and *Desire*. The release in 1997 of his sombre, world-weary, hauntingly eerie *Time Out of Mind* brought him the greatest critical acclaim he had enjoyed in 30 years and earned him a Grammy. The release of *Love and Theft* in 2002 demonstrated the eclectic character of his music more fully than any previous single album, drawing as it does on the American musical heritage that saturated his youth: rock and roll, jazz, blues, bluegrass, country and folk. *Modern Times* (2006) continued Dylan's revival as a cultural icon, as a significant figure in rock music and as a masterful interpreter of a range of American popular music. It was his fastest ever selling album. The release of alternative versions and leftover gems from the period spanning *Oh Mercy* to *Modern Times* on *Tell Tale Signs* (2008) confirmed Dylan's late return to form. His contemporary public pre-eminence has been supported by his emergence as a DJ of flair, knowledge and wit and by the making of interesting and celebrated film biographies: *No Direction Home* by Martin Scorcese and *I'm Not There* by Todd Haynes.

The phases that are associated with the continuously changing Dylan are not, however, easily subject to distinct and discrete periodisation because concurrent with the changes there was continuity, an identity in difference or unity in diversity. The large number of retrospective albums and the official bootlegs, not to mention the unofficial recordings, ensured that at any one moment the multifaceted Bob Dylan is continuously projected. The performing Bob Dylan, with the exception of his fundamentalist religious phase, always relied heavily on his back catalogue. Todd Haynes' film *I'm Not There* makes the elusiveness of the various Dylans of past and present its central theme.

In what remains of this Introduction we give a brief overview of the arguments of each chapter. The three chapters 'The Drifter's Escape' by Andrew Gamble, 'Bob Dylan's Critique of Judgement: Thinkin' about the Law' by Richard Brown and 'Dylan and (Post)Modern Times' by Gary Browning are linked in that they review Dylan's work as a whole. They see all of his work as casting light on the political world. These chapters recognise Dylan's enduring critique of the political condition, its judgements and values, while they acknowledge and distinguish the changing forms and styles of critique that Dylan adopts. The chapters by Lawrence Wilde and Michael Jones take as their starting points an emblematic moment in Dylan's career, namely the infamous 'Judas' accusation during the concert at the Free Trade Hall, Manchester, for many decades wrongly known as the Albert Hall Concert. From the same starting point they move in very different directions. Wilde relates Dylan to Adorno's aesthetic and theory of artistic commitment, whereas Jones sets Dylan in the ideological context of folk music in Britain, contrasting it with its American counterpart. Chris Brown's chapter focuses upon Dylan's performance at Live Aid, where his opening remarks disturbed the overt political theme of the concert. Elizabeth Brake's chapter is concerned with interpreting Dylan's generally overlooked film, *Masked and Anonymous* in the light of his late preoccupation with an older man's concern over how self-realization and freedom fit with personal, cultural and political pasts. David Boucher concludes the volume by looking at different modes of interpretation spanning the whole of Dylan's career, and suggests that asking the appropriate questions of the different types of lyric is crucial to sound appraisal. In this respect he offers us an exercise in meta-interpretation.

Gamble's chapter, 'The Drifter's Escape', opens by reflecting on the title of Dylan's 1990s album of traditional songs, *World Gone Wrong*. He takes the severity of its judgement on the political to be emblematic of Dylan's persisting standpoint. Politics for Dylan is a world gone wrong. Gamble goes on to reflect upon Dylan's song 'Political World' on the album *Oh Mercy,* where politics is construed as a world of unremitting bleakness. Gamble reviews Dylan's acerbic judgements on the political via a number of interrelated themes. Dylan's sense of the alienation of the political world, its estrangement of the self from its authentic standpoint, is highlighted. This notion of alienation is seen to be ever-present in Dylan's work, though the changing styles and viewpoints of Dylan songs reflect differing senses of alienation. Gamble distinguishes between songs of redemption and songs of survival, with the latter conveying a bleaker assessment of the possibilities of changing or redeeming the political world. Dylan's identification of alienation is seen to go along with his adherence to an American dream of rural simplicity that is set against Old World complexity. Dylan's adherence to a fundamentalist Christianity in the late 1970s is seen to inflect his sense of alienation from the political world with an Augustinian view of the corruption of the fallen ungodly world. The power of Dylan's critique of an alienated world of politics is sharpened by his persisting vision of an impending apocalypse. Dylan's reference to the imminence of destruction through hard rain, flood, storm and earthquake underlies the urgency of his critique of politics. 'All Along the Watchtower' is seen to be the masterly, economical expression of the apocalypse, where the enigmatic lyrics include reference to the Biblical horsemen, who are harbingers of catastrophe.

Gamble observes how Dylan persists in using arresting metaphors of the political condition. He notes how Dylan sees the world as a prison and as a graveyard in songs such as 'George Jackson', 'Hurricane', 'Highway 61 Revisited' and 'Tombstone Blues'. Gamble reads Dylan's songs of the mid-1960s as heightening his satire on the political system, which is seen as absurd and perverse. He notes Dylan's image of an 'Insanity Factory' to convey the lifelessness and absurdity of contemporary America, where capitalism produced a consumerist, militaristic and nationalistic culture that destroys authenticity. Dylan's mid-1960s songs are seen as exploring the absurdity of the political system via a variety of deliberately discordant means, including allegory, deliberate obscurity and satire. 'It's Alright, Ma, I'm Only Bleeding' and 'Desolation Row' probe deeply into the disoriented world of modern America. In the latter, society is teetering on the abyss and the only refuge from the madness is no refuge at all; it is Desolation Row. As a counterpoint to his critique of the political system, Dylan is recognised to embrace the romantic counter-image of the outlaw or drifter.

Richard Brown's chapter, 'Bob Dylan's Critique of Judgement: Thinkin' about the Law', takes another approach to the theme, which nevertheless resonates with key aspects of Gamble's analysis. He begins by recognising the senses of Dylan's work that are explicitly political, the criticisms of distinct aspects of contemporary American economy and society that are featured in the early songs. Again, Dylan's mid-1960s songs are held to harmonise with a new, youthful, radical counter-culture consensus. Brown observes, though, that what is particularly engaging about Dylan's treatment of politics is the question of the ways in which it may be said to be political. Like Gamble, Brown attends closely to the relatively neglected but provocative late song, 'Political World'. He reads the song as attesting to Dylan's disturbing postmodern sense of extreme post-industrial alienation. He highlights the mediatised hollowness of Dylan's image of the political. He remarks that the unreality of the modern political world, for Dylan, is felt rather than discursively comprehended. This feeling of the unreality of the political world points to Dylan's counterposing of the aesthetic to the political. This foregrounding of the contrast between the aesthetic and the political world of ordered judgement serves as a prelude to Brown's complex and engaging review of Dylan's sense of politics via Kant's critique of the faculty of judgement. The way in which judgement itself is experienced by feeling, for Kant, is non-categorisable and is different from the judging of items of experience in terms of categories. Brown takes this contrast between feeling and intellectual judgement according to rules and categories to apply to Dylan's exploration of politics.

Brown undertakes a considered review of one of Dylan's most celebrated political songs, 'The Lonesome Death of Hattie Carroll', pausing along the way to consider Marqusee's elaborate contextual reading of the song and Ricks' contrasting non-contextual and concentrated textual analysis. Both of these interpretive strategies highlight the politics of Dylan's critique of the plight of the poor black victim of injustice, Hattie Carroll. Brown, though, attends to the song's abjuring of philosophical judgement and observes its evocation of an authentic feeling of injustice that is not to be measured or categorised. Brown goes on to highlight Dylan's deprecation of the institutions of justice and judgement and his valorisation of non-discursive feeling in his lovesongs and in his songs of social commentary. He relates the many jibes Dylan makes at the expense of judges, and his countervailing appreciation of outlaws, who are manifestly outside the conventional political world of judgements. Brown connects Dylan's radical perspective on politics and ethics to Badiou's notion of a disorienting event that enables a movement away from conventional judgements.

Following from Brown's exploration of the different ways in which the political is expressed in the songs of Dylan, Michael Jones explores the political in what has become one of the most infamous incidents in Dylan's long career. The wounding accusatory charge of 'Judas' directed at Dylan during the legendary Manchester Free Trade Hall concert. The concert is analysed in terms of its impact on Dylan and his audience from both a personal and a political perspective. It is Heideggerian in acknowledging the situatedness of the performer in the particular context of the accusation and the situatedness of the author at the time, and also in looking back on such a defining moment over 40 years later. Jones shows how, even though folk music had left-wing tendencies in both America and Great Britain, the composition of those tendencies was very different, to a large degree represented by the attitudes of Pete Seeger and Ewan MacColl.

There was, of course, much that Seeger in the United States and MacColl in Britain had in common. They had the moral strength of their own convictions, reinforced by a belief that history was on the side of the people in the struggle against the oppressors. They were almost messianic in conjuring up an imagined vision of the future arising out of the imagined past and constructed present. Music was a wonderful medium through which to convey this vision and was inclusive because of the communal or participatory character of the songs. Commercial music constituted a threat to the authenticity of the transformative power of the collective music-making experience. Despite the ideological congruency, Jones argues that features peculiar to the British context help explain why members of a British audience at a Dylan concert would react in the way they did, knowing what they were about to encounter and yet paying good money to register their disgust.

In particular, it was Ewan MacColl who, with his inauthentic name, drew the demarcation lines of what was authentic in British folk music. From the point of view of the Stalinist MacColl the betrayal by collaboration, selling out to commercialism, symbolised by the electric guitar, was indicative of American capitalism and its cultural imperialism, which were threatening to engulf traditional British culture. The most significant tension between MacColl's commitment to a 'folk revival', resurrecting the truly traditional aspects of English and Celtic culture, and Seeger's political campaigns, fought in song, was that much of MacColl's work was largely negative. It was against American music in all its forms, and not just against American popular music. MacColl, and the ideology that he represented, rejected Dylan from the start, whereas for Seeger, Dylan for a while represented the redemptive power of political song. Jones suggests that the reaction against Dylan, and the accusation of betrayal, were ill judged and held the American responsible for views of which he could not be expected to be the custodian.

The author reflects in a personal way on how Robert Zimmerman, the man behind the many masks, was in fact unmasked, wounded and disarmed by the shout of Judas, and how he betrayed not his audience, but an uncharacteristic weakness, underlying the cool persona he had until then so successfully projected. This realisation forces Jones to confront the limitations of his personal 'consumption' of Dylan. Dylan had constructed himself first as a 'folk-singer' and then as a temporary 'rock star'. Viewed from the vantage point of an overview of Dylan's entire career it becomes apparent that his use of metamorphosis is key to understanding what has remained stable in all his incarnations—the expressive and 'analytical' power he has continued to draw from 'traditional' music in his desire and determination to explore the 'human condition'.

Lawrence Wilde begins his essay by taking the same incident that Michael Jones analyses. By using the theoretical work of Adorno, Wilde wants to show that in going electric Dylan had not become another Rock-a-Day Johnny, but instead had transformed the political protest medium into a higher level of expression. Adorno and Dylan are an unlikely combination, given that the former viewed popular music with disdain. Despite this, Wilde contends that Adorno's writings on commitment in art serve as a conceptual tool for appraising the revolutionary artistic power of Dylan's disturbing imagery exposing the underlying corrosive pillars of modern society, greed, hypocrisy and corruption. Principally, but not exclusively, the songs are to be found on *Bringing It All Back Home* and *Highway 61 Revisited*. The songs in this genre conform with Adorno's severe criteria for an autonomous aesthetics of protest, and so constitute an art of resistance that aggressively resists assimilation into the social forces that it confronts and condemns. For Adorno the German Expressionist Movement of the early twentieth century epitomised revolutionary art. Wilde contends that Dylan's work of this period resurrects Expressionism in a novel and popular form.

The work of this period renounces traditional narrative form and abjures the conventions of popular song. They are a fusion of the poetic technique of modernism and a relentless social critique. They conjure up an alternative and subversive ethical community, comprising a challenge to prevailing moralities. Wilde is not suggesting that the early German Expressionists had a direct influence on Dylan, merely that there are strong affinities in the manner in which content and structure are constructed to provoke the receiver emotionally to confront the dominant values. Wilde contends that Dylan outgrew the folk music idiom because it ceased to be an adequate vehicle for the new form and content of his songs. The controversy surrounding the acoustic versus electric debate disguised the transformation of his songwriting, which ultimately was of greater artistic significance. Of the songs that provide the focus for Wilde, only 'Ballad of a Thin Man' has electric backing. The songs are the product of a brief transition in his careeer, although their artistic strength is enduring.

Developing the theme, Wilde goes on to address Adorno's theory of commitment in art with a view to discerning the manner in which Dylan rejects the 'official' politics of the day, enabling the American to develop a more sophisticated songwriting style characterised by a more forceful radical rejection of late capitalist social structures and values. Following from this, Wilde examines the development of social expressionist songs in terms of form and content, from 'A Hard Rain's A-Gonna Fall' to 'It's Alright, Ma (I'm Only Bleeding)', and illustrates the point that the most extreme and hard-hitting social expressionist songs in Dylan's catalogue are 'Ballad of a Thin Man' and 'Desolation Row'. By way of conclusion Wilde establishes the distinctiveness of this brief period in Dylan's career, maintaining that he created a revolutionary aesthetic of powerful dramatic proportions that was radical in scope and displayed lyrical panache. The songs are a searing denunciation of surrendering to the allure of money and power, and of the conservative reverence for order and the fear of freedom. These songs have enduring significance in a world that continues to be profane.

Chris Brown focuses on yet another controversy in which Dylan became embroiled. Dylan's plea at Live Aid in the States to divert a proportion of the money to help American farmers and save some of their farms from being repossessed was severely castigated by Bob Geldorf for being stupid crass and nationalistic. Losing one's livelihood pales into insignificance when compared with losing one's life. Brown challenges this characterisation. While acknowledging that in a certain respect Dylan's comments were nationalistic, he contests the claim that they were crass and stupid. Dylan's comments reflect and illuminate important debates in contemporary (international) political theory. Brown takes Dylan to be saying not that charity should be bounded by a national moral community, and that we have no obligations beyond those boundaries, but instead that a charity that does not begin at home ought not to be taken seriously. Nothing in Dylan's plea intimates or implies that we need not concern ourselves with the interests and needs of 'distant strangers'. Brown contends that what Dylan implies is that our concern for distant strangers should not supersede or trump our concerns for those of our compatriots closer to home. Our obligations to those closer to home are stronger than those towards strangers and to juxtapose the loss of livelihood with the loss of life raises much more complicated issues than Geldof acknowledges.

Following Brown's discussion of the issues raised by Dylan's impetus in establishing Farm Aid, Gary Browning broadens the perspective by reviewing Dylan's corpus as a whole. He takes as his starting point Dylan's recent album *Modern Times*. His chapter, 'Dylan and (Post) Modern Times' discerns a postmodern emphasis upon ambiguity, elusiveness and the complexities of identity in Dylan's work and notes parallels between Dylan's career and art, and the disconcerting postmodernism of the philosopher, Lyotard.

The sceptical perspectivalism of postmodernism brings into focus Dylan's extraordinary career, his complex simultaneous engagement with a variety of objects; the burdens of celebrity, the distortions of the media, the opacity of personal relationships and the alienating world of politics. Moreover, the greatness of Dylan's lyrics and his singing weave together postmodern themes in ambiguous performances that attest to aesthetic insight while renouncing intellectual, discursive explanations. The focus on the changing styles and standpoints of Dylan's career as a singer and songwriter and his self-conscious engagement with the burdens of his own celebrity are taken to be central to an understanding of Dylan and to Dylan's political and personal concerns. His firsthand appreciation of the idiot wind orchestrated by the media infecting personal relationships and of the cost of the struggle to be innovative and expressive testify to what is at stake in resisting the power of the political world. Dylan, like Lyotard, is seen to question the nature of the political, and in critiquing aspects of its impact, is recognised as seeing the struggle to achieve authentic self-expression as taking place against the backdrop of a diverting and constraining political world. The postmodern aspects of Dylan's politics, though, should not be taken as a label that excludes other readings. Lyotard, the arch-postmodernist did not take postmodernism to exclude preceding perspectives and indeed drew significantly upon Adorno so that Browning's postmodern reading of Dylan is not opposed to Wilde's recognition of Adornian themes in Dylan's expressionist songs of the mid 1960s.

Brake's chapter, '"You can always come back, but you can't come back all the way" Fate and Freedom in Dylan's Recent Work', discusses how Dylan considers freedom in his most recent work. She builds upon a previous reading of Dylan as moving beyond a concept of negative freedom. In this piece she reflects upon how Dylan in his latest work reconsiders freedom from the standpoint of someone who has experienced much and who now has to confront the identities he has himself expressed. She is surely right to recognise the maturity of Dylan's recent songs, their power in expressing an older man's reflections on identity and freedom. She sees Dylan's late songs to be about connecting with the past and the senses of recovery with which engagement with them might achieve. She observes how Dylan also revisits the American past, relishing and drawing upon its musical and lyrical styles and achievements but also looking at its failures and omissions. But Brake does not take Dylan to be simply looking for recognition in the land-scape of personal, cultural and political pasts. She senses that he is looking for more, namely a recovery of creativity and authenticity. She sees these themes in Dylan's largely underrated film, *Masked and Anonymous*, identifying and illuminating its interweaving of the themes of personal renewal, artistic integrity and political commentary.

In the final chapter, David Boucher engages in an act of meta-interpretation. He categorises the predominant modes evident in the unsettled surface of Dylan interpretative studies. He attempts to show how commentators have interpreted Dylan and detects what he takes to be some evident and obvious flaws. The commentators, Boucher suggests, lack a vocabulary to discern what questions might pertinently and appropriately be asked of different songs or lyric poems. Questions are crucial in interpretation and different types of question may arise in relation to different songs. The way to interpret hinges upon asking the right sort of questions.

The author distinguishes three predominant modes of interpretation. The first is distinguished by the search for referents in places, peoples and objects. The second by the search for referents in influences, both poetic and musical. The third mode of interpreting Dylan's lyrics the author calls the 'emotional response'. Here the establishing of meaning in relation to the historical or literary context is rejected in favour of understanding, or experiencing the capacity of the images to resonate emotionally in the psyche of the hearer. All three modes of interpretation posit different types of question, and view the purpose and object of interpretation differently. Boucher wants to formulate a theoretical basis for the appropriateness of asking particular questions of the particular types of lyric or poetry to be found in Dylan's *oeuvre*. He does this by presenting three aesthetic theories: those of R. G. Collingwood, Michael Oakeshott and F. G. Lorca. The crucial point is distinguishing between those lyrics that may be taken as propositions about the world and whose contexts may illuminate them, and those that are non-propositional and about which it makes little sense to ask whether they are right or wrong, and for which the search for meaningful contexts detracts from their poetic imagery. It is suggested that different types of lyric poetry are characteristic of Dylan's various styles, and that the theoretical conclusions help us to distinguish what types of questions may be asked of them. It is not suggested that Dylan's career may conveniently be divided into different phases characterised by these different types, though it maybe possible to argue that one or other dominates and recedes at one time or another, without losing sight of the fact that they run concurrently with one another throughout his career.

## References

Dylan, Bob (2004), *Chronicles vol. one*. New York, London Toronto, Simon and Schuster.

Feinstein, Barry (2008) *Real Moments*. London, Vision On: Omnibus Press.

Gill, Andy (1998) *My Back Pages: Classic Bob Dylan 1962-69*. London: Carlton.

Jerome, Jim (1975) 'Bob Dylan: A Myth Materializes with a New Protest Record and a New Tour', *People Magazine*, 10 November. Reprinted in *The Bob Dylan Companion*, ed. Carl Benson. New York: Schirmer Books, 1998.

Meisel, Perry (1999) *The Cowboy and the Dandy: Crossing over from Romanticism to Rock and Roll*. New York: Oxford University Press.

Ricks, Christopher (2003) *Dylan's Visions of Sin*. London, New York, Viking.

Ricks, Christopher (2008)'A lesson in Dylan Appreciation', an interview with Leva Lesinska, *Rigas Laiks*, *Eurozine*. http://www.eurozine.org/articles/2008-04-11-ricks-en. html accessed 15 October, 2008.

Santelli, Robert (2005) *The Bob Dylan Scrap Book 1956-1966*, London, Simon and Schuster.

Williamson, Nigel (2004),*The Rough Guide to Bob Dylan*. London: Rough Guides.

Andrew Gamble

# The Drifter's Escape

One of Dylan's albums in the 1990s was called *World Gone Wrong*. The title has a wider resonance. It expresses the particular conception of politics and the political which informs so much of his work. Many of his songs depict a world which is fundamentally disordered and from which, as a consequence, people are alienated and disaffected. Alienation is one of Dylan's major themes, but his account of how human beings become alienated and his recommendations as to how we should respond to it are many-sided and complex. There is no single perspective or attitude which he consistently presents. The changes through which his work has passed and the constant reinventions of himself have contributed to this, but the ambivalence goes deeper and is reflected in songs at every stage of his career.

Alienation has a long history in Western thought, in both the Judeo-Christian tradition and in the secular social theories which grew out of it (Marcuse 1955; Meszaros 1970; Ollman 1971). Its oldest meaning is estrangement, the experience of the world as alien. Individuals become divorced from their essential nature and from authentic existence, and begin to live in inauthentic ways. The source of this alienation is alienation from God and from the ways of God, brought about by Original Sin and the Fall of Man. Disobedience to God's commands led to the expulsion of human beings from the Garden of Eden and the loss of innocence. The attempt to understand and overcome this estrangement between God and Man lies at the centre of Judeo-Christian teaching and its parables about human existence, and has always been a deep influence on Dylan's songs, not just in the Christian albums.

The Judeo-Christian tradition also shaped the secular ideologies and social theories of the modern period, including liberalism and socialism, which proclaimed the possibility of a redemption for the human race through the reordering of society. Rather than being alienated from the ways of God, human beings in the modern world were seen as alienated from nature, from both the physical world and their own human nature. They experienced feelings of estrangement, powerlessness, insecurity and anxiety arising from political and social structures which denied equality and liberty to their citizens. The two great authors of secular theories of alienation, Jean-Jacques Rousseau and Karl Marx, helped shape the traditions of ideas and feeling on which Dylan draws in his songs.

At the heart of Rousseau's thought, for example, is a contrast between nature and civilisation. Human beings are naturally good and free, but corrupted by civilisation, which separates them from their own nature and imprisons them and condemns them to live inauthentic lives, in thrall to useless and pointless desires (and 'useless and pointless knowledge' as Dylan puts it in 'Tombstone Blues', 1965). Vice and evil are the product of the institutions of organised societies. 'Man is born free but is everywhere in chains', Rousseau proclaims at the beginning of *The Social Contract*. These chains are the chains of institutions, of civilisation, of cities, of industry and of states, in short of modernity itself. What civilisation has produced is an artificial and inauthentic being in place of the natural and original human being. The revulsion against the complexity and corruption of the modern world and the beliefs and processes that underpin it, and the corresponding desire for simplicity, for a return to nature, for goodness, for truth and beauty, and for authenticity — these are themes which resonate in the American romantic tradition of Emerson and Whitman (Salusinzky 1994), and became an important strand in the sensibility of modern America, and in the counter-culture of the 1960s. Dylan articulated this sensibility more searchingly than any of his contemporaries, and explored the alienated world of late twentieth-century America, a civilisation recognisably descended from the civilisation condemned by Rousseau and Emerson, but on a hugely expanded scale, and vastly more complex and more corrupt than anything they could have imagined.

A second major meaning of alienation is associated with Hegel and Marx, and draws on the legal meaning of alienation as the process by which individuals divest themselves of property. They alienate their property by transferring the ownership to another. As such, alienation is built into the structure of market economies which rely heavily upon individual exchange and upon buying and selling all goods and services which have a use, including the labour power of individuals. Society appears as a vast collection of commodities, the products of alienated labour. The conversion of everything into commodities, the treatment of nothing as sacred, the subordination of all values to the laws of supply and demand, were essential aspects of the secularisation of society and the creation of the great wealth-creating institutional nexus of modern capitalism. The idea of everything being for sale, and therefore everything being in principle commensurable, is fundamental to commercial society and the formation of capitalist relations of production, and as such provided the basis of Marx's critique of alienated labour and exploitation, his analysis of the relationships of power and oppression which arise from them, and his moral condemnation of capitalism as denying true emancipation, the possibility of a true human community (Ollman 1971). Dylan's songs, drawing on the folk and blues traditions, and the political ferment of the 1960s, are suffused with this understanding of the modern world as one of unjust power and the denial of human potential (Marqusee 2003).

In the Judeo-Christian tradition there has always been much theological dispute as to whether Original Sin and the alienation of Man from God is a sentence which defines the human condition and from which there is no escape, or whether it is possible for individuals to achieve release from the burden of Original Sin and be saved, by renouncing their sinful ways to live in accordance with the ways of God, and by so doing increase their chances of reaching paradise after death. Is redemption and the creation of a Christian society possible on earth? For the secular doctrines of progress which were deeply imbued with the same eschatological visions as Judaism and Christianity, there was no question. Paradise could be realised on earth, if human societies were reordered so that they corresponded with the true nature of human beings. True human emancipation meant that alienation could be overcome.

In Dylan's work, now spanning four decades, the theme of alienation is ever-present, but the theme is treated very differently in particular songs and particular periods. Dylan has written and performed many different kinds of song, but there are some distinct recurring patterns, one of the most important of which is the distinction between what might be called songs of redemption and songs of survival. Songs of redemption reflect a 'committed' gaze and their primary motif is change, the possibility of transforming the world and human beings, while songs of survival reflect a 'sceptical' gaze, a much bleaker assessment of the world, and their primary motif is escape. But I hope to show that they have a common conception of politics and the political, what Dylan calls 'the political world', which for him is an alienated world.

## Alienation and the American Dream

The theme of alienation is there in Dylan's earliest songs, and finds expression in both the songs of redemption and the songs of survival. What Dylan almost never offers is a straightforward accommodation to the world as it is, certainly not the political world. Instead, his starting point is always a 'world gone wrong', a world which fails to live up to or match its ideal. As many commentators on Dylan have noted, this is an ideal of America, and Dylan belongs in an American romantic tradition which was inaugurated by Emerson, and includes Thoreau, Whitman and Melville

(Pichaske 1987), but which also has deep roots in American Protestantism. The idea of the American people as God's Chosen People, in the same way that the Israelites had been, became closely allied to the sense of America as a new beginning, a break with the past, particularly the old European past, and the birth of a nation which was forever young and forever capable of renewing itself (Longley 2002).

This possibility of renewal was never a matter of cautious, incremental reform but a moral revolution, a cleansing of the nation's soul, stripping away the pretences, corruption and lies, casting down the false idols and returning to a life of simple purity and goodness. This ideal is contrasted with the actual world of complexity, of 'mixed-up confusion', of corruption and greed. Entanglement with this world means that individuals themselves become corrupted, alienated from their true selves and their true potential. To escape from this entrapment individuals must either find redemption or escape. If they find neither they become victims, and Dylan's catalogue has numerous examples of victims, from Emmett Till and Davy Moore to Hattie Carroll, George Jackson and Rubin Carter.

Dylan's ideal of America has been fairly consistent. In the early days he drew much of it from Woody Guthrie, and the folk tradition and radical politics that he represented. He constantly contrasted the purity of the country with the corruption of the city. 'I'll take all the smog in Cal-i-for-ne-ay/ 'N' every bit of dust in Oklahoma plains/'N' the dust in the caves of the Rocky Mountain mines/It's all much cleaner than the New York kind' ('Hard Times in New York Town', 1962). This went along with the myth of the Wild West, the independent, rugged, self-reliant pioneers who extended the frontier and built new communities. Dylan has always been attracted by the persona of the drifter, the outlaw, the vagabond, 'hard-travellin' with no fixed commitments or fixed abode. His songs frequently celebrate such characters — some fictional like the Jack of Hearts in 'Lily, Rosemary and the Jack of Hearts' (1974) and The Man in the Long Black Coat' (1989), some (often loosely) based on actual historical figures, such as John Wesley Harding and Billy the Kid (Whithouse 1987).

This mythical America of the frontier has such a hold on the American imagination because of its moral starkness and simplicity, and because the special American virtues of liberty, equality and independence can flourish there without impediment. This is also the ideal Whitman championed of the archetypal American setting out on a voyage of self-discovery down the open road into a future where anything might happen (Ford 2003: 129). At the same time, it is understood as a fragile space which was doomed to be destroyed by the forces of modern urban civilisation, the application of its laws and its systems of economy and politics. These signal the dominance of what Dylan calls 'the political world', which destroys the true America and makes it forget its true self. The task of the singer is to keep alive this tradition by celebrating its heroes and its outlaws, and to call for their values to be recognised once more as the values of America. Emerson himself had denounced the state of American culture and prophesied the arrival of a genius who would transform America (Ford 2003).

This sense of an older, better America runs through Dylan's work, and it projects an image of an America that is unalienated, in which human beings can be honest and simple and true, no longer estranged from themselves or from their society. This determination to strip away complexity and embellishment is a desire to return to an original state of simplicity and purity. In Dylan's songs this idea is often expressed through nakedness. 'In Ballad of a Thin Man' (1965) Mr. Jones is alarmed to see someone naked, and exclaims, 'Who is that man?'. He cannot adjust to the unexpected situation in which he finds himself, cannot understand what is happening. Similarly, in 'Bob Dylan's 115th Dream' (1965) Dylan the hobo sailor searching desperately for help to free his friends runs into a bank: 'They asked me for some collateral/And I pulled down my pants/They threw me in the alley' — as well they might. Nakedness here signifies being authentic, real values over the values of the straight world (which, from the standpoint of the ideal

America, is really the crooked world). In 'It's Alright Ma (I'm Only Bleeding)' (1965) Dylan declares (to wild applause when he performed the song again during Nixon's Watergate crisis), 'Sometimes even the President of the United States must have to stand naked'. Standing naked is to stand stripped of all honours, offices, titles, the attributes of wealth and power, naked before God. In the liner notes for 'The Times They Are A Changin'' (11 Outline Epitaphs) Dylan writes: 'I never eat, I run naked where I can/my hobby's collectin' airplane glue ... that is the bare hungry sniffin' truth'.

During Dylan's Christian period the hobo/outlaw tradition of the authentic America appeared to be supplanted by fundamentalist Christianity, but a closer reading of his work shows that the Judeo-Christian themes had always been present in his songs (Cartwright 1991; Gray 2000, ch. 7). His embrace of Christianity, full-hearted though it was for a time, did not fundamentally alter his vision of America or what was valuable about it. But it gave him another way of expressing his faith in a morally pure America and his disgust at how it had fallen into the abyss. His apocalyptic warnings of imminent doom for America were echoes, if rather starker this time, of warnings he had delivered in his earlier songs. What unites the three Christian albums (*Slow Train Coming*, *Saved* and *Shot of Love*) with the 'protest' albums (*The Free-wheelin' Bob Dylan* and *The Times They Are A-Changin'*) is that in both Dylan is singing songs of redemption, proclaiming that America could be saved if it realised its errors and repented.

### Apocalyse Now

One striking characteristic of Dylan's view of alienation has been the constant warnings in his songs and public utterances of a coming apocalypse (Herdman 1981). This is present very early in 'The Times They Are A-Changin'' (1964), with his call to his fellow Americans to 'admit that the waters around you have grown' and that they had 'better start swimmin' or you'll sink like a stone'. These are predictions of a sudden cataclysmic event, like Noah's flood, which will also be a day of reckoning, and those who are not prepared will not survive. Dylan returns to it again and again, even entitling one of his live albums *Before the Flood*. His songs are scattered with dark hints at apocalyptic events, travelling the 'crooked highways', 'sad forests' and 'dead oceans' of 'A Hard Rain's A-Gonna Fall' (1963). He sees newborn babies surrounded by wolves, black branches with blood that kept dripping, guns and sharp swords in the hands of young children, a young woman whose body was burning, people starving, and hears 'the roar of a wave which could drown the whole world'.

This sense of impending doom is nowhere better expressed than in 'All Along the Watchtower' (1968), one of Dylan's most complete songs.

He adapts lines from Isaiah, which prophesy the appearance of two horsemen signalling the destruction of Babylon:

> Prepare the table, watch in the watchtower, eat, drink: arise ye princes and anoint the shield ... And behold here cometh a chariot of men, with a couple of horsemen. And he answered and said, Babylon is fallen, is fallen and all the graven images of her gods he hath broken into the ground (Isaiah 21: 5–9).

The first two verses of Dylan's songs have the two riders, two archetypal drifters, the Joker and the Thief, conversing, with one gravely aware that 'the hour is getting late'. The third verse then identifies them (although not directly) as the riders of Isaiah, and therefore as the harbingers of catastrophe, expressed in the song by the growl of a wild cat (a lion in Isaiah) and the wind beginning to howl.

This theme is picked up again in much later songs, such as 'Things have Changed' (1999). But not much has changed for Dylan, it seems. He sings 'Standing on the gallows with my head in a noose/Any minute now I'm expecting all hell to break loose'; and later, 'I've been walking forty miles of bad road/if the Bible is right the world will explode'. There is a similar theme in 'Shelter from the Storm' (1975). The storm is both the pressures of celebrity from which Dylan (briefly) escaped in the 1960s, and also the biblical flood once again. For a moment Dylan, 'burned out with exhaustion' and escaping from a world of 'steel-eyed death and men who are fighting to be warm', imagines he has found sanctuary: 'Try imagining a place where it's always safe and warm'. But before long he was on the road again and confronting once more another major change in his life, the acceptance of God. In 'Senor' (1978) which appeared on *Street Legal*, the last album before the Christian albums, the sense of an apocalyptic moment in Dylan's life and the approach of the Last Judgment is palpable. 'Senor, Senor, do you know where we're headin'?/Lincoln County Road or Armageddon?/Seems like I been down this way before'. He had been down this way before, and would be again: 'This place don't make sense to me no more./Can you tell me what you're waiting for, senor?'.

What was waiting for him was what he had already predicted in 'Shelter From the Storm' (1975): 'In a little hilltop village, they gambled for my clothes /I bargained for salvation an' they gave me a lethal dose'. These lines are reminiscent of the ones in 'Stuck Inside of Mobile with the Memphis Blues Again' (1966) when the rainman gave him two cures and said '"Jump right in"/The one was Texas medicine,/The other was just railroad gin/An' like a fool I mixed them/An' it strangled up my mind/An' now people just get uglier/An' I have no sense of time'. The dose of salvation Dylan got also strangled up his mind, and led to his decision for a while to stop performing any of the songs written before his conversion at concerts, and also produced the long, rambling monologues in which he warned his audiences to prepare to face their Maker:

> How many people are aware that we're living in the end times right now? How many people are aware of that? Anybody wanna know? Anybody interested to know that we're living in the end times? How many people *do* know that? Well we are. We're living in the end times. That's right. I told you that the times they are a-changing 20 years ago and I don't believe I ever lied to you. I don't think I ever told you to vote for nobody; never told you to follow nobody... Well let me tell you now, the devil owns this world — he's called the god of this world. Now we're living

in America. I like America, just as everybody else does. I love America, I gotta say that. But America will be judged. ...

You just watch your newspapers, you're going to see — maybe two years, maybe three years, five years from now, you just wait and see. Russia will come down and attack in the Middle East. China's got an army of two million people — they're gonna come down in the Middle East. There's gonna be a war called the Battle of Armageddon which is like something you never even dreamed about. And Christ will set up His Kingdom, and He'll rule it from Jerusalem. I know, far out as that might seem this is what the Bible says (Heylin 1992: 144–5).

But Dylan, as so often before, did not stay convinced by fundamentalist Christianity for very long. He was soon distancing himself from it and recovering his more usual sceptical, detached pose. In 'Sweetheart Like You' (1983) he sings rather poignantly, 'There's only one step down from here, baby,/It's called the land of permanent bliss'. Dylan had been there and it had failed to satisfy.

But although his religious ardour notably cooled in the 1980s it did not disappear, because at root the religious vision is only a more extreme version of the American vision to which Dylan has always subscribed. Religious imagery of doom and destruction continues to form an essential backdrop to his songs and to his understanding of the American predicament. Two recent examples will suffice. In 'Shooting Star' (1989) Dylan sings: 'Listen to the engine, listen to the bell/As the last fire truck from hell/ Goes rolling by, all good people are praying/It's the last temptation/The last account/The last time you might hear the sermon on the mount/The last radio is playing'. Dylan has always believed that we are living in the last days, though not always in the very literal sense as foretold in the Bible. It is what has given many of his songs their edge. The same sense of apocalypse is there in 'Caribbean Wind' (1985): 'Every new messenger brings evil report/ 'Bout armies on the march and time that is short/And famines and earthquakes and train wrecks and the tearin' down of the walls.... And them distant ships of liberty on them iron waves so bold and free/Bringing everything that's near to me nearer to the fire'.

## The Political World

With his apocalyptic vision that we are living in the last days and are soon to be judged, and with his ideal of a lost America, it is hardly surprising that Dylan should have a jaundiced view of the role of politics. Indeed, he regards the political world as the antithesis of the world of love, community and authenticity. The political world is the alienated world which individuals must decide whether to seek to overthrow, to survive within or to escape from. There is not much room in his vision of politics for cautious, piecemeal reform of institutions and policies. Things are too far gone for that.

He displays this anti-politics in many ways. Almost every reference to politics and politicians in his songs is derogatory, from the 'drunken politician leaps' in 'I Want You' (1966) to the reference in 'Summer Days' (2001): 'Politician got on his jogging shoes/He must be running for office, got no time to lose/He been suckin' the blood out of the genius of generosity'. In 'Stuck Inside of Mobile with the Memphis Blues Again' (1966) the Senator is wandering about 'showing off his gun'. Politicians are treated marginally better than judges, but are generally seen as part of the same axis of evil and corruption. In 'Union Sundown' (1983) Dylan states: 'Capitalism is above the law/It say "It don't count 'less it sells ... Democracy don't rule the world ... This world is ruled by violence"'.

The reason for Dylan has always been plain. 'We live in a political world', he sings, where 'Love don't have any place/We're living in times where men commit crimes/ And crime don't have a face' ('Political World', 1989). Wisdom is thrown into jail, mercy walks the plank, courage is a thing of the past, it's all a stacked deck, in the cities of lonesome fear, where suicide is one of the kinder options. Unrelieved bleakness is often characteristic of Dylan's view of modern America. It is there in the 'Song to Woody' (1962), where he sings about the world being sick, hungry, tired and torn. In another very early song, 'Train A Travelin'' (first published 1968), he sings: 'There's an iron train a travelin' that's been a-rollin' through the years/With a fire-box of hatred and a furnace full of fears/ ... Did you ever stop to wonder 'bout the hatred that it holds? Did you ever see its passengers, its crazy mixed-up souls? ... Does the raving of the maniacs make your insides go insane/ ... Do the kill crazy bandits and the haters get you down/Does the preachin' and the politics spin your head around?' And he asks rather plaintively, 'Did you ever start a thinking that you gotta stop that train?' The train is the train of Southern White supremacy, but it stands as a metaphor for the whole political world as Dylan came to see it.

In some moods Dylan is fiercely condemnatory of the political world; in others he is more reflective. In 'Slow Train' (1979), for example, he declares 'Sometimes, I feel so low-down and disgusted' and he goes on to rail against man's inflated ego, his outdated laws which no longer apply. He depicts modern America as a land where people starve when grain silos are bursting: 'You know it costs more to store the food than it do to give it...They talk about a life of brotherly love, show me someone who knows how to live it'. This style can be contrasted with one of Dylan's greatest songs 'Blind Willie McTell' (1983), where the history of slavery in America is evoked with masterful economy and haunting images. From the very first line, 'the arrow on the doorpost' signals that 'this land is condemned' and the theme is continued through the images of burning plantations, the cracking of the whips, the sweet magnolia blooming, the ghosts of slave ships, the tribes a-moaning, the undertaker's bell and the chain gang on the highway.

At the end of 'Blind Willie McTell' Dylan chooses to make a more general statement from his vantage point in the St. James Hotel: 'God is in his heaven/And we all want what's his/But power and greed and corruptible seed/Seem to be all that there is'. That sums up Dylan's view of the political world — it is a bleak Augustinian vision of sin, in which only power and greed and vulnerable sinful human beings (corruptible seed) exist. But although as in this song Dylan is often to be found gazing out of the window, reflecting on the infirmities and perversities of the political world, he is also fascinated by this world, and in his extraordinary output of songs he has explored it vigorously. Among the many metaphors he uses to describe it three will be drawn on here: the political world as a prison; the political world as a graveyard; and the political world as the Insanity Factory.

### The Prison

Dylan's songs contain many references to the world as a prison. It is there in 'George Jackson' (1971): 'Sometimes I think this whole world/Is one big prison yard/Some of us are prisoners/The rest of us are guards'. This idea that all of us are part of the prison system is echoed elsewhere in his belief that it is impossible to tell the sane from the insane. He has often written about prisoners, and the effects of prison, for example in songs like 'The Walls of Redwing' (1963) and 'I Shall be Released' (1967). Dylan tends to see the inmates of prisons as victims, as in 'The Ballad of Donald White' (1962) many of whom, like Rubin Carter, have been falsely imprisoned on trumped-up charges.

Many of Dylan's more committed songs treat the political world as sanctioning oppression. Special opprobrium is reserved for judges, who are seen as bending the rules to favour vested interests, and protect the wealthy and privileged, as most famously in 'The Lonesome Death of Hattie Carroll' (1964). Dylan here satirises the gap between the ideology of the courts and their actual practice:

> In the courtroom of honor, the judge pounded his gavel/ To show that all's equal and that the courts are on the level/And that the strings in the books ain't pulled and persuaded/And that even the nobles get properly handled/ Once that the cops have chased after and caught' em /And that the ladder of law has no top and no bottom/ Stared at the person who killed for no reason/Who just happened to be feelin' that way without warnin'/And he spoke through his cloak, most deep and distinguished/ And handed out strongly, for penalty and repentance/ William Zanzinger with a six-month sentence.

Now is the time for your tears, Dylan tells his audience. A similar pattern of miscarriages of justice involving the imprisonment of the innocent like Rubin Carter in 'Hurricane' (1975) 'For somethin' that he never done', or excessive punishment of a defendant as in 'Percy's Song' (1964).

Dylan sees law for the most part as coercive, part of a structure of power which disadvantages the poor and the weak, and is used systematically against them. Much of this stemmed from the experience of the Civil Rights Movement, as Mike Marqusee has shown in *Chimes of Freedom*, his major study of the political background to Dylan's songs of the 1960s (Marqusee 2003), and the systematic denial of black rights and frequent murder of black activists. Dylan wrote many songs about the civil rights struggle, including 'Oxford Town' (1963) and 'Only a Pawn in Their Game' (1963). Dylan may have told Joan Baez that he only wrote his protest songs for the money, but as Marqusee points out, this does not ring true either with the songs themselves, or with the fact that he was to return on several occasions to these themes in his later career, most notably in 'Blind Willie McTell'.

## The Graveyard

A second metaphor for the political world and one quite strongly related to the first is that of the graveyard. This informs above all the many anti-war songs, which include 'John Brown' (1963), 'Masters of War' (1963) and 'With God on Our Side' (1963). These are songs about the consequences of war and the evil motivations of those who prosecute and profit from it, and the hypocrisy of the ways in which war is justified. War is regarded in these songs as an ultimate evil, which destroys lives, and with them communities, and the ideal of an America, which wants to be at peace, and a model of peace, harmony and community for the rest of the world. War is the means by which all the worst elements of American society come out on top, and transform the United States from a loose confederation of isolationist, pacific and independent states into a centralised, federal state, and by degrees a world power and an interventionist power.

Marqusee notes that Dylan hardly ever mentions Vietnam directly in his songs. There is one brief reference in the liner notes to *Bringing it All Back Home*. In the 1990s he added a verse to 'With God on our Side' to include Vietnam, but he studiously refused to be drawn on the issue in the 1960s, even though it was convulsing America and in particular Dylan's fans, and Dylan's songs articulated the sensibility and political awareness of so many in his generation. Dylan was unwilling to be cast in the role of a leader and to 'sound a battle charge', but his 1960s songs do refer obliquely to Vietnam and to the desperate morass into which America was sinking. 'Highway 61 Revisited' (1965) and 'Tombstone Blues' (1965) are dark satires on the mentality promoting the war in Vietnam. The first begins with the willingness of fathers to sacrifice their sons, and ends with the 'rovin' gambler' trying to create the next world war: 'He found a promoter who nearly fell off the floor/saying I never engaged in this kind of thing before/but yes I think it can be very easily done'.

'Tombstone Blues' has the memorable image of 'John the Baptist after torturing a thief/Looks up at his hero the Commander-in-Chief/Saying "Tell me great hero, but please make it brief/Is there a hole for me to get sick in?"/The commander-in-chief answers him while chasing a fly/Saying "Death to all those who would whimper and cry"/And dropping a bar bell he points to the sky/Saying, "The sun's not yellow it's chicken"'.

'Tombstone Blues' also contains the lines which have often been taken to be a direct reference to the escalating war in Vietnam: 'The King of the Philistines his soldiers to save/Puts jawbones on their tombstones and flatters their graves/Puts the pied pipers in prison and fattens the slaves/Then sends them out to the jungle', from where many did not return. The sequence is continued in 'From a Buick 6' (1965) which concerns 'this graveyard woman' who 'if I go down dyin', you know she bound to put a blanket on my bed'. It ends with the plea for 'a steam shovel mama to keep away the dead', 'a dump truck mama to unload my head'. Images of death, destruction, desperation abound in the song, reflecting the experience of so many young conscripts, disproportionately poor and black, thrust into the inferno of Vietnam.

These satires mark a bridge between the more conventional anti-war songs which Dylan wrote at the beginning of his career and his new sense of the absurdity, disorientation and perversity of modern America, which he expressed in *Bringing it All Back Home, Highway 61 Revisited* and *Blonde on Blonde*. This will be explored further in the next section, but as with the prison metaphor, the graveyard metaphor for the political world has continued to be employed by Dylan and to shape his understanding of the nature of politics.

### The Insanity Factory

One way in which it particularly did so was in influencing his conception of the political world as an 'Insanity Factory', a place of death and inauthenticity. Lifelessness was one of its abiding characteristics, and it was the spreading of lifelessness which Dylan regarded as the great scourge of modern America, the attitude which more than anything undermined independence, self-reliance, creativity and vitality. What it left was a profound sense of emptiness, a feeling Dylan has often written about in his love songs — 'Felt an emptiness inside to which he could just not relate' in 'Simple Twist of Fate' (1974) — but which he also treats as a major symptom of political and social alienation.

The Insanity Factory is a phrase used by Dylan in the liner notes to *Highway 61 Revisited*. He proclaims there that 'Lifelessness is the Great Enemy' and associates it with calls to 'go save the world' and 'Involvement! That's the issue'. Liberal activism is no longer enough; for Dylan it has become part of the problem. It cannot understand the seriousness of the situation. He states: 'We are singing today of the WIPE-OUT GANG—the WIPE-OUT GANG buys, owns and operates the Insanity Factory—if you do not know where the Insanity Factory is located, you should hereby take two steps to the right, paint your teeth & go to sleep'.

What Dylan means by the Insanity Factory is the peculiar institutional character which American capitalism had come to assume in the second half of the twentieth century, with its aggressive consumerism and market imperialism, its militarism and nationalism, and its deep racial and social conflicts. Dylan's instinctive anti-authoritarian streak and his roots in the Emersonian tradition made him a strong critic of developments in modern America, but the growing dislocation occasioned by the assassination of President Kennedy, the race riots and, above all, the Vietnam War transformed his attitude from one of wanting a moral reform and the cleansing of his society to one of despairing that this society was reformable at all.

In his exploration of modern America, Dylan uses satire, anecdote, allegory, free association and deliberate obscurity to try to capture aspects of this weird and complex culture. The starting point is that the lunatics have taken over the asylum, and that sane people, or those that want to remain sane, had better watch out. In this way, as will be shown in the next section, Dylan provides a series of commentaries and notes on how to survive in modern America. In some of his earlier songs such as 'Bob Dylan's 115th Dream' the satire is quite good-humoured, although with a sharp edge. America is a weird place in which hypocrisy and self-serving behaviour abound. The building with a sign advertising brotherhood turns out to be a funeral parlour and the undertaker is only interested in Dylan's imprisoned friends if they die. He knocks on a house displaying the US flag and asks for help, only to be told: 'Get out of here/I'll tear you limb from limb/I said "You know they refused Jesus too"/He said "You're not him"'.

The general picture repeated in many other songs is of a society driven at best by selfishness, at worst by crazed prejudice. At first Dylan seems to have thought that the crazies were confined to particular groups of racists and bigots, such as the John Birch Society, with their obsessions with communism, blacks and Jews, which he memorably satirised in Talking John Birch Society Blues'. But subsequently his mood becomes darker and he appears to believe that insanity has spread to all those in charge of the society. In songs such as 'It's Alright Ma (I'm Only Bleeding)' (1965) and above all 'Desolation Row' (1965) Dylan probes deeply into the perversities of America.

A constant theme is the corrupting power of markets which seek to turn every human attribute into a commodity in order to exact a profit. In this way traditional values are subverted: 'Made everything from toy guns that spark/To flesh-colored Christs that glow in the dark/It's easy to see without looking too far/That not much/Is really sacred' ('It's Alright Ma'). Dylan here draws on one of the classic themes of alienation—everything has become for sale. Balzac satirised the France of his day in which 'even the Holy Spirit has its quotation on the stock exchange' (Meszaros 1970, 33). Dylan does the same for America. The loss of the sacred means also that individuals are defenceless against the tide of consumerism: 'Advertising signs that con/You into thinking you're the one/That can do what's never been done/That can win what's never been won/Meantime life outside goes on/All around you' ('It's Alright Ma'). The members of this society are trapped, 'For them that must obey authority/That they do not respect in any degree/who despise their jobs/Their destinies' are forced to 'gargle in the rat race choir, bent out of shape from society's pliers'.

Dylan's classic song about the Insanity Factory and about modern America is 'Desolation Row' (1965). It combines the apocalyptic 'They're selling postcards of the hanging/They're painting the passports brown' and 'the *Titanic* sails at dawn' with a succession of images of the threatening, the absurd and the freakish, from the restless riot squad and the superhuman crew rounding up 'everyone that knows more than they do' to Dr Filth and his sexless patients, Einstein the former electric violin player bumming cigarettes, and Ophelia whose sin is her lifelessness. This is a society portrayed as on the edge of the abyss, where everybody's shouting 'Which side are you on?', an old socialist anthem, as if political action of any kind could redeem and save this world. Dylan's response is to state that the only refuge from this madness is no refuge. It is Desolation Row, but it is the only place to be (Crotty 2003).

## The Outlaw

Dylan's achievement in his extraordinary run of albums in the 1960s from *Freewheelin'* (1963) up to and including *John Wesley Harding* (1968) was to take the persona of the drifter and the outlaw from the folk and radical tradition personified by Woody Guthrie and translate them into the very different world and experience of 1960s urban America. What Dylan takes in particular from the Guthrie tradition is the idea of the outsider, the drifter who is always travelling, 'travellin' hard', always on the move, driven by that 'restless hungry feeling' ('One Too Many Mornings', 1964), never content to be tied down. These drifters, the vagabonds, the hobos, the jugglers, the clowns, the gamblers, the hustlers, the jokers and the thieves are the true Americans, or at least the ones that are keeping alive the true American spirit and the possibility of a different America. Dylan plays endlessly throughout his career with the myths of this other America, and its favourite images, such as the railroad. The obsession with the railroad in all its forms is ultimately nostalgic and locates this America firmly in the past (Pichaske 1987: 103). There are hardly any references in Dylan to aeroplanes, (apart from bombers), except for the rather plaintive 'Time is a jet plane, it moves too fast' on 'You're a Big Girl Now'.

The American ideal of a life of self-creation and self-discovery is a central motif in Dylan and draws on a particular ideal of American masculinity, typified by such figures as James Dean, Jack Kerouac, Jim Morrison or Marlon Brando. Along with these Dylan is said to be part of a 'masculine iconography of white, rebellious America' (Hodson 1990: 187). Dylan's songs and parables are said to be primarily about men, and to exclude women, by treating them in fairly standard ways, as 'bookends' to the innovative, creative, life-enhancing, challenging male experience. Dylan, it is argued, has contested many aspects of the dominant culture, but not its preferred styles of masculinity (Hodson 1990: 187). That a particular narrative of male experience is one of the sources of Dylan's songs is undeniable, but just as Dylan drew hugely on the folk tradition, he was not confined by it, and he succeeds in providing much more than just a male view of the world (Thurschwell 2003). Many of his later songs, including 'License to Kill', 'Floater' and 'Highlands', demonstrate greater self-knowledge and a more complex view of male/female relationships and of female experience. Dylan is too subtle and ambivalent an artist ever be to satisfied with one way of looking at the world.

What Dylan began to do during that extraordinary surge of creative energy which possessed him in the 1960s was to explore an alternative sensibility and an alternative model from that of the folk tradition — the moralist with one foot in the American past, confronting contemporary America with its fall from grace. Although Dylan proved exceptional in that role, it failed to satisfy him, and instead he began to explore what it meant to experience contemporary America as a drifter. As he puts it much later in one of the greatest of his recent songs 'Highlands' (1999): 'Feel like I'm drifting/drifting from scene to scene/I'm wondering what the devil could it all possibly mean'. These lines capture the sense of the drifter constantly moving on, never satisfied, never fixed, but also permanently confused about the meaning of existence. As he put it in 'Visions of Johanna' (1966): 'We sit here stranded though we're all doin' our best to deny it'.

Dylan has always denied that he is a leader or that he wants people to follow him, or that he has any useful advice to give them. That has certainly become true. But it was different in the 1960s, and in part because even when he had consciously abandoned the role thrust upon him of being spokesman for his generation, and setting out the moral challenges facing it, he was still seen as providing 'road maps for the soul'. His songs no longer preached, but they did show others how to live and how to survive in modern America; how to evade authority, how to watch out for the traps laid by conventional society, how to keep running and keep independent and true to oneself. The song where all this came together was 'Subterranean Homesick Blues' (1965).

From its very first lines ('Johnny's in the basement/Mixing up the medicine/I'm on the pavement/Thinking about the government') this song conveys a mood of urgency and menace: 'Look out kid/It's something you did/God knows when/but you're doin' it again'. This is a world as nightmarish and threatening as Desolation Row; the phones are tapped, busts by the authorities are imminent, the repeated advice is to watch out, otherwise you will be hit, 'users, cheaters, six-time losers' are looking for a new fool—and you could be it. No one can be trusted, you are on your own. Dylan insists 'Don't follow leaders', they will always let you down or lead you astray. Instead trust your instincts, just look around you and you will see what is going on: 'You don't need a weatherman to know which way the wind blows'. This eerie echo of 'Blowin' in the Wind' (1962) shows how far Dylan had moved in two short years. The wind was blowing, but no longer promising progress and hope for a better world. In saying these things, however, and in so concentrated and powerful a way, Dylan was providing his own lead to many in his generation. He was saying, this is how it is, this is our experience, and you have to draw the right conclusions if you want to stay out of trouble. In his satire on the American Dream in the final verse, Dylan lists the things that are expected of everybody as they grow up, but look out kid, they keep it all hid, 'Twenty years of schoolin' and they put you on the day shift'. The realities of the production line in modern America snuff out opportunity and individuality. The only way out is to escape: 'better jump down a manhole'. Don't draw attention to yourself, keep on the move. In a last enigmatic line, with its hint of resistance to authority and the crushing conformity of modern American life, Dylan wrote 'The pump don't work/ 'Cause the vandals took the handles'.

Dylan is renowned for his strong opposition to established authority of any kind and his refusal to fit in with people's preconceptions. Along with the often surreal press conferences, a mine of disinformation, one of the most notorious incidents came when accepting the Tom Paine award from the Liberal Establishment just after Kennedy's assassination, he stated that he saw something of Lee Harvey Oswald in himself (Marqusee 2003: 88–9). The audience booed. Another instance was at the climax of the Live Aid Concert in 1985 when he asked for some of the money being raised for famine relief in Africa to be given to help the farming crisis in America (Marqusee 2003: 281–2). In both cases it was not what he was supposed to have said — he punctured expectations and disappointed his friends. But then Dylan has always been puncturing expectations and disappointing his friends, always restless, never content to be categorised and taken for granted. Even when he has accepted the embrace of the Establishment, as when he received an honorary doctorate of music from Princeton, he sent up the ceremony afterwards in 'Day of the Locusts' (1970).

In his early career he did deliberately cultivate the image of the hobo, with his tales of running away from home, hitchhiking and living rough, in songs like 'Long Time Gone' (1963) and also in interviews and liner notes ('My Life in a Stolen Moment'). Joan Baez, in 'Diamonds and Rust' (1975), later depicted the young Dylan as bursting on the scene 'Already a legend/The unwashed phenomenon/The original vagabond'. As many at the time and since have pointed out, Dylan was not actually the vagabond he pretended to be. In songs like 'Guess I'm Doin' Fine' (1964) Dylan sings, 'I been kicked and whipped and trampled on/I been shot at just like you', which could be doubted. But in the same song he also shows awareness of both the pose he is adopting to make his way as a singer and the grimmer reality beyond: 'My road might be rocky/But some folk ain't got no road at all'.

In many of his early songs Dylan slips easily into the persona of the hobo, a standard identity of the folk tradition. But he soon turned it into something quite different, especially in those songs in which he uses it to explore not the America of the past but the America of the present. These songs, which include 'Bob Dylan's 115th Dream' (1965) and 'Motorpsycho Nightmare' (1964), depict Dylan encountering the absurdities, the cruelties and the prejudices of modern America. The gun-toting farmer of 'Motorpsycho Nightmare' is reassured when Dylan tells him he's a doctor, 'A clean cut kid/And I've been to college too'. In order to escape from the house Dylan's ruse is to shout out 'I like Fidel Castro and his beard'. It has the desired effect and Dylan is chased out, with a Reader's Digest, Bible of middle America, flung after him and the farmer's curse: 'You unpatriotic/Rotten doctor Commie rat'. As the last line of the song observes, 'Without freedom of speech we might be in the swamp'. The same persona is developed further in Dylan's Candide-like odyssey through America in 'Bob Dylan's 115th Dream'. The contrast is between America as it pretends to be and America as it really is. The hobo sailor fails to find anyone to help him, and is adrift in a corrupt and self-interested society.

What the outlaw has to do is survive. To do that she has to have higher standards than the society around her. 'To live outside the law you must be honest' ('Absolutely Sweet Marie', 1966). She has to learn 'how to live out on the street', like a rolling stone. Dylan's famous chorus 'How does it feel/To be all alone/With no direction home/A complete unknown?' is both a taunt and injunction. Being like a rolling stone is the only way to be. 'When asked to give your real name never give it', was Dylan's advice to Geraldine (Dylan 1987: 124–5), advice he faithfully followed. He told one audience in 1964, 'I have my Bob Dylan mask on' (Wilentz 2003: 290). Throughout his career he has had his Bob Dylan mask on, or rather one of his many Dylan masks. Many of his characters are enigmatic and mysterious, like the 'Man in the Long Black Coat' (1989): 'He had a face like a mask'. Occasionally, this has approached caricature, as when Dylan was cast as Alias in Peckinpah's film *Pat Garrett and Billy the Kid* and coyly responded, 'That's a good question' when asked 'Who are you?'.

Dylan's long catalogue of outlaw songs contains many western heroes, but also some modern ones, such as Lenny Bruce. Not only did Dylan write a song to Bruce, there are also several references to him in his liner notes and other writings (for example 'Some Other Kind of Songs' on *Another Side* and '11 Outlined Epitaphs' on *The Times They Are A-Changin'*). In the song 'Lenny Bruce' (1981) Dylan quite possibly is addressing himself when he sings: 'He was an outlaw that's for sure/More of an outlaw than you ever were'. What he admired about Bruce was his uncompromising opposition to established authority. He lived outside the law and was honest: 'Never robbed any churches/ Nor cut off any babies' heads'.

One of Dylan's strongest allegiances is to what the Japanese call the floating world, the world which is outside straight society and peopled by jugglers, clowns, vagabonds, criminals, misfits of all kinds, beats, bohemians, hippies, the world of Desolation Row and the St. James Hotel, where people apply different standards and higher levels of honesty. One of his late songs is even called 'Floater' (2001), its lyrics influenced by a Japanese novel, *Confessions of a Yakuza* by Junichi Saga. Yet while no one has explored the floating world of modern America more searchingly than Dylan, he is also ambivalent about it. In 'Man in the Long Black Coat' (1989) Dylan criticises the notion of just floating and drifting, treating life as a joke and never taking life-and-death decisions: 'There are no mistakes in life some people say/And it's true, sometimes, you can see it that way/But people don't live or die/People just float'. The implication is that those who do live their lives on the edge are not like the majority of people who never consider doing anything that would risk them making a mistake. Most people accept the dull conformity of an alienated life, and never glimpse the possibilities of anything different.

A final prevalent image in Dylan's self-creation as outlaw is his persona as the Thief. This operates on several levels. Dylan is the thief of other people's music and other people's words as he transforms them into his own highly personal narratives. The title of his 2001 album *Love and Theft* is taken from Eric Lett's book on American blackface minstrelsy during the Civil War (Wilentz 2003). Dylan has always seen himself as working within the broad tradition of American song, drawing at will from its many strands and refusing to be categorised as belonging to a single branch. To be a thief in this sense is necessary in order to interpret a tradition and to develop it. But Dylan is also not just a thief but *the* Thief, a mask he assumes to signify that in a corrupt world the honest man must live outside the law. When Allen Ginsberg asked him at a news conference in 1965, 'Would there ever be a time when you'll be hung as a thief?' Dylan replied, 'You weren't supposed to say that' (Wilentz 2003: 298). There are numerous reference to him as a thief, for example, in 'Sad Eyed Lady of the Lowlands' (1966) ('Now you stand with your thief), and many references to thieves in his songs, above all, the archetypal figures of the Joker and the Thief in 'All Along the Watchtower' (Pichaske 1981).

The opening lines 'There must be some way out of here/Said the Joker to the Thief/There's too much confusion/I can't get no relief' crystallise the sense of being trapped and the yearning to escape, which are such powerful themes throughout Dylan's work. The representatives of the alienated world from which the Joker and Thief seek to escape are the oppressive figures of the ploughman and the businessman (also present, as it happens, in 'Sad Eyed Lady of the Lowlands'—'the farmers and the businessmen'). None of them knows 'what any of it is worth'. It is the Thief who then tries to calm the Joker ('No reason to get excited') and who suggests that treating life as a joke is no solution either. Things are too serious for that—'Let us not talk falsely now'.

Yet as always with Dylan there is ambivalence. Desolation Row is the place to be and the place not to be. 'She knows there's no success like failure, and that failure's no success at all' ('Love Minus Zero No Limit', 1965). Stealing and thieves are often condemned in Dylan's songs as expressions of corruption and power. In 'Changing of the Guards' (1978) on *Street Legal* he talks of 'merchants and thieves, hungry for power'. Elsewhere he sings, 'You're on your own, you always were/In a land of wolves and thieves'. In 'Sweetheart Like You' (1983) he observes, 'Steal a little and they throw you in jail/Steal a lot and they make you king'. Dylan is aware that taking the persona of thief as a badge of honour has its own difficulties.

He continues to have a deep regard for those striving to live outside the law according to their own codes, although at times, as in 'Joey', one of his least successful songs, he ends up romanticising a brutal gangster (Bangs 1990). But he is more sure-footed in dealing with the numberless anonymous victims of arbitrary systems of justice. 'Drifter's Escape' (1968) portrays one archetypal Dylan figure, the Drifter himself, about to be sentenced but still unaware of what he has done wrong, in a manner reminiscent of 'Subterranean Homesick Blues': 'It's somethin' you did/God knows when/But you're doin' it again'. The judge sorrowfully advises the Drifter not even to try to understand what is happening to him. There is the atmosphere of a lynching with the crowd stirring and the jury crying for more. But just at that moment lightning strikes, and in the confusion the Drifter escapes. It is a parable for modern America and for Dylan's own life.

Ultimately, despite bursts of indignation and injunctions to action, Dylan's political message is one of resignation but not of conservatism. The world cannot be fundamentally changed, but individuals can still survive if they are bold and independent enough to go against the 'idiot wind' and 'live outside the law'. The world is meaningless—'I think also/that there is not/one thing any place/anywhere that makes any/sense' he wrote in his liner notes to Another Side of Bob Dylan. The world is also endlessly confusing: 'There's too many people/And they're all too hard to please/ … I'm looking for some answers/But I don't know who to ask' ('Mixed Up Confusion' 1962). At the same time, it exerts stifling pressure for conformity: 'Well, I try my best/To be just like I am/But everyone wants you/To be just like them' ('Maggie's Farm', 1965). In his most recent albums Dylan's mood of resignation has deepened as he confronts ageing and disillusion, and his sense of a lifeless, alienated world increases: 'I'm walking through streets that are dead' ('Love Sick', 1997). In 'Trying to Get to Heaven' he wonders 'If everything is as hollow as it seems'. He has been walking 40 miles of bad road, he tells us in 'Things Have Changed' (1999), 40 years of song-writing, and at times he feels there is nothing left: 'The party's over, and there's less and less to say' ('Highlands', 1997). Yet at the same time he is still yearning for escape: 'Well, my heart's in the High-lands at the break of day/Over the hills and far away/There's a way to get there, and I'll figure it out somehow/But I'm already there in my mind/And that's good enough for now'.

## References

Bangs, Lester (1990) 'Bob Dylan's Dalliance with Mafia Chic', in Elizabeth Thomson and David Gutman (eds) *The Dylan Companion*. London: Macmillan, 210–21.

Bauldie, John (ed.) (1992) *Wanted Man: In Search of Bob Dylan*. London: Penguin.

Cartwright, Bert (1991) The Bible in the Lyrics of Bob Dylan, 1985-1990', *The Telegraph*, 38, 53–90.

Corcoran, Neil (2003) Do *You, Mr. Jones? Bob Dylan with the Poets and the Professors*. London: Pimlico.

Crotty, Patrick (2003) 'Bob Dylan's Last Words', in Neil Corcoran (ed.) Do *You, Mr. Jones?* London: Pimlico, 307–33.

Dylan, Bob (1987) *Lyrics: 1962–1985*. London: Cape.

Ford, Mark (2003) Trust Yourself: Emerson and Dylan', in Neil Corcoran (ed.) Do *You, Mr. Jones?* London: Pimlico, 127–42.

Gray, Michael (2000) *Song and Dance Man III: The Art of Bob Dylan*. London: Continuum.

Gray, Michael and John Bauldie (eds) (1987) *All Across the Telegraph: A Bob Dylan Handbook*. London: Sidgwick & Jackson.

Herdman, John (1981) *Voice without Restraint: Bob Dylan's Lyrics and Their Background*. Edinburgh: Paul Harris.

Heylin, Clinton (1992) 'Saved! Bob Dylan's Conversion to Christianity', in John Bauldie (ed.) *Wanted Man*. London: Penguin, 141–7.

Hodson, Paul (1990) 'Bob Dylan's Stories about Men', in Elizabeth Thomson and David Gutman (eds) *The Dylan Companion*. London: Macmillan, 183–90.

Longley, Clifford (2002) *Chosen People: The Big Idea that Shaped England and America*. London: Hodder & Stoughton.

Marcuse, Herbert (1955) *Reason and Revolution: Hegel and the Rise of Social Theory*. London: Routledge & Kegan Paul.

Marqusee, Mike (2003) *Chimes of Freedom: The Politics of Bob Dylan's Art.* New York: The New Press.

Meszaros, Istvan (1970) *Marx's Theory of Alienation.* London: Merlin.

Ollman, Bertell (1971) *Alienation: Marx's Conception of Man in Capitalist Society.* Cambridge: Cambridge University Press.

Pichaske, David (1981) *The Poetry of Rock: The Golden Years.* Peoria, Illinois: The Ellis Press.

Pichaske, David (1987) 'Bob Dylan and the Search for the Past', in Michael Gray and John Bauldie (eds) *All Across the Telegraph.* London: Sidgwick & Jackson, 98–106.

Salusinzky, Imre (1994) 'Chimes of Freedom Flashing', *The Telegraph,* 49, 23–37. Thomson, Elizabeth and David Gutman (eds) (1990) *The Dylan Companion.* London: Macmillan.

Thurschwell, Pamela (2003) 'A Different Baby Blue', in Neil Corcoran (ed.) Do *You, Mr. Jones?* London: Pimlico, 253–74.

Whithouse, Chris (1987) 'Alias, Pat Garrett, and Billy the Kid', in Michael Gray and John Bauldie (eds) *All Across the Telegraph.* London: Sidgwick & Jackson, 107–26.

Wilentz, Sean (2003) 'American Recordings: On 'Love and Theft' and the Minstrel Boy' in Neil Corcoran (ed.) Do *You, Mr. Jones?* London: Pimlico, 295–306.

Richard Brown

# Bob Dylan's Critique of Judgement 'Thinkin' about the Law'

## The Category of the Political

Even if it wasn't so conspicuously the case that rock-and-roll music as a medium could be said to voice the political and cultural aspirations of the generation that grew up in the 1960s and 1970s as much or more than any other cultural medium, much of the lyrical content of Bob Dylan's work is explicitly political and in some of the most direct of senses—loudly critical of war, of racial prejudice, of the nuclear threat, of aspects of contemporary commercial society, of right-wing political movements in particular, of political leaders in general and of injustice. Dylan's political personae urge and empower his audience to refuse to be exploited, not to work on 'Maggie's Farm' and to get stoned in various, I assume at least partly symbolic, ways rather than submit to the potentially entrapping forces of conventional authority, or reason, or bourgeois hypocrisy. The work memorably invites its audience to experience and explore how it feels to be homeless or exiled, like a no-moss-gathering dead-beat or drop-out rolling stone (which has been no less valuable an invitation as parts of this audience have become more affluent and secure). In at least one song, the potentially revolutionary Dionysian radicalism and frustrated anger that can be sensed in the rock-and-roll medium is voiced in a specific invitation to make a righteous act of subversive destruction, to disconnect cables and overturn tables, like Christ in the Temple with the money changers. That is 'Senor' (Street Legal, 1978).

Yet the distinctive character let alone the discursive diversity of the *oeuvre* surely dictate that we ask not so much what the politics of Dylan's work are as in what ways that work is or may be said to be political. Such a question invites several kinds of answer at a time when literary-and cultural-critical discourses often claim to offer political readings as a way of confirming what they do and when political theorists may also turn towards the reading of the literary text. Some of the typical answers that arise may seem mutually exclusive or self-contradictory or may depend on narratives that require us to accept big changes in the attitudes or tendencies of the work. Dylan's work has been read as political in the sense that rock-and-roll (especially his folk-protest branch of it) and the decade of the 1960s mapped out a new, youthful, radical political consensus. As that argument goes, it may now have lost much of its original radical charge, by virtue of its changes of style and position, its persistence, its commercial success, its middle age. Alternatively, the work has been read as being most political in that it avoids politics, at least in the conventional sense, as it flirts with ambiguity, as it refuses to *stand for* anything other than its own playfulness and as it only offers such political programme or instruction as we might find in the much-quoted anti-advice: 'Don't follow leaders and watch your parking meters' from 'Subterranean Homesick Blues' *(Bringing it All Back Home,* 1965). Here, the argument may go on to lament the apparent lapse into the more directly didactic modes voiced in parts of the gospel albums, for example, or else some aspects, for instance, of the apparently extreme, time-serving triviality and regressiveness of parts of the later work.

It may then be especially appropriate that Dylan's lively but critically neglected song 'Political World' *(Oh Mercy,*

1989), one of the songs from the late 1980s revival that doesn't really fit with either of these narratives, where he most explicitly names the political, may also be said to be a song where he most calls the political as a category into question. Browning (2004) has argued that it may be dangerous to attempt to define Dylan's sense of the political given the changes that have taken place over the past half-century. Yet reading this song seems to require us to take that risk. The world the song describes may be seen as one that is political in a succession of highly dynamic, unstable and intriguing glosses on that term. It is said to be 'political' in that it is loveless, in that criminality is prevalent but has become faceless. The world is political in that the weather is icy and cloudy, in that wisdom is imprisoned and inaccessible, in that mercy and courage and peace are absent or have even been maliciously excluded from it. It is 'political' in that death may be both imminent and terminal, in that one may live in a condition of fear or uncertainty in one's own knowledge, but that one is also 'under the microscope' of the surveillance of others. Travel or escape or freedom may be merely a matter of having enough rope with which to hang oneself. It is a world of sleeplessness and evasion where everything is owned and where one might wish to call upon a deity, but without being sure of its name. There are some more apparently positive terms thrown into this almost haphazard mixture of negatives such as the fact that wedding bells ring and angels sing, but these items seem rather sentimentalised or idealised in the context of what surrounds them. The song works rather to name or to suggest in terms of their absence or negation a not unfamiliar set of positive human values—including love, the human face, elsewhere, mercy, wisdom, wanting children, peace and, perhaps above and behind them all, freedom. Qualities are so compromised and mediated in the contemporary world (life is said to be 'in mirrors') that they may only be nameable by their absence or negation.

   This mind-bogglingly awful situation seems as much dis-ethical or even psycho-pathological as it is political in the usual senses—though perhaps its materialistic nastiness, environmental and cultural toxicity and Kafka-like expressions of entrapment suggest that it may be a social or at least more general condition of psycho-pathology rather than merely a personal one that is defined. Inasmuch as the song names death it invokes a condition that is so general as to be that of mortality rather than politics. It may be a definition of the extreme experience of the contemporary that has close analogies with the sense of the world given to us in much postmodernist theory with its characteristic diagnoses of post-industrial alienations (Jameson 1992) and critiques of enlightenment modes of knowledge (Lyotard 1986). That knowing and uncertainty, secrecy and surveillance, seem to be presented as aspects of empowerment and victimisation may echo the menacingly political senses of knowledge that appear in the work of Louis Althusser or Michel Foucault. There's more than a little hint of the world of mirrors and mediation that we find in much postmodern theory. Moreover, where the post-Lacanian consciousness or the hypermediated worlds of Jean Baudrillard or Umberto Eco are often said to consist in an absence or displacement of the 'real', Dylan's postmodern dystopia is here one that is, perhaps, all the more paradoxically alarming in that it is one that we can 'see and feel' and all too readily 'know for sure that it's real'. Internal rhyme gives emphasis to the word 'feel' and may make it seem as important in this song as it is, by virtue of its straining cadence and repetition (usually taken up as a defining anthem by the whole audience in a final encores in live performance) in 'Like a Rolling Stone'.

The 'unreality' of this 'political' world is the one thing that we do know is real about it. To that extent one might perhaps say that the experience of the song is about feeling this experience and is therefore as much aesthetic as it is political in the usual sense. At any rate the representation is of the world as feeling unfeeling, as a loveless, valueless, uncomprehending, material jungle where the enclosure, isolation, expropriation and harassment of the individual seem almost to preclude the possibility of the political as a mode of analysis let alone as one of willed agency or redress. Perhaps this is one reason why the song is so unloved or else neglected even by those of Dylan's critics who one might expect to treat it. It deserves more attention in these terms, even if no others, as a definition of what the political had apparently come to mean in the contemporary world of the 1980s and 1990s: an experience of inhumanity characterised by the pervasive diseases of disempowerment and denial.

In this song at least, the alternative aspects of the common-sense political reading of Dylan I sketched at the start are not as incompatible as they may at first seem. We are, perhaps, reminded by it that any cultural or aesthetic product must typically make a variety of kinds of appeal of which a subtle or complex rather than a simple political message is likely to be the result. In my previous writing on Dylan, for example, I may have sensed the political in the work without directly naming or addressing it. Indeed, it may be this very reluctance to name it that enabled me to explore ways in which the love lyrics may be said to voice a distinctively masculine kind of emotional vulnerability at a time of social change and also to attempt to articulate the vision of a symbolic contemporary American *polis*, part-political, part-mental state, which Dylan's naming and sense of place might be said to chart (Brown 1990, 2002).

Yet the question of the political as such is always also resurfacing as 'another side' of the work, a quasi-ethical obligation which it seems to place upon its audience. It's an element that, we may feel, *deserves* more direct treatment and sometimes gets it, for example, in Marqusee's recent, well-researched historical study of Dylan in his 1960s political contexts, *Chimes of Freedom: The Politics of Bob Dylan's Art* (2003). For Marqusee, the context of Dylan's emergence and the continuing contexts of his performances are important aspects of what defines the political nature of his art: from the political marches and organisations of the American 1960s protest movement to the gesture of singing 'Masters of War' in the wake of 11 September 2001. In such arguments Dylan is the American 1960s protest movement and the story of his alignment and misalignment with a more or less organised and consensual political group in America is the true story of his artistic development. Not much from the later work (with the notable exception of 'Blind Willie McTell') gets much crediting and it is especially inspiring and committing to this reading to place 'Chimes of Freedom' (*Another Side of Bob Dylan*, 1964) in the centre of the Dylan canon. Here, as Marqusee's reading usefully demonstrates, Dylan reads out of the symbolic anger of a sudden thunderstorm a cast-list of the underdogs and the dispossessed of modern urban society that sketch out an ideologically undefined but nevertheless identifiable constituency of social exclusion and injustice. The song lists socially marginalised characters whose characteristic plights or positions are mixed, awkward and even somewhat contradictory, disruptive not only of orthodoxy and authority, but also of social or ideological boundaries that might locate their place of resistance. They are all, perhaps, definable as opposites to an ideal of freedom that the song's title suggests. Yet rarely in Dylan's works does a cast of characters so coalesce into a recognisably political constituency as it does here and, at least in retrospect, there also seems something quite elegaic or nostalgic in the song that may emerge from its sense of politics as well as it does from the slow waltz of its music and from the distinctive and emotional American image of its title.

The characters in 'Chimes of Freedom' are called into being through labels for their social roles rather than by their proper names that, as Danny Karlin has suggested, form such an intriguing part of Dylan's linguistic adventurousness (Karlin 2003). We might contrast them, then, with the much larger but much more diffuse and polyvalent concatenation of disembodied ghosts (who are sometimes real people, but are also often apparently called into being merely by the surreal weirdness of their names) that he was to dream up in his novel *Tarantula* a couple of years later. The characters in the novel are at once more personal to the writer and more estranged from him, at once more individual in themselves and yet more abstracted and yet they are equally, if not more distinctively Dylanesque. In fact, they can shadow Dylan-the-writer himself, voicing his anger at the ignorance of his critics, as Christopher Ricks shows in his use of the passage about the butter sculptor 'Snowplow the Floater', who rails against the critics of his work in a passage from chapter 39 of that book in his study *Dylan's Visions of Sin* (Ricks 2003). But they don't easily add up to a constituency in the political sense that the characters of 'Chimes of Freedom' might, and, to take account of this difference, a more complex sense of the category of the political in the work, or of the relation of the work to the category of the political, one which is more representative of the work in all its diversities, is no doubt required.

## The Critique of Judgement

I want to argue here that one might seek to find that more complex and universally engaging sense of the political in the expression of the feeling of injustice and indeed what one might call the critique of judgement itself that the experience of the world and of the characters in it that recurs in Dylan's writing so commonly demonstrates.

For a critic like Marqusee, it might be said, the category of the political functions as a principle of discursive economy, allowing him to give special weight to some kinds of meaning over others and to give a welcome and serious clarity to his reading of the songs — a sense of meaning and priority to what he says about them in the terms of reference which he brings to them.

This is nowhere more evident than in his reading of the song that is one of Dylan's most powerful protest songs of the 1960s, a political song in the sense that it most powerfully defines a sense of injustice and one of Dylan's songs that has been most rewarding to criticism: 'The Lonesome Death of Hattie Carroll' (*The Times They Are A-Changin'*, 1964).

Marqusee's reading of the song depends throughout upon an informed sense of its context in a reconstructed history that surrounds it. His account (though he says of the song 'we don't need to know anything more than we are told') offers in fact a good deal more, constructing a contextual metanarrative that begins with the Washington protest march of August 1963 and the reactionary racist bombing of a black church in Birmingham three weeks later, in relation to which Dylan's song, recorded on 23 October of that year, becomes a kind of flashback to a single representative incident that had taken place during the previous February. Marqusee compares the song to what 'actually happened' according to the contemporary newspaper report. He's not entirely insensitive to the song's 'literary' form or technique or to its generic placing, invoking as his main intertextual referent the folk ballad 'Mary Hamilton'. He runs through the narrative sequentially, verse-by-verse, in about 500 words, commenting concisely on things like its rhymes, glossing some of its distinctive word usages and pointing to aspects of what it says as opposed to what it doesn't say, and hinting at the theatricality of its 'last act', though making silence seem like omission on Dylan's part and failing perhaps to suggest the extent to which, for instance, in its refusal to name race, class, age and gender as such, there may be aspects of one of the song's most clearly Brechtian, and therefore also most politically theatrical, of strategies.

It is most important for Marqusee to prioritise the link between language and reference to its context outside and beyond the language used in the song itself. He tells us, for instance, that the 'real' Zanzinger was really called Zantzinger and uses this version of the name throughout his discussion of the song, which reaches its goal when the conclusion to his reading becomes about the real Zantzinger himself (who he was and what has happened to him since the song) rather than, for instance, offering a statement about Dylan's naming of him as Zanzinger, or a generalisation about literary language, or even the subsequent history of the opponents of racism (Marqusee 2003: 78–84).

Christopher Ricks, on the other hand, *in Dylan's Visions of Sin*, demonstrates a rather different sense of discursive economy. Whereas the song itself is some 400 words in length, Ricks, in an extraordinary and exhausting *tour-de-force* of detailed textual scrutiny, provides more than ten times that number of words in his sustained reading (and almost as many more elsewhere in the book), only a few of which point outside the song to its historical or political contexts at all. Though he says of the song that it is Dylan's 'most political song in that everything in it is under the aspect of politics' (Ricks 2003: 221–33), it seems perhaps more accurately to represent for him no more nor less than a kind of lyrical omniscience and perfection. Ricks is consequently a scourge of misplaced contextualisation, castigating Alex Ross for mentioning the possibility that the waltz tempo of the music may re-enforce the sense of social exclusion in the song by alluding to the fact that the Baltimore hotel society gathering to which it refers may have been a Spinsters' Ball (Ricks 2003:15–18). Even the music of the performance is outside Ricks's sphere of apparently legitimated interest: there's so much for him to say about the nuance of sound and rhythm in the words themselves, not least in the by now well-known revelation of the extraordinary way that the biblical subtext of the Cain and Abel story haunts the song's emphatic rhyming structures with an ineluctable ethical eschatology. One cannot but join with him in his amazement at and ability to articulate the way in which the song's rhymes and repetitions and its sustained contrasts and correspondences between Hattie Carroll the poor black woman victim and Zanzinger her killer are articulated through, for instance, a stunning contrast between the moral and social hierarchy in the song implied in the contrast between moral and social meanings in the word 'gentle' and the powerfully egalitarian politics implied in the idea of the two characters being 'on a whole other level' from each other, and of the fact that the courtroom should be 'on the level' but is not—re-enforced by the fact that this pun itself operates within an American beat vernacular rather than a more official register of the word 'level'. One could say that there is a great deal that is said about the politics of Dylan's art and about the art of the politics in such relentless attention to the words of the song. Ricks also gives much attention to the idea of justice in the song, seeing it as both a criticism of the particular judge and an expression of justice as an absolute ethical ideal.

Ricks sees the racial politics in the song's use of the doubled negative ('never done nothin') in black American English rather than in the context of a protest movement external to it. He glosses the crime and its real-life perpetrator with the 't', but chooses rather to play with the naming that is there in the song itself. For him Zanzinger is a significant version of the name because it somehow includes the letters of the word anger in sequence within it. Of course, it's not impossible to make fun of Ricks's extreme enthusiasm for the nuance of potential meaning in this way and of the way in which his reading of the song comes to its own telling mode of closure. The name may also, for example, be said to contain, by anagram and English and romance-language sound-sense, such elements as *'San'*, 'sin' and 'singer' (holy sin singer?), and *'sans'* and 'sense' and 'range' not to mention 'ringz', 'rage', 'raze' or inverted 'reazzin' (though it would probably be uneconomical of me to point that out). He concludes by saying that the song 'shows something perfect everywhere' — a statement that can seem an absurd over-justification of Dylan's obvious and delightful beat casualness and spontaneity. It is almost as evasive as it is circular and self-justifying when it is taken out of context in this way and it certainly loses political agency by offering an universalising *carte blanche* (Ricks 2003: 233). Similarly, his ethicalising of the idea of justice seems to take political force from the critique of the justice system as a particular social practice that may be complicit with corruption in a variety of very specific ways.

It may, no doubt, be easier to be clear about how the category of the political operates in Marqusee and Ricks than to be precise, still less original, about what the political is or how it works in the song itself. But clearly one way of glossing this is to point to connections between the senses of criminal and political or social justice that the song so powerfully underscores as it shifts the attention from Zanzinger to the justice system that sentences him at the close and to the way in which the song's searingly direct address to its audience attacks not just those who administer corrupt or false justice but also those who 'philosophise disgrace'. To 'philosophise', it would seem here, is not to seek truth but to rationalize, justify or explain away, to miss the ideal human obligation to feel an emotional response to such a sense of outrage. So the song adds to its devastating condemnation of the crime of racial killing and of the criminal who perpetrates it and to its swingeing critique of judge and criminal justice and social system, an uncompromising exposure of the issues of race, class, age and gender and an overwhelming assault on the intellectual complacency to which its audience might be subject were they not to respond to it in this way. It is an aesthetic response that is demanded of us—one of feeling as opposed to judgement—or perhaps more precisely one of aesthetic judgement as opposed to rational judgement—that the suspended transformation of the repeated refrain of the song until its conclusion surely implies. This is profoundly poetic in that it implies that such a truth of feeling is more unerringly accurate in its politics and ethics than a false or self-justifying kind of philosophy could ever be. Marqusee may, then, be wrong to imply that the politics are to be found somewhere outside the text in something called history; and Ricks is also off the mark in offering too immaterial or a-politically transcendental a sense of where the ethical absolute of justice may be said to be located and in saying that everything in the text sits under the political when, in a way, the political effect of Dylan's song may be to re-enforce the extent to which the political is to be located not above but within such poetic feeling as the text can produce.

Now, the differences between Dylan's critique of judgement and *The Critique of Judgment* that is the third of the philosophic critiques of the eighteenth-century German philosopher Immanuel Kant may at first sight be too great and too many for them to be compared or even very productively juxtaposed here. For one thing, a 'critique', in the Kantian sense, is a thorough intellectual review of an area of knowledge and does not necessarily imply the alternative radical stance that we might associate with the more contemporary use of the word or the alternative critical pose of a Bob Dylan. For another, the Kantian notion of judgement (approachable through the German term *Urteilskraft*) consists more in the matter of fitting things to their proper categories (or of seeing things through the necessary categories attendant on the act of rational cognition) than it does in the conventional contemporary sense of a socially sanctioned exercise of morally evaluative and punitive authority of the kind that Dylan's lyrics here criticise.

On the other hand, if judgement is to be understood as the faculty which mediates between pure and practical forms of reason, as it is in Kant, between the categories and what it is they may be said to categorise, then there is perhaps a connection with the anger at those who 'philosophise' and the questioning of and resistance to categorisation that we can find in Dylan's lyrics. Moreover in Kant's sense that in the judgement of the aesthetic and the sublime we can observe the workings of the faculty of judgement in its purest form, we may intuit a correspondence with the critique of the compromised or limited nature of the judicial by means of the prioritisation of the aesthetic that we may find at the root of the sense of the political in this song and this is Kantian or post-Kantian, not least in that the very foundations of rationality are called into question by its operation.

In some ways, furthermore, the displacement of the legal by the aesthetic may call to mind a significant characteristic of literature itself as a category which has been highlighted by Jacques Derrida in his essay on Kafka's short story 'Before the Law'. According to Derrida, it is of the very essence of the law that makes something literature that each act of literature is to be seen as a unique event whose impact conforms to a law of nonconformity (Derrida 1979, in Attridge 1992). To that extent we may record that the special impact of the song is not just that it is aesthetic or that its aesthetic is suddenly political, so much as that both its aesthetic quality and its being political in precisely the way that it is make it distinctive enough to be characteristic of Dylan's work as a whole.

## Thinking About the Law

On a simpler level, aspects of this complex intellectual shift by which Dylan prioritises the aesthetic over the judicial in his radical political sense can be seen in the consistent ways in which the songs hold up, demystify, stigmatise or even make fun of judges and the judiciary; another may be the sense in which he repeatedly re-enforces the claim of the outlaw or socially marginal to experience an unmediated access to the kinds of ethical absolute or ideal that is denied to those in power. A further ramification of this may be seen in the way that Dylan's political discourse appeals to a generalised sense of injustice that is very closely connected to the personal feelings of injustice which the lover-persona voices in the love songs which keep pace in number with the political ones during the 1960s and after.

Dylan's songs of the 1960s frequently re-enact a sense of political protest and outrage that is based on opposition between the representatives of justice and the outcast. This can foreground questions of racial inequality ('Oxford Town' or 'Hollis Brown') or religious complacency ('With God on our Side') or the worker's sense of exploitation by the employer ('Maggie's Farm') or the ways in which an individual can be the victim of a system for which nobody admits responsibility ('Who Killed Davy Moore?'). Occasionally, in a way that can suggest a mixture of the idiom of the American blues and the characters of the Western, Dylan may choose to identify specifically with the figure of the 'outlaw'. In 'Outlaw Blues' this is extended so that the figure in question is Dylan's Chaplinesque, comic-surreal urban misfit persona, who is neither an outlaw in any legal sense nor especially comes into conflict with figures of authority as such. Dylan's songs of the mid-1960s explore such paradoxes of the alternative culture and include such great 'outsider' songs as 'Desolation Row' or *Highway 61 Revisited* and 'Gates of Eden' or *Bringing it All Back Home,* whose complex language and imagery do much to invoke the experience of this condition as well as to define and legitimate it. In the later developments of the outlaw idea we have the songs about Lenny Bruce and Rubin Carter, who aren't outlaws in the usual senses, as well as 'Joey', a song about someone who was.

An appeal to freedom chimes through these songs and in such attempts to explore or define aspects of freedom as may be found in the comic surreal narratives 'I Shall Be Free No. 10' and 'Motorpsycho Nightmare'.

The writings are full of memorable references to law, rules, crime and to the criminal. Their characteristic accumulation of judges and juries and the outlaws they attempt to constrain is often reminiscent of an American Western narrative, not least in that the frontiers of sympathy are consistently shifting and being redrawn between them. We might say, in effect, that the representation of law and judgement particularly becomes an aspect of Dylan's radical politics when his sympathies are made to sit strongly with the outlaw and against the judge.

So we have the 'false-hearted judges' who are 'dying in the webs that they spin' in 'Jokerman' *(Infidels,* 1983) and the judge in 'Hattie Carroll' and the one in 'Seven Curses' (who like Angelo, the deputy in Shakespeare's *Measure for Measure,* seeks to exploit his power for sexual victimisation). The judge in 'Hurricane' (whose authority is contemptuously dismissed as that of 'some fool's hand') and whoever it is that puts wisdom in jail in 'Political World' are of a piece in being the objects of Dylan's political anger. There are also songs where the fragility of the position from which the singer makes his critique of judgement is more strongly felt, such as 'Percy's Song', where the intractable power of the judge and the surreal arbitrariness of his 99-year sentence on the singer's friend for whom he pleads is greeted only by the singer's sense of defeat and, in a song of 'turning', defines the aesthetic response of his 'turn' away from the courtroom and towards playing the guitar. Then there is 'Bob Dylan's Blues' where the political example set by the comic drop-out protagonist consists in asking his audience to rob banks and then to 'tell the judge I said it was alright'. The judge in these songs is frequently a fallible individual whose only power is his office, and the arbitrariness of his individual authority is contrasted with that of the disempowered individual that he may judge or sentence. There's a black humour in the arbitrary acts of sentencing in the traditional song 'Delia' which he recast in 'Joey'. There's also a surreal and satirical comedy in his drama-tisation of the endless struggle between the law and the outlaw. I've tried to argue that a song like 'Tombstone Blues' offers a sense of Dylan's symbolic America as a kind of frontier town torn between law and lawlessness and this may be as relevant to the experience of law in the postmodern world as it is to the formative wildernesses of the modern nation during the twentieth century (Brown 2003). One might add that the two alternative directions named in Dylan's symbolic geography in the song 'Senor' are Lincoln County Road (Lincoln County, New Mexico was the home of Billy the Kid) and Arma-geddon, suggesting a place that is symbolically caught between law and lawlessness yet still presided over by a transcendental doomy eschatology.

In these songs Dylan shows justice as a social practice rather than as an ethical ideal, one that is quite strongly inflected by an American linguistic idiom and by a sense of the American history and mythology of the frontier. It is, then, no surprise to find that one of Dylan's most intriguing vehicles for thinking about the law should be a comic-surreal-Western-theatre-crime-narrative song like 'Lily, Rosemary and the Jack of Hearts' (*Blood on the Tracks*, 1974).

This is one of Dylan's liveliest narrative songs, a chaotic and opaque story that begins with the arrival in the town cabaret at the end of a festival of a mysterious outsider who, with a touch of Lewis Carroll, is partly an outlaw character and partly the playing card, the Jack of Hearts. His rival, Big Jim, owns the town's diamond mine and also, apparently, both of the two women of the song, Lily and Rosemary (Lily has his ring, Rosemary plays the role of his wife) though not very secretly they both prefer Jack. Like Zanzinger, Jim has a cane. There's a poker game in progress on all kinds of lit-eral and symbolic levels (the King of Diamonds, two Queens and a Jack?). All is dark and mysterious and the backstage manager of the cabaret has a walk-on part to explain that 'there's something funny going on'. Both Jack and Lily and Jack and Jim seem to have a 'past'. Jack and Lily take off to a back room together. (Could it be Jack himself, or a surreal intruder who is the mysterious actor dressed as a monk?). Jim bursts in with possibly murderous or at least vengeful intent (we can't be sure whose cold revolver it is that clicks) but he ends up being stabbed in the back (presumably by Rosemary who goes to the gallows calmly) whilst we discover that the whole event has apparently been a distraction perpetrated by Jack while his accomplices rob the bank next door. Lily is left alone at the end of the song 'thinkin' about the law', leaving us to ask what kind of law it is that she is thinking about.

The song gives us another judge who personifies this idea of law to some extent. He's a 'hangin' judge' (who dispenses an ultimate pre-set punishment rather than one that fits the crime). He arrives at the cabaret to be wined and dined so that when he is needed to enforce the rule of law he is too drunk to act and doesn't seem likely, willing or able to investigate or intervene in any of the actions the song describes. On the other hand, when it comes round to 'hangin' day', he is sober and therefore apparently all too ready to punish Rosemary, especially since she is present on the gallows and 'the only person on the scene missin' was the Jack of Hearts'. Such law is arbitrary and yet insistent, both too capricious and too pedestrian in its working and it seems inevitably to miss the main event. No less than in 'Political World', life is seen as a poker game where you can, as with the elements in this story, draw different combinations of cards; though the game is arbitrary it is not fair since the card game is played with a 'stacked deck'. It's a world where brute bullying power is in seemingly unassailable control ('This world is ruled by violence', as Dylan says in 'Union Sundown'), but where everyone has their real sympathies with the quick-witted underdog who can often win against the odds, despite everything after all. Jack is another kind of 'Jokerman' for whom the law is that there is only an archaic retributive system or else no law at all, for whom:

> ... the book of Leviticus and Deuteronomy,
> The law of the jungle and the sea are your only teachers
> (Infidels, 1983).

Since the judge leaves before the end, the song's final judgement seems left to Lily who makes a judgement that reflects a truth of the heart as much as a truth of abstract morality.

### 'To Live Outside the Law you Must be Honest'

The judge in 'Most Likely You Go Your Way (and I'll Go Mine)' isn't an objective one either. On the contrary, his judgement emerges from the rule of rhyme as much as from that of reason and what he voices may be said to emerge more from a one-sided kind of resentment than it does from a position of balance or objectivity. In this song, as elsewhere with Dylan's thoroughly unidealised notion of judgement, 'The judge, he holds a grudge'. Law is not so much an enduring category as it is a series of disconnected events. The song is, moreover, not directly about judgement or about politics in themselves, but is rather one of the love songs on *Blonde on Blonde* (1965) in which Dylan's lover-persona seems as often to voice the resentments of breaking up as the joys of affection between lovers. The lovers are parting and inevitably there seems to be a wrangle about who is to blame, who is leaving whom, who has 'fallen' and 'who's been left behind' and the 'judge' is a biased one invoked by the lover's resentment, one who is programmatically dysfunctional, but none the less dangerous for that:

> ... he's badly built
> And he walks on stilts,
> Watch out he don't fall on you.

The mixed image suggests some kind of carnival or clown performer but also perhaps the doomy retribution of the statue that falls on the guilty lover in the story of Don Juan and especially the *Don Giovanni* version of it.

Whether about parting or being together, Dylan's love songs are, perhaps, especially romantic in that they typically depend on a kind of confederacy between the lovers whose affection is perceived as all the more intense and true because it is unique to them and beyond social convention or sanction. In this way they are frequently political in the sense of voicing injustice and offering a critique of judgement that I have tried to outline here. The 'love' in 'Love Minus Zero/No Limit' 'knows too much to argue or to judge'. Elsewhere, lovers are conceived as outlaws and the contractual nature of their loving tryst depends to some extent on their outlaw condition, just as the 'truth' of the outlaw or the outsider in the more explicitly political songs seems to be inevitably posited upon their being 'outside'. This paradox is voiced perhaps most strongly as a statement with paradoxical ethical-political implications in the unforgettable aphorism that 'to live outside the law you must be honest' from 'Absolutely Sweet Marie' on *Blonde on Blonde* (1965).

It is, no doubt, quite hard enough to define the law without trying to define the human condition as being outside of it and then working to legitimate that condition and yet, in as much as that is a political position, it may be approached as one that has been recently defined in the postmodern *Ethics* of Alain Badiou. According to Badiou, since knowledge systems are already bound up and determined by systems of power, the subject only has access to the possibility of truth or change by means of an 'event' that both circumscribes and evades these structures of power, by an act of extreme self-separation from the norm. Such an event of truth he defines as the only kind of good. However, it is also an 'event' whose reality must be shared and confirmed by its participants and one that only becomes true or retains the character of truth by virtue of a process of a continuing fidelity to it on the part of those participants, just as the continued agreement and fidelity between lovers may be what confirms their love as love. For Badiou, ethics is a wide realm to do with our being in the world, our perceived relation to what is going on, a political realm, in effect. Ethics is not to be understood by appeal to abstract categories such as the human or human rights, but rather by the way in which the subject relates to 'situations', both of which terms are to be understood, according to the postmodern paradigm, as to some extent discontinuous and unique to themselves. Likewise communities are characterised only by their continuing to be together; to name them and define them would be what Badiou calls an 'evil'. Antigone (who refuses to conform to the law and morality of her uncle and king, Creon, and the state in which she lives in order to respect the higher moral law that her brother should be honorably buried) is a representative figure for this kind of ethics of subject, situation and persistence. Hamlet's alienation from the norms of rationality that surround him in order to 'remember' the ghost of his father may be another useful paradigm.

Badiou's English translator, Peter Hallward, usefully identifies the extent to which this thinking depends upon a Kantian notion of the separation of true acts of judgement from those that are contingent on circumstances, but also constitutes a radical break with the Kantian ethical imperative that 'I ought never to act except in such a way that I could also will that my maxim should become a universal law', inasmuch as each ethical truth event is of its nature unique to its situation. He also explains some ways in which Badiou's notions of the subject build on and from those of Jacques Lacan and Slavoj Zizeck and that his ethic of truths and events is to some extent both engaged with and to be radically distinguished from a Levinasian ethic based on notions of the other and of difference (Hallward, in Badou 2002: xx, xxv-vi).

It seems especially appropriate, then, that the song in which this decisive Dylan line appears is not a song of the political outsider or any kind of crime, outlaw or Western frontier story so much as a resentful and frustrated love song, which wittily complains about the failure of the beloved to honour, respect or reciprocate the intimate and personal trust that is associated with love—even in the context of a fleeting love affair.

The 'absolutely sweet' Marie of the song is anything but absolutely sweet. In fact (judged from the perspective of the extreme emotional need of the lover's love), she is a classic bitch who keeps him waiting and is always promising things she doesn't deliver. The lover conceives of himself as being locked out of her affections (by her 'railroad gate' or outside her house and 'can't unlock it'), but he is also locked inside the condition of being a lover, like a criminal, in 'jail' and in a 'penitentiary' and this condition is 'hard' in at least two of the more obvious senses of the word. The implication would be that he has engaged in some moral or social transgression (made himself an 'outlaw') for her, but that she has not been prepared to join him in the way that their transgressive pact had promised, one that ultimately might legitimate as well as gratify them both by mutual confirmation. Rather than join him in the jail of both their making, she has abandoned him, taken off somewhere else. Whether this is to another 'illegitimate' desiring liaison or to some supposedly legitimate act that is still a betrayal of their affection is not clear. He can only ask, rather accusingly, 'Where are you tonight?'.

Dylan's songs contain such complaints about ungenerous or neglectful women from Jesse Fuller's funny blues grouse 'You're No Good' — the very the first track on Dylan's first album — right up to songs like 'Honest With Me' and 'Sugar Baby' on *Love and Theft* (the first album of the new millennium). Dylan's ability to capture a lover's sense of being slighted or of emotional injustice is acute and can be powerfully articulated through the surreal estranged idiom of the beat or deadbeat poet of social disadvantage, or else through the blues of the racially marginalised and emotionally neglected man. It was not just the one-man-band style of playing harmonica on a neck-brace that (as Shelton records) he learned from the black San Francisco blues performer, but also a distinctive mixture of the melancholic and the comic-satiric-surreal that applies particularly to a sense of gender relations and is reanimated by the hints of cultural difference in the norms of gender relations implied by Fuller's African-American roots. A comic picture of a woman's cruelty to her lover is the result, but then so is the broader political inflection of some of these love songs.

A character called Marie also occurs as one of the most frequently appearing figures in Tarantula. She is a Spanish-speaking Mexican girl whom we see first, like Cleopatra, on a barge associated with a variety of Madonnas and *prima donnas*, then see as an emotionally demanding 'Unpublished Maria' and as a destructive 'Maria Nowhere'. She seems to be a desired but profoundly demanding and infuriating lover to whom a character called 'water boy' eventually addresses a 'last letter'. Law and legality sometimes surround her or the address to her in the book (such as in the letter written by 'The Law' to someone called 'Mervin' in the 'Hopeless and Maria Nowhere' section and the demand for a lawyer in the letter from 'Froggy' completes the 'Paradise, Skid Row & Maria Briefly' section of the novel), (Dylan 1972, 27–8, 32–3, 46–8, 59–61, 78–9, 115–17).

The refrain from 'Absolutely Sweet Marie' recurs over a decade later in Dylan's work in 'Where Are You Tonight? (Journey Through Dark Heat)', the most intense of the songs on *Street Legal*, which Dylan produced at the end of the 1970s and on the eve of his conversion to evangelical Christianity—a song Shelton describes as a work of triumph over suspicion through faith, though its ending (suspended between the euphoric 'I can't believe I'm alive' and the more melancholic 'without you it just doesn't seem right') may be a good deal more ambiguous. The song is also one of lovers' separation, more deeply painful than touched with the kind of blues comedy that we find in the earlier song. There's been a separation, though not quite the same sense of the lovers being outlaws and the separation being a betrayal of their outlaw confederacy. Law and legality are also of course a key issue on this album and in this song. The title of the album (indicating the minimum standard required by a racing car or motorcycle in order for it to be usable on the road) seems to connect, albeit indirectly, to the woman's father's warning that the lover will need to be 'more than street-wise' to live with her and perhaps also to the sense that the lover-persona is back, as it were, out of the domestic idyll and on the street which has its own laws and where he is victim to 'horseplay and disease', whilst the law, neglectful this time rather than over-intrusive, 'looks the other way'.

More than the invocation of a judge who can offer redress for the lover's sense of being slighted or ignored and more than the outsider's perennial complaint about the law, the song suggests a profound sense of instability in the border-lines between the legitimate and the illegitimate, the moral and the immoral, that might make up the kind of alternative society that many people — in fact, almost all young people in the 1960s — were trying to establish or explore that has turned, in so many ways, into the accepted norm of the more mixed and plural society of our time. To investigate the love songs in these terms may be to help us register the emotional or aesthetic character of Dylan's ethics and politics and may also be to help us get beyond the narrowness of their reference as love songs in some ways.

## Ethical Absolutes and Confederacy

In Dylan's February 2003 song 'Cross the Green Mountain' (contributed to the soundtrack of the American Civil War historical film *Gods and Generals*) we find a song that is, as I see it, partly written in character through the persona of a dying Confederate soldier, though no doubt is also partly readable as an apologia for Dylan himself. He sings in his own defence:

> Let 'em say that I walked in fair nature's light
> And that I was loyal to truth and to right.

Now, this is a huge claim even for a dying soldier to make of himself, let alone a distinctively evasive contemporary popular musical performer, and yet it is an appeal that anyone may want to make on his own behalf and it does pose a question and a challenge to the critic which sits beneath this question of the political in this quasi-ethical sense, and that is to ask in what ways we can claim to have said something like this of his work or in what ways could we say that this was true of it in some way? In its Civil War context the song may especially present itself as an expression of the heartlands that are the American South and of the deep ideological fissures that American Civil War history must inevitably attempt to revisit. Its double pull consists in that the appeal of the underdog or of the defeated underscores our sympathy for the plight of the Confederate soldier and his loyal attachment to the losing side must be respected, perhaps revered as a prototype of American loyalty to home and to value and to territory. On the other hand, one asks, how could the confederate soldier stand for these things when he fights an appropriately doomed cause on behalf of, amongst other things, a social system based on slavery?

This is a question that Dylan, in his voicing of the plight of the 'underdog soldier' of 'Chimes of Freedom' along with his powerful credentials as a voice for the exposure of the American racism against which the Civil Rights Movement took up arms in the 1960s, may be especially qualified to ask. And he answers it in the song through an appeal not just to such unmediated ethical absolutes such as 'truth' and 'right', but also to the loyalty that at least according to Badiou could define them as such. There is much in the song that would invite us to transcend the immediate historical or ideological context in a way that may often be invoked in the discourse of the elegy. The inevitable tarnishing of the ideals of truth and right in their context arguably only adds depth to the elegiac feeling here. At any rate the positive ethical implications of the confederacy or loyalty itself may perhaps partly even overcome the negative ethics of what the confederate may be said to be confederate to.

Throughout Dylan's work ethical absolutes are invoked with a boldness that is rare, especially in the lyrics of popular music, though that sits alongside a profound instability of all such absolutes in his work. I have tried to argue here that what legitimates his claim to them and makes his encounter with the ethical into a political thing is often the sense that it is only through the experience of the outlaw or the social outsider that access to such truths can be had and it is the confederacy of such outsiders and both his and their remarkable persistence, their determination to go on, that confirms this as a kind of truth.

At any rate the 'political' in Dylan's work is not to be easily recuperated or named and reclaimed by ideology

without doing violence to the very questionings and insta-
bilities that may be thought to make it political in the first
place. Alongside the many songs in which Dylan's voice is
obviously political it would seem especially appropriate to
register the extent to which that political sense emerges
from a sustained enquiry into law and legitimation, one that
is conducted through numerous judges and judgements in
particular and that amounts to a critique of judgement
itself. And we can note the extent to which this complex feeling of injustice is parallel in his work to the feelings of injustice there might be between lovers in conflict with each
other or in a position of romantic confederacy against the
world.

The old question of whether Dylan is a poet or not may
find a different kind of answer through this approach, since
it reveals the extent to which the senses of justice and of the
political are linked to the sense of the aesthetic in his work.
And if since Plato's *Republic* the poet has been exiled to the
margins of political community because his discourse is
'untrue', Dylan responds by constructing a poetic discourse
in which truth can be perceived only by one exiled from a
necessarily corrupted and untruthful community.

That is to leave aside or unanswer the other question of
whether the political is a category—even when stretched
and distorted by its several multidisciplinary contemporary agendas—that is, a category large enough for all the
complexities of Dylan's lyric discourse to fit into. We might
rather say that the category of the political is an enabling
and even necessary one, but hardly a sufficient category for
the fully nuanced explanation of the aesthetic potential of
these songs, whose politics consists in that their impact is
ethical and aesthetic after all. On the other hand, the political may be said to occur in them precisely when the legal
and ethical come into conflict in their aesthetic impact, and
that may be when the aesthetic becomes most truly itself, in
its most potent form.

# References

Badiou, Alain (2002) *Ethics: An Essay on the Understanding of Evil,* trans, and intro. Peter Hallward. London and New York: Verso.

Brown, Richard (1990) '"I Want You": Enigma and Kerygma in the Love Lyrics of Bob Dylan', in Ann Massa (ed.) *American Declarations of Love.* Basingstoke: Macmillan.

Brown, Richard (2003) 'Highway 61 and Other American States of Mind', in Neil Corcoran (ed.) *'Do You Mr Jones': Bob Dylan with the Poets and Professor.* London: Pimlico.

Browning, Gary K., this volume, chapter 6. Day, Aidan (1988) *fokerman: Reading the Lyrics of Bob Dylan.* Oxford: Basil Blackwell.

Derrida, Jacques (1979) 'Before the Law', in *Acts of Literature,* ed. Derek Attridge. New York: Routledge, 1992.

Dylan, Bob (1972) *Tarantula,* London: Granada.

Jameson, Fredric (1992) *Postmodernism, Or the Cultural Logic of Late Capitalism.* Durham, NC: Duke University Press.

Kant, Immanuel (1952) *The Critique of Judgement,* trans. James Creed Meredith. Oxford: Clarendon Press.

Karlin, Daniel (2003) In Neil Corcoran (ed.) *'Do You Mr. Jones': Bob Dylan with the Poets and Professors.* London: Pimlico.

Lyotard, Jean-Francois (1986) *The Postmodern Condition: A Report of Knowledge.* Manchester: Manchester University Press.

Marqusee, Mike (2003) *Chimes of Freedom:The Politics of Bob Dylan's Art.* New York: The New Press.

Ricks, Christopher 2003. *Dylan's Visions of Sin.* New York and London: Viking Penguin.

Shelton, Robert (1987) *No Direction Home: The Life and Music of Bob Dylan.* London: Penguin Books.

Michael Jones

# Judas and the Many 'Betrayals' of Bob Dylan

In 1998 I heard Bob Dylan's 1966 'Royal Albert Hall' concert
for the first time. Released by Sony as 'Volume 4' of the
'Bootleg Series', I found the entire performance both affecting and disturbing. For some reason I had never heard the
actual 'bootleg' recording of this performance — though, of
course, I had heard and read references to it for almost 30
years before its eventual 'official' release. We know now, as
many have always known, that the 'Albert Hall' show was
in fact a recording of a performance at the Manchester Free
Trade Hall on 17 May 1966, several days before Dylan's UK
tour ended with two London appearances. Further, we
recognise this as one of the most notorious performances in
Dylan's career because this was the night that one of his
abusers was captured on tape issuing perhaps the worst
insult of all: 'Judas!'.

Abuse of Dylan during live performance had begun the
previous year. Again, the story is a familiar one: at the 1965
Newport Folk Festival Dylan is reported to have outraged
the 'folk music' community by playing a handful of songs
on electric guitar accompanied by a conventional 'rock'
line-up of bass, drums and keyboards. From that point
onwards — until his disappearance from public view following a motorcycle crash in 1966 — Dylan's performances
were organised as two 'sets', which took the form of a solo,

acoustic rendition of fairly recent material followed after an interval by his taking the stage with an electric band with whom he played a mixture of new material and radically rearranged versions of older songs. At each performance and incessantly — city-by-city, country-by-country — 'Newport' was reprised: some audience members loudly booed him, others clapped enthusiastically, while still others (probably the majority) judged the shows on their merits and perhaps remained bewildered by the tensions surrounding them.

If the 'Albert Hall' performance is 'notorious', then, it is so in part because of the vehemence of the reaction of a proportion of the audience at that particular event (distilled in the infamous 'Judas!') but it is 'notorious' also because of what the recording captures and has preserved. As the near-final date of his first 'world tour', what the 'bootleg' conveys so graphically is the scale of the anger Dylan had provoked in a considerable number of his supporters and the degree of polarisation he engendered within his audience *as a whole* by his conscious and substantially public break with his former incarnation. He had been until this time — and by a very great distance — the leading songwriter and singer of not just the 'folk revival', but of the more diffuse 'protest movement'. It seems impossible now to imagine a singer who could fill large auditoriums internationally, yet sell tickets to people who came to denounce him. Further, it seems impossible to imagine a music performance at which so much would appear to be at stake. For example, Eminem is a controversial writer and performer but his gigs have never been the battlegrounds that Bob Dylan's were in 1965 and 1966; that they were has continued to lend Dylan a popular cultural status decades later.

As a 'Dylan fan' in those years I was too young to appreciate the significance of the stages in his self-development as a singer and as a writer: I saw, for example, no conflict between 'The Times They are A-Changin' and 'Positively 4th Street'. There were no 'different' Dylans for me. Consequently I could not then have conceived of him as a betrayer; quite simply, I lacked the cultural context and the degree of personal investment in a version of 'Bob Dylan' for any song in his recorded and publicly available reper- toire to offend me in any way. This is not to make some pious point; rather, it is to comment on how, in the days before instantaneous and 'global' mass communication, cultural distances were often far greater than physical ones: my 'Bob Dylan' was a composite of disparate, dislocated and discontinuous 'facts', images and opinion. I relied for information on him as did, I am sure, the vast majority of my peers, through occasional radio plays of his material (mostly on Radio Luxemburg and pirate radio stations), on snippets in the mainstream music press, and on the good offices of friends and acquaintances who might be cajoled to lend you a Dylan album for a brief period. All the possible responses to new information of whatever kind would be rehashed and worried at through perhaps hundreds of hours of conversation, joint listening sessions and, as the months and years passed, in front room and local folk club renditions of Dylan songs by close friends and even closer rivals.

In 1966, had I been five years older, I might have had far more invested in the 'protest' 'Bob Dylan' and, conse- quently, been hostile to the emergent 'existentialist' one (to quote Irwin Silber [1990: 103], one of Dylan's primary detractors in those days). As it was, apart from being vaguely pleased that he had offended some people, I knew very little of the 'Newport' incident; The Byrds' version of 'Mr. Tambourine Man' was, and remains, one of my favour- ite records, and I had absolutely no knowledge that anyone, anywhere, had shouted 'Judas!' at Bob Dylan in perfor- mance. In later years, hearing about the incident could not have prepared me for the impact that actually hearing it did; but, by the time I did hear the record I was of course a differ- ent person, with far more cultural experience to draw on and with which to contextualise the confrontation which climaxes with 'Judas!' And I use 'climax' here in a dual sense—not only does the shout prepare the climax of the particular show (Dylan's verbal engagement with the shouter seems to add enormous extra significance to 'Like a

Rolling Stone', the final song) but it carries the far greater weight and import of seeming to climax the entire, painful process of Dylan's break with the folk revival.

With all of this in mind, when at last I listened to the 'official bootleg' the strength of my emotional response to the incident took me by surprise; and I wondered why. After some time I concluded that I found the calling out of 'Judas' to be disturbing because I felt a sense of complicity in it; and I found the recorded moment 'affecting' because I felt that Dylan's reply to his accuser—'I don't believe you. You're a liar'—uttered in the way that it was, told me more about Bob Dylan (and, to an extent, about myself as a Dylan fan) than I had ever known before. On this basis I intend to discuss the Manchester event first as a 'disturbing' one, then as an 'affecting' one, before drawing conclusions from both dimensions of my response to the record.

## Being 'Disturbed'

My reason for finding the performance 'deeply disturbing' was, ultimately, the Judas shout itself. Not so much for its racism—though clearly the term derives its force from 2,000 years of Christianity-inspired anti-Semitism—but for its distilled intolerance. Judas's kiss is a synecdoche for betrayal, the blank cheque that helped, in part, to underwrite Crusader pogroms, the Spanish Inquisition and the ghastli-ness of Auschwitz; and Dylan himself had used the reference in this way in his own song, 'With God on Our Side'. To heap all of this negativity at the door of Keith Butler (the reputed shouter), then a 22-year-old student at Keele University—or at that of John Cordwell who (bafflingly) volunteered that it was his shout—would be harsh in the extreme: the word 'traitor' is reported to have been shouted at Dylan at Forest Hills in New York, his first gig after the Newport festival and the opening date of the tour that would culminate at the Albert Hall—and perhaps 'Judas!' had been shouted elsewhere, we cannot know if it was or was not. Yet the recorded instance of it being shouted occurs in England—a long way from the immediate circle of people who might have felt 'betrayed' by Bob Dylan. Further, it occurred over a year after the Newport Folk Festival of 1965 and months after the release of Dylan's second 'electric' album, *Highway 61 Revisited*. Why, after having had a considerable interval (as well as two albums) to absorb Dylan's new music, were people still determined to pay to insult him? And why also should this be the case in the UK, the last stop on a tour that had begun nine months earlier? The answer does not lie in Butler's or Cordwell's psychopathology (or not entirely); it lies in the context of how new, radical identities were formed and sustained in the mid-1960s.

'Judas' is not just a substitute for 'traitor'; it is, for a Jew especially, the ultimate insult — at least from outside Judaism. It is fair to assume that Butler's/Cordwell's motive and intention were neither racially derived nor driven by racism yet, somehow, this makes the choice of the 'ultimate insult' even worse: 'worse' because it is used deliberately and yet almost casually. I write 'casually' because there is something so petulant in the shout — like a child who expects one dish and has been served another. Of course, much more seemed at stake at the time and the booing and cat-calling was 'justified' (or at least endorsed subconsciously) by those who protested because of the Manichean complexion of radical politics in the 1960s — and because, also, *protesting* was synonymous with the political practice of the radical Left in the period. Bob Dylan had 'crossed the line', had 'joined the other side', and all the evidence anyone needed was present in his concert appearances. It is this reductionism which disturbs me because I recognise it from my own behaviour in later years but what concerns me here is why Dylan should appear to be the worst kind of traitor *beyond* the immediate context in which the persona he appeared to be destroying had first been created.

## The Folk Revival and its Contradictions

It is superfluous here to attempt some potted 'history' either of the 1950s and early 1960s or of the 'folk revival' itself: I would recommend Cantwell (1996) for the US revival and Brocken (2003) for the experience in the UK. What both these texts have in common (apart from being exceptionally well written) is that neither is afraid to point out the contradictions of the revival itself. Embodied in the US by Pete Seeger and in the UK by Ewan MacColl (who married Seeger's sister, Peggy), what both men represented — though, ultimately, in decisively different ways — was a determined and determinate attempt to articulate and help sustain existing radical politics through music. That their manner of doing this coincided as a fierce resistance to any hint of 'commercialism' in music created the ideological straitjacket from which Dylan fought to free himself; at the same time, though, there was a decisive difference between the two projects, and between the two men, that helps to explain why an English person might come to feel particularly betrayed by Bob Dylan fronting an electric band.

Pete Seeger, although a pacifist, is someone it is easy to imagine in another era fighting in the American War of Independence or French Revolution — against arbitrary rule and for the ideals of liberty, fraternity and equality. He embodies the tradition of US radicalism that continues to resonate today in the politics of 'anti-globalisation', to which he has lent support — as he has done to a substantial number of causes since the late 1930s. Seeger joined the American Communist Party in 1942 and remained a member for eight years but he was not then, and never became, a Marxist fundamentalist. Instead, Seeger's politics were, and remain, closer to the radical communitarianism of the Levellers and the Diggers familiar from the English Civil War but leavened, in the spirit of modern times, with a greater awareness of the needs of the natural environment in the face of corporate industrial despoliation and indifference. In these ways, his commitment has always been to the needs of 'the people' over and above those of 'the system' in all its guises and dimensions. In this reading of history, 'the people' are constantly those who are oppressed by whatever form (arbitrary) authority takes; they are the poor majority who resist their oppression in order to survive it and who express their accumulated experiences together with the values and codes of their resistance through song.

Both as a solo performer (and songwriter) and also as a member of enormously influential political musical ensembles (The Almanac Singers, The Weavers), Seeger has been tireless in seeking to promote the people's cause through what has been historically, he would argue, the people's medium of choice (and necessity) — music; but not any music. Rather, Seeger's commitment has always been to *participatory* music. In this interpretation of the place and power of music, music which expresses the needs and goals of the people and is sung *together* has an almost alchemical force wherein seemingly alienation itself (as separation from one's fellow men and one's own identity) can be overcome. In this way, the people's music could not issue from 'Tin Pan Alley', because no music written for profit would be up to the task of focusing and sustaining struggles against oppression, of whatever kind; instead, it perforce consists of an amalgam of existing or new songs written to express particular or general social grievances or political goals; together with songs that have been appropriated from other sources but re-inscribed by being put to new, collectivist ends and so transformed into vehicles to rally and inspire those in struggle. In this way, what came to be called 'folk singing' was always, for Seeger, a diluted misnomer. The 'folk' is a cosy, conservative notion, 'the people' is a far more dynamic and proactive designation of a social entity which always foots history's bill and carries its can: so much so that the people's music exists almost as an immense dry battery which the oppressed can at any time tap into for energy, resolve, example and explanation. Equally, the discoveries, adaptations and new material generated in the present can be passed on, through collective singing, as a *living tradition* of oppositional music: there are no dilettantes, divas, passengers or poseurs in this musical arena.

Ewan MacColl was also a communist and, in the UK especially, to be a Communist Party member from the 1930s onwards was to be a Stalinist. Even though he left the Party in the early 1950s, MacColl was and remained a Stalinist

and a particularly intractable one at that, if that is not a tau-
tology. What he represented and what drove him was a
fierce but very partial reading of 'working-class history'
characteristic of British communism in all its variants and
persistent to this day. In this story there was a time, before
industrialisation, when workers were 'the people', proud to
be Saxons and, especially, Celts. What capitalism had done
to 'the people' was to enslave them, to break their bodies but
not their will. What was required was an empathetic but
robust guidance to help restore to 'the people' (or, since
industrialisation, to 'the workers') a sense of what they had
lost in the rise of wage labour and what they had to gain if
only they could reconnect with their potential power to
effect radical change. In this historic pursuit MacColl was
convinced that what the workers possessed was a living but
substantially unrecognised 'memory' of their own potential
where this 'memory' resided in 'working-class culture' and
its traditions—in collective activities, in the supportive
behaviour of communities, in the 'camaraderie' evident in
the dangerous environments of coalmining and seafaring (to
name but two) and, ultimately, in the songs that were sung
about the 'way of life' of which these were all component
parts.

Consequently, what was required for radical change to be
effected was a reversion to, and an overhaul of, exactly this
culture in the face of the 'alien' forms of cultural expression
workers came increasingly to engage with (magazines,
pulp fiction, Hollywood cinema, 'pop' music, and so on).

Seeger and MacColl, then, had much in common: both
drew energy from the moral force not simply of their own
convictions but from the underpinning and 'guaranteeing'
sense that 'history' itself was on their side; a sense reaf-
firmed on every picket-line and every march; in every
working-class community and in every confrontation with
authority. They both worked tirelessly in the present by
urging that an imagined future could be created from materials which were, simultaneously, recoverable from the
(imagined) past but also retrievable from a (substantially
imagined) *present*—just so long as the tides of commercial

music could be driven back and quietened long enough for the people's music to be heard, for traditional music to be embraced and for the transformative power of collective music-making to be experienced. In all of this both men (and aspects of the 'revivals' on both sides of the Atlantic) were ideologically congruent: but it is possible to argue signal differences below this congruence which, in part, help explain why UK audience members at a Dylan concert would feel specifically aggrieved.

## Mass Culture and 'the Masses'

The primary tension between MacColl's efforts at 'folk revival' (truly the restoration to full health of English — and Scots, Welsh and Irish — 'traditionalism') and Seeger's various projects was that much of MacColl's work was defined in the negative — by what it was *against* rather than what it was for: *American* music and, ironically, not just US pop music. As he explained to Robin Denselow (1990) many years later:

> I became concerned ... that we had a whole generation who were becoming quasi-Americans, and I felt this was absolutely monstrous! I was convinced that we had a music that was just as vigorous as anything America had produced, and we should be pursuing some kind of national identity, not just becoming an arm of American cultural imperialism (Denselow 1990: 25–6).

The notion of 'American cultural imperialism' is what so divides MacColl from Seeger and, with it, the political dimension of the separate revivals from each other. There is an almost tangible despair in MacColl's reflection that 'we had a music': what he wants this to mean is that 'we' (the UK) *possessed* a music — then, in the 1950s — but what he implies is that *at some time in the past* 'we' had this music and that now it was (virtually) gone. What makes his observation particularly ugly is that the term 'quasi-Americans' can also be taken to include people *inspired by* the very music that he had, at first, endorsed and that Seeger continued to champion in the same period (for example, the folk blues of Leadbelly which had become chart material in the hands of

Lonnie Donegan). MacColl's response continued to be to seek out 'traditional' songs and to insist that singers at the Singers' Clubs he inspired to form around the country remain in and with 'their' traditions—wherein Scots sang Scottish songs, and so on. Further, he controlled a repertoire which was, simultaneously, a canon—to which would be admitted songs either he wrote himself or contemporary songs he, and his coterie, *approved*. In this way, MacColl's project was, then, congruent more with that of F. R. Leavis than it was with Pete Seeger wherein MacColl exercised an authority over the cultural field of the UK 'folk revival' (or at least sections of it) that not only mirrored but actualised Leavis's own desire to arbitrate the field of cultural production, in general.

The true contrast between the US and UK folk revivals is not just that Seeger's and MacColl's angle of address to their separate (though historically connected) traditional music differed, but that Seeger could claim a closer connection to a *living* tradition. If we take Woody Guthrie as a touchstone for this contrast, Guthrie was not someone who collected traditional songs in the way that MacColl and A. L. Lloyd did (and as Cecil Sharp and Percy Grainger had done, for very different reasons, in an earlier epoch). Guthrie was involved in political struggles and campaigns—he sustained himself this way. And when he wasn't singing songs he had just written he was drawing on a repertoire consisting predominantly of songs of largely recent origin and wide currency—notably the songs associated with the International Workers of the World (the IWW, or 'Wobblies') and especially those by Joe Hill—together with songs of more recent provenance again, ones that came from the heart of the often extremely violent US labour disputes of the 1930s.

The anarcho-syndicalist 'Wobblies' were formed in 1905. Still in existence today, the organisation reached a peak of 100,000 members during the First World War. Concerted government action in the wake of US entry into the war largely neutralised the IWW, but its example and influence persisted throughout the 1930s. Songs associated with the

Wobblies (who issued the *Big Red Songbook* to members on joining—a source of Seeger's belief in the power of collectivist music) continued to play a part in union disputes up to the Second World War. Further, the practice of singing as an act of solidarity and morale-raising (often in the face of severe physical intimidation and assault) characterised disputes during the 1930s. Consequently, when the Almanac Singers sang 'Which side are you on?' they were singing a *contemporary* song that had been written by Florence Reece, wife of a union official, during the Harlan County coal dispute of 1931. Similarly, 'I Don't Want Your Millions, Mister' was written by Jim Garland, half-brother of Aunt Molly Jackson, another activist from a mining community who herself wrote 'union' songs in the 1930s. Taken together, while MacColl would need to search hard for examples of this kind of songwriting and, more pertinently, song *use* in Britain, Seeger could immerse himself in it and, concurrently, was able to play and perform with the greatest political troubadour of them all—Woody Guthrie.

What bearing the contrasts between MacColl and Seeger's experience of traditional or peoples' song would have for the hostile reception to the 'electric' Bob Dylan in Britain derives from the differently composed ideologies of the two men (and the influence each exerted in their own movements or 'revivals'). While Seeger was completely enamoured of Dylan, from the outset MacColl claimed to be unconvinced by him—where this in turn may have contributed a circumspection to the esteem that Dylan came to be held in by a proportion of his audience. There is no evidence that Keith Butler or John Cordwell had any direct connection with MacColl or his views, but that MacColl's views (especially in establishing which music could be considered 'radical', which not, and why) helped create the 'common sense' of the young radicals whose social life was simultaneously their *political* life where both (according to one of my respondents) consisted of CND meetings, Young Socialist activities, as well as regular folk club attendance. In this atmosphere, what was at stake was a new, collective, identity—one organised around 'folk' music in the US and the UK, but one, arguably, that was inflected differently between the two countries.

## Minutemen and (Tolpuddle) Martyrs

Cantwell (1996) provides an especially useful and sympathetic account of the changes in US society in the post-war years. These years, he argues, witnessed the creation of a numerically significant white middle-class generation of young people whose lives took shape in a US that was considerably different (for young white middle-class people) from the divided and desperate society of their parents (1996: 319). His conclusion to a detailed overview of the many new facets of the cultural context which helped give birth to a generation distinguished by their 'fastidious social self-awareness' (1996: 323) is that, in their hands, the folk revival became a 'restorative' rather than a 'revolutionary' project (1996: 325), one in and through which

> Young people ... sought and believed in ... the blessing of the parent generation—for its high purposes were precisely the return on the moral, cultural, and indeed financial investment that generation had made in its children (1996: 324).

While this representation of the motivation of young supporters of the folk revival might at first sight seem difficult to square with union militants singing 'Casey Jones' inside General Motors plant at Flint, Michigan while fists and rocks flew outside—and also with Seeger's veneration of Guthrie and his own, continued militancy—we need to reflect on the substantial historical differences between US and British radicalism. In the US, following the War of Independence, the break with the Crown was complete; consequently, what US citizens were also able to break from was the British class system. That another, equally powerful, class system rose in its place does not concern us here, what does is the fact that what Britain's own radicals faced *from the Restoration onwards* was that the sanctity surrounding the right of the ruling class to rule (whatever hard-won democratic modifications were made to government) was sanctioned by a symbolic authority (and a real state power) that derived from an almost feudal sense of the fitness of the wealthy to dominate society.

In the US, the place of radicalism (its character and also its limits) remains rooted in the sense of what it is to *be* an American — entitlement to the freedoms and guarantees of the constitution. In the UK in the mid-1950s the social and cultural contexts within which a parallel generation of young people began to imagine their 'New Left' was not the comparatively 'enabling' one described by Cantwell — for all the determination to resist civil rights and to root out 'communism'. At least the young American 'folkniks' had room to move and manoeuvre — from the suburbs into the cities; from 'suburbia' to 'bohemia'; from the East Coast to the West Coast and back again; and from all surrounding locations into the Deep South and, barring murder there, out again. In Britain there was no equivalent sense or experience of social, cultural and geographical 'space'. Instead, what there was was the Labour Movement and its shibboleths wherein 'protest' could only gather momentum beneath their shadow and by their prescriptions and proscriptions. These limits were eventually exceeded — as were the limits set on the US movement (if only for a short time as it transpired) — but while they held sway, when he plugged in his Telecaster, Bob Dylan could be measured by them to have repudiated the values associated with the (different) radicalisms of the UK and US. What complicated the issue was, though, that while Dylan could be accused of 'betraying' the folk movement and the 'protest' movement for a set of reasons common, roughly, but never completely, to both sides of the Atlantic, in Britain, in the constituency that contained Butler and Cordwell as well as MacColl, he was deemed 'guilty' of betrayal by a further, and distinctive, measure. In this way we can identify three main 'betrayals' underpinning the hostility to Dylan *in Manchester*.

1. In the US, Seeger had helped make 'acoustic' (guitar and banjo) music the authentic voice of American radicalism (as MacColl had made it permissible for 'traditional' performance in the UK). On this basis, by appearing not just with a 'non-standard' and clearly

non-acoustic instrument Dylan had broken a central
code of what was acceptable to the folk revival—the
people's music could not be played on an electric guitar because 'the people' (notably in the US) used
acoustic guitars. They used acoustic guitars because
they could not afford and had no need of amplification—the voice was the important instrument because
the words were what was important: 'the people'
were not in the entertainment business. (There is also a
sub-text here of valuing the rural over the urban—as
iconic of 'poor' over 'rich', 'natural' over 'contrived',
and so on).

2.     Again, for the revivals on both sides of the Atlantic,
what the electric guitar also and decisively symbolised was 'commercialism'—'Tin Pan Alley', the music
industry, and with it 'mass culture' and the cultural
subjugation of 'the people'. Dylan's adoption of an
electric instrument was a particularly bitter pill, for
Seeger especially, to swallow. In all of the early,
approving references to Dylan published in *Sing Out!*
(the main US magazine of the revival), together with
reviews and album sleeve notes, he was represented
as a 'boy wonder', almost as the return of Woody
Guthrie himself (the recording of the 1963 Newport
Folk Festival documents this in an especially moving
way). When Dylan appeared at Newport with an electric guitar so incensed was Seeger that he is reported to
have threatened to take an axe to the main power cable
(although whether the audience was equally outraged
is moot). For those *not* at Newport, the 1. reported
'confrontation' between Dylan and Seeger would
have become the 'preferred reading' of events and as
such would have transmitted a sense that the former
had crossed a crucial 'line', had joined the camp of,
and thus become, 'the enemy'. Which side are you on?
Indeed.

3.     As we have noted, by the time Dylan reached the UK
in 1966 both *Bringing it All Back Home* and *Highway 61
Revisited* had been available for some months. Most of
the theatre audiences would have had knowledge of
these records; many would have been conversant with
them. The hostility to him can, then, only have been

substantially premeditated and contrived. Before discussing this in any more detail, it follows that his third 'betrayal' is that Dylan arrived in Britain to play not just *American* music but apparently the worst kind of American music—the amplified pop we would soon come to call 'rock music'—music MacColl later described to Denselow as 'politically suspect ... very venal ... very corrupt' (1990: 28). Again, this is not how Butler for one represented his shout ('I think what really sent me over the top was what he did to those lovely songs....') but it is unlikely that Butler or Cordwell would have been motivated to shout at all if it had not been *de rigueur* to abuse Dylan and had not the level and the extent of the heckling grown incrementally throughout the electric set during that evening. Paul Williams (1990) gives a gripping and convincing reading of this but, for the key moment itself, Greil Marcus (1997: 36) puts it best:

> And then, as if he had been waiting, well informed as to the precise order in which Dylan played his songs, a person rises and shouts what he has been silently rehearsing to himself all night. As over and over he has imagined himself doing, he stands up and stops time. He stops the show: 'JUDAS!'.

## Divided by a Common Language

Whether Keith Butler or John Cordwell shouted 'Judas' at Bob Dylan is irrelevant; what counts is that a broad constituency within the British folk revival was opposed to Dylan's decision to transform his music. Prominent within this constituency would have been Communist Party members, along with those other Marxists in far smaller organisations together with young, left-wing trade unionists, left Labour Party members and 'non-aligned' individuals in and around the central 'campaigns' of the day (notably, but not solely, CND). This is not at all to argue some kind of 'communist conspiracy'; rather, it is to reflect that, in the historical formation of the British Far Left as a whole, there was, and remains, a marked tendency to adhere to a one-dimensional view of the working class—its nature, culture and needs.

What existed strongly in the 1950s Far Left (and continues to exist in some quarters to this day) was captured in Richard Hoggart's *The Uses of Literacy,* published in 1957. Hoggart's work exhibits a nostalgic and deeply conservative reverence for the working class. It is the habit of the Far Left to reduce the working class to a handful of occupations—notably those with strong trade union representation—and, further, to represent as pernicious all cultural artefacts and practices deemed to originate from beyond the cultural 'boundaries' of that class. Considered in this way, it is no accident that MacColl's views coincided with those of F. R. Leavis—in the years following the First World War nostalgia for a 'lost' Britain and a vanished national integrity characterised a far wider range of cultural and political projects than just those of the Scrutiny group and of the Communist Party—and it was a response clearly not confined to Britain, alone. What, then, came to 'unify' these essentially reactionary projects (for all their declarations of the need to reconstitute Britain *progressively* in some way) was an open scorn for, and hostility to, the products of the new, substantially US-owned and dominated, 'culture industries'.

That the 'threat' of 'American cultural imperialism' should, in an always unacknowledged way, 'unite' left- and right-wing tendencies across Europe from the 1930s onwards is one of recent history's great ironies—where, worse still, it is but a short step (in some political demonologies) to argue *Jewish* control over these same industries (especially film and music). Consequently, the sense of 'complicity' I experienced when listening to the Manchester recording for the first time drew from an uncomfortable admixture: the self-recognition of my later practice of the Manicheanism (the 'reductionism') of the Far Left; together with a recognition of the fundamentally conservative and *conformist* politics this underscored (which reprised the questions not so much of what we were fighting for, but *how*). But what also surfaced was a memory of how the need to *conform*—to conform to some vision of 'the workers' and to what can only be described as an innate *morality* attributed to them (think of the published work of Tony Benn and E. P. Thompson in this context) — was prevalent in the experience of the left for many years after Dylan's appearance at 'the Albert Hall'. As someone who grew up working-class and Methodist I still flinch when I remember how often I (and many others like me) were forced to account for our 'Bohemianism' — tastes in music, clothes, reading matter and so on — by a new set of 'ministers', the 'officer class' of whatever tiny sect we happened to find ourselves in. It was as if there was a cold piece of Ewan MacColl lodged in every communist (along with an echo of Seeger's evangelism) and we come too close, far, far too close, to the demonisation, the 'Jewification', of the factories of *popular* culture when we hear that infamous shout.

In summation, then, Bob Dylan truly 'betrayed' no one — whether at the Albert Hall, the Manchester Free Trade Hall, Forest Hills or Newport. As a songwriter and a performer, Bob Dylan was not responsible for the 'world views' of members of his audience. The abuse of Bob Dylan in 1966 cannot be compared, for example, with the disruption of the 'Miss World' contest at the Royal Albert Hall in 1970 — the latter is a political act (an attempt to draw attention to the institutional oppression of women); the former is simply a peeve, and a cowardly one at that (Dylan was a 'soft' target). This is partly why I found Dylan's reply to the shout of 'Judas' so affecting — he sounds hurt and vulnerable — and being 'allowed' to hear it smacked of 'voyeurism' (whatever the distinction between 'hearing' and 'seeing' that which should remain 'hidden'). This was also an uncomfortable sensation but it was not, or not entirely, what affected me; rather it was the way in which Dylan's tone — more than the words he said — which caused me to wonder whether, if Bob Dylan had not betrayed anyone, perhaps Robert Zimmerman had.

### Being 'Affected'

Hearing about the 'Albert Hall' bootleg meant trying to imagine the confrontation; rooting for Dylan as he uttered the words 'I don't believe you'. It could only have been devastating—for the shouter—because, in my composite version of him, Bob Dylan seemed not just cool and powerful, but 'all-powerful' and 'all-cool'. In my mind's eye I saw a larger-than-life figure, in complete control, guitar slung like a weapon, inflecting the words with the kind of venom apparent in confrontations with journalists in D. A. Pennebaker's film of his 1965 UK tour, *Don't Look Back*. And, oddly, this is exactly how Dylan is almost always depicted in accounts of the incident—he is the acid-tongued victor whose reference to his song of the same title is dripping with 'absolute contempt' (Marcus 1997: 36). It is as if the majority of commentators, Dylan fans almost all of them, *will* the event to unfold to a script that they, too, have imagined—with their hero vanquishing his critics in one, devastating verbal flourish—even when writing to the bootleg recording itself.

One of the key problems with the recording, even in its official release as 'a fresh mix straight from the three-track master tape' (Sony album jacket), is that, following 'Ballad of a Thin Man', the penultimate number, the only shout from the audience that is truly intelligible is 'Judas', itself. There is one remark, which precedes it, and several that follow. It is not possible to determine whether the latter are also addressed to Dylan or are shouts back at the shouter; and neither is it possible to determine whether, if shouts to the shouter, these are in support of or in opposition to the accusation made. Further, as there are shouted comments from the audience audible from the end of the second song ('I Don't Believe You', itself) we have to allow that the audience has created a dialogue within itself, so that shouts have taken on the form of a conversation or argument. Certainly, Dylan appears defensive from his spoken introduction to 'I Don't Believe You' (there is no introduction to 'Tell Me Mama', the first song, or to the set itself). This is evident in *what* he says—'This is called "I Don't Believe You", it used to be like that but now it goes like this'—but much more so in *how* he says it—in a kind of uninflected monotone unlike natural speech but with an unnatural extension of the second syllable of 'believe'. This is Dylan exercising 'cool' authority (or the authority of cool). He expects trouble and his apparently unemotional delivery (matter-of-fact to the point of disengagement) is, in its *disrespect* for his audience, a symbol of defiance.

That Dylan was, indeed, expecting trouble is unquestionable, and for reasons that are completely understandable, he had experienced opposition from this point onwards on almost every night of the tour. What he had *not* experienced was an insult of the magnitude of 'Judas!' He clearly hears the shout — it would have been impossible to miss it — but it takes him almost 20 seconds to reply. When he does, his voice is significantly different from the two previous times he speaks to the audience — the introduction to 'I Don't Believe You' and (following 'Leopard-Skin Pillbox Hat') the remarkable routine he uses to silence the evidently large number of slow-handclappers. By mumbling an apparent 'story' into the microphone Dylan forces the noisy section of the crowd to desist as they strain to listen to what he is 'saying' to them. Once he has their complete attention, and without breaking the rhythm of his nonsense words, he delivers the line: 'If you only just wouldn't clap so hard'. This is clearly a set-piece, no one is slow-handclapping at the time; he 'tunes' an already in-tune guitar essentially provoking his opponents to renew their assault which he then turns to his advantage with an enormously skilful piece of verbal 'judo'.

It is this kind of 'battle' that so much of Dylan's reputation — as a remarkably cool, knowing, fearless and astute cultural figure — was based on and the reason he *remained* a potent figure for so many, even as he freed himself from the grip of his earliest advocates. In its most 'positive' form, when demolishing the wooden questions of mainstream journalists, Dylan comes across as the quintessential rebel and much of the cocktail of comparisons to 'Brando', 'Dean' and even 'Chaplin' — served up, again and again, in hagiographies of Dylan — are born in these encounters. Bob Spitz (1989: 323, 333) recalls a more sinister Dylan, though, one who, urged on by Bob Neuwirth, devastated Phil Ochs and Brian Jones amongst a host of 'lesser' names in reportedly unprovoked and brutal bouts of this same 'judo'. Dylan could be a bully or, more accurately, *Robert Zimmerman* could use his 'Bob Dylan' identity to bully others as well as to defend himself. If he was sometimes indiscriminate in his use of the public powers he developed then we can attribute this to his youth and to the licence that extraordinary acclaim (and extraordinary ability) makes difficult to refuse. But what we must not lose sight of is that 'Bob Dylan' was, indeed, a fictional character and he is in full flow in Manchester, as the first two comments to the audience attest; what concerned, and concerns, me is the third time he speaks — in the far plainer, far less mannered voice of the man behind the character.

## *Out of Character*

Robert Zimmerman invented 'Bob Dylan' no earlier than 1959. He had played guitar and sung from the early 1950s. His first attempts to write songs were, understandably, derivative:

> The songs I wrote at that age were just four chord rhythm and blues songs. Based on things that the Diamonds would sing, or the Crewcuts, or groups like this (Dylan, in Miles, 1978: 15).

The 'doo-wop' groups that Zimmerman listened to were popular from the mid-1950s onwards but his first 'love' was Hank Williams. Williams died on New Year's Day 1953 at the age of 29. In the previous four years he had registered a string of country music hits. At the time of his death his personal life and career were in steep decline, although he continued to have hit records. Even more hits followed his death and the young Zimmerman was very much a fan:

> I started singing after I started writing. I started that when I was about ten. Ten or eleven — and started out country and western — Hank Williams, Lefty Frizzell kinda things. Hank Williams ... had just died and I started playing sometime around there ... I tried to sing everything he would sing ... Hank Williams was the first influence ... I guess for

a longer period of time than anyone else (Dylan, in Miles 1978: 15).

I do not intend to argue that *all* that Robert Zimmerman wanted to do as a young man was to emulate Hank Williams and that 'making it' as a folk musician called 'Bob Dylan' was his way of accomplishing this ambition; but Zimmerman did more than change his name — he invented an entire autobiography and learned an entire, and entirely new, repertoire and what he achieved through this brilliant disguise was staggering in its scale. As a 19-year-old, on his own initiative, he left home for New York City. He visited Woody Guthrie in hospital and began to play Greenwich Village folk clubs. As Robert Shelton (1986) indicates, between March and September 1961 (when Shelton published his landmark review of Dylan for the *New York Times;* Shelton 1986: 111) Dylan had gone to the heart of the New York folk scene — and also to the heart of those in Boston and Cambridge. He knew every influential person there was to know and had become a 'face' on the three key East Coast folk scenes. He had places to stay and places to play — in nine months he had gone from complete obscurity to being hailed as the 'bright new face in folk music' who was going 'straight up' (Shelton 1986: 111). And this at a time when the folk revival was well established with the majority of its key performers in place. This is not 'luck', it is *strategy;* not 'independence', it is *focus;* not 'talent' (or not just), it is *business.* Robert Zimmerman wanted to become a star; not only wanted to but needed to, and this 'need' is what is achingly apparent the night he, and we, heard someone shout 'Judas!' in the Manchester Free Trade Hall. As Dylan put it in an interview in 1965 (Ephron and Edmiston 1965, in Miles 1978: 46): 'I became interested in folk music because I had to make it somehow', and, as he said in other interviews in that same year, on the same tour that would reach its climax in Britain,

> I didn't go into folk music to make any money, but because it was easy, you could be by yourself, you didn't need anybody.

And:

> I used to play rock and roll … when I was 15 … and by the
> time I was 17 you just couldn't make it anymore at all
> unless you wanted to be a sideman … I couldn't make it that
> way … and I discovered a thing called folk music. And I
> did that for a while and then I stopped doing that and
> started writing the songs myself and I always wanted
> accompaniment you know but I just couldn't afford it …
> now when its happened I don't really think about it one
> way or the other. Its, I like it more this way.

At the very least, Robert Zimmerman wanted to be the
leader of a band, someone in the spotlight singing his own
songs. This would not be viable again in popular music
until the arrival of The Beatles and their aftermath. Meanwhile, in the folk revival, there were no 'bands'; there were
earnest ensembles like the Rooftop Singers but there was
nothing like Hank Williams and his Drifting Cowboys.
Consequently the fees paid were not sufficient to support
permanent 'accompanists', so Zimmerman compromised
for a while — and mainly for logistical reasons — but he did
not compromise cynically or for reasons of 'bad faith'.

### Taken For a Ride?

What the shout of 'Judas!' exposes like an open wound is
that, for many, Robert Zimmerman appeared to have taken
them personally, and the folk revival itself, together with all
of the ideals it represented, for a brutally cynical ride.
Again, as someone who came to Dylan through a discontinuous patchwork of sounds and images, I had no framework
within which to register him as a cynic. What affected rather
than disturbed me when I heard the exchange with the 'Judas' shouter was that it made me realise that Robert
Zimmerman was attempting to accomplish far more with,
and as, 'Bob Dylan' than I had ever been aware. It was not so
much that Dylan 'losing his cool' diminished him for me (if
anything, this added to the legend), it was the unmasked
voice that made me realise there was a *person* behind my
version of the 'cool Dylan' in exactly the same way that
there was a person behind the 'folk Dylan', the restored
Woody Guthrie whom the folk revivalists were determined
not to let go. This, then, in turn had the effect of forcing me to

confront the limitations of my own 'consumption' of Dylan—as a temporary 'rock star' rather than an individual engaged in a coherent, life-long artistic adventure. In all of this, I do not believe I was taken for a ride by a cynical Robert Zimmerman, and neither was the folk revival: the greatest 'affect' was attempting to understand why. Ian MacDonald makes the strongest case for the *integrity* of the Zimmerman-Dylan transformation—arguing, essentially, that what the folk revival got for its indulgence of Zimmerman's often absurd lies about his folk credentials was a star of a brilliance they could only have dreamed about:

> From a standing start in two and a half years, he turned himself into the most convincing and compelling folk performer in America. Only genuine musical talent, real creative ability and formidable self-belief could pull *that* off. The carefully studied counterfeit character who turned up … to record his debut album … was anything but a straightforward fake. Rather, he was the real thing in folk drag, made powerful, indeed unforgettable, by his innate resources of artistry and personal intensity (2003: 16).

MacDonald is 'almost there' in this assessment, but what he just misses is what the folk revival critics of Zimmerman/ Dylan missed by a mile: Robert Zimmerman did not want simply to be a 'star', he wanted to be a star *on his own terms*— and this is the root and the anchor of the integrity of his project throughout its course. What Robert Zimmerman set out to do, and succeeded in doing, was to create and maintain a character who in turn would attract the level of acclaim (and with it the income) that would allow Zimmerman—the man behind the mask(s)—the place of privilege to *explore*. Once recovered from the enormous effort of achieving the prominence that allows (the still delimited) space to create, and only to create, Bob Dylan (he changed his name from Zimmerman in 1962) has spent his life on the paying stage worrying and working away at the conundrums embedded in what inspired him in the first place in the form of Hank Williams and his music—the bare but minutely intricate fact that, in Williams' lyric, *(we'll) never get out of this world, alive.*

When Irwin Silber (1990: 103) accused Dylan of dealing in 'existentialist philosophy' (and attempted to blackmail him emotionally in his 'open letter' published in *Sing Out!* in 1964), he was missing the point in exactly the way the cry of 'Judas!' was the same epistle in a single word. Silber failed; the folk revival failed; Keith Butler and John Cordwell failed; and I failed too, to recognise that, in Dylan's engagement with life as a puzzle with a fatal outcome, it is not that change or reinvention is *integral* to that engagement, it is that change is the *form* of the engagement itself. Considered in this way, Dylan did not take the folk revivalists for a ride, he had to begin somewhere and he began there; and, in doing so, he gave the revival a prominence it would never otherwise have enjoyed. In this elevation of the folk revival to 'global' significance, what revivalists did not anticipate was a contingent, dual effect of 'success through Bob Dylan': first, in going 'straight up' Dylan was only ever likely to go by one route—the route of *popular* music and this meant that the folk revival would indeed be 'spread' but only by its popularisation. 'Popular' music is not the 'people's music', in Seeger and MacColl's reading of that term, but neither is it 'mass culture': pop involves a negotiation of meaning. In this way it can be a medium through which to explore alternatives, a site of pleasure, a means of individual and collective affirmation, even a place to *restore* community. By taking folk into popular music (from which it had never been as isolated as Seeger and MacColl would claim and have preferred), Bob Dylan helped to open up the field as a popular resource—an achievement of great significance and one far from the dilution of its 'message' and abandonment of its 'sanctity' of which he was accused. Second—and ultimately because of their ungenerous and conformist approach to their political goals—the revivalists failed also to recognise that not only was Dylan *not* abandoning 'traditional music', but that he had found a power within it that was greater than the one offered simply by singing it together.

To look more closely at the first of these two points, what we first need to consider is that in the early 1960s the music industry was not the 'global' marketing and distribution infrastructure it is today. In fact, it was Dylan himself who laid the foundation for an industrial logic that is only now beginning to collapse. Put simply, his success with the 'album' form encouraged The Beatles to concentrate on album-length works, to which they took—at least for *Revolver* and *Sgt. Pepper's Lonely Hearts Club Band*—their tremendous gift for writing hit *songs*. The enormous sales, and concomitant cultural impact, of The Beatles was then consolidated and regularised by adaptation into a set of business practices geared round the studio production of albums and the subsequent promoting of the album through the release of a sequence of heavily-marketed singles—wherein the profit margin on albums was considerably higher per unit than it was on singles, with the added bonus that the same recording could be sold *twice*. Once record companies geared up to mass marketing albums, what they sold—what they were glad to sell—was a new type of commodity. That this commodity was also someone's distinctive 'art' project was immaterial to them—in the same way that it was substantially immaterial to Bob Dylan that his work should be treated as a commodity: as long as he received money for making records and giving performances he was able to carry on the work of exploration—where his 'tools' and his inspiration were exactly those he found in traditional music.

Returning to MacDonald's observation; if, right at the outset of his career, Dylan's 'artistry' and 'intensity' could not be faked, then neither could the energy and the mystery that he found in traditional songs be faked—whether these were of 'European' or African-American provenance. As Dylan described it in an interview with Nora Ephron and Susan Edmiston, again in 1965:

> I became interested in folk music because I had to make it somehow. Obviously I'm not a hard-working cat. I played the guitar, that was all I did. I thought it was great music. Certainly I haven't turned my back on it or anything like that. There is—and I'm sure nobody realizes this, all the authorities who write about what it is and what it should be, when they say keep things simple, they should be easily

> understood—folk music is the only music where it isn't
> simple. It's never been simple. It's weird, man, full of leg-
> end, myth, Bible and ghosts. I've never written anything
> hard to understand, not in my head anyway, and nothing
> as far out as some of the old songs. They were out of sight ...
> "Little Brown Dog". I bought a little brown dog, its face is
> all gray. Now I'm going to Turkey flying on my bottle. And
> "Nottemun Town", that's like a herd of ghosts passing
> through on the way to Tangiers. "Lord Edward", "Barbara
> Allen", they're full of myth (Dylan, in Miles 1978: 46).

Throughout his work, Greil Marcus has made much of the
power of traditional music for its rehearsals of the potentiality of America as a site of renewal for settlers and immigrants, forced and unforced, and for its ability to speak to
and for the fierce trials relocation brings. In *Invisible Republic*, his extended work on Dylan's *Basement Tapes* (the music
Dylan made with The Band in his exile from the music business following the 1966 tour) Marcus concludes in this way:

> Those who had left their stages as betrayers of immemorial
> traditions discovered deeper traditions, and in a room
> without mirrors refashioned them. The traditional people,
> still living, were laid to rest and raised up with new faces.
> The cuckoo turned into a floorbird (1997: 223).

Perhaps it was the case that the unceasing hostility vented at
Dylan during 1965 and 1966 in the name of tradition itself
caused him to consider tradition more fully, to confront it
more nakedly and to mine it more deeply than in his first
encounter with it when, to an extent, he had used it fortu-
itously rather than opportunistically to *become* 'Bob Dylan'.
Whatever the motivation behind the period of playing and
recording in his basement in Woodstock, from his return to
recording with John Wesley Harding in 1968, onwards, Bob
Dylan has continually drawn energy and insight from the
music beyond Tin Pan Alley.

Instructively, each time he has returned to the well of
American traditional music Dylan has come away in a new
guise, rather than as a new man—we need only consider the
consistencies in the form and, substantially, the content of
his song lyrics when set against his changes in vocal style, in
the arrangement of old material, in the switching between

musical genres, and even his oscillating allegiance to belief systems, to recognise not just that change in identity is emblematic of his life's work but that his life's work is change itself. In an 'endless tour' that is now deep into its second decade, Dylan plays around the world, constantly, night-after-night, as if through the public performance of his songs he will remain in touch with the power of the archetypes from which they draw — where this power is the power to reconcile the extremes and the absurdity of being alive, at all.

## Conclusion

What affected me most when I listened to the 'Royal Albert Hall' concert for the first time was the sheer beauty and power of Dylan's music, evident in both sets. To hear 'Judas' shouted at the climax of this concert was disturbing and affecting, indeed — disturbing for the reasons I have given, but affecting also because he chose to reply to his adversary with the words *I don't believe you* — not so much in the sense of 'I don't believe you could be so stupid' (although he does mean this) but more as 'I don't believe you can't understand what we're involved in here'. The shouter, whoever he was, stood for all those who felt betrayed by Bob Dylan, but not only was Bob Dylan not the embodiment of their hopes and dreams, he was not the embodiment of their *purpose* – or if he was, it was not in a way that could be grasped easily by the radicals in the folk revival. As someone who joined those same radicals and then went on to write (hit) 'political' songs, myself, what really affected me was that, after years of playing Bob Dylan records, I had failed to grasp that there was a man, a man working at something, behind *my* version of Bob Dylan. Instead, I had been disconcerted by the changes in vocal style, dismayed by *Slow Train Coming* and *Saved*, outraged by 'Wiggle, Wiggle' — yet I continued playing those early albums and drawing a fake 'power' from them (or, perhaps, a real power for fake reasons).

## Coda

While preparing to write this paper I happened to attend a Bob Dylan concert—at Wembley Arena on 15 November 2003, another night on the 'endless tour' and I was disappointed by it; not so hugely that I would never want to see Dylan 'live' again or so profoundly that how he sang and played made me want to re-evaluate my love for his work, but disappointed even so. In this concert he played electric piano throughout. At the end of each song he would teeter around the keyboard in a loop that took him in front of the lead guitarist to a halt before the drum-riser. There some words would be exchanged with the drummer. He would then teeter back towards the keyboard and begin the next song. But what that song was hardly mattered; some combination of his piano-playing style (pounding chords on the beat) and the desire to front what amounted to a bar-band (rocking, loud, with no sense of light, shade or restraint) meant that melodies were abandoned for a constant rhythm. Consequently each lyric was squeezed into this unrelenting pattern and seemed neutered as a consequence.

I became so disenchanted with this performance that, at one point, after Dylan had (for me at least) mangled 'Mr. Tambourine Man' and beaten 'Every Grain of Sand' half to death, I felt like shouting 'Which song are you going to murder next?' And there was a space to do it—just before 'The Lonesome Death of Hattie Carroll'. I would not have shouted—I am not that reckless—and in an arena with a capacity of 11,000 he would not have heard me, but the irony that I had been on the verge of shouting 'Judas!' was not lost on me; in fact, it was what helped consolidate my responses to my listening to the Manchester recording in 1998.

The purpose of this vignette is to raise further questions: What do we expect, what are we *entitled* to expect when we buy a concert ticket? If Dylan is our Picasso, should we expect him to repaint *Guernica*, brush-stroke-for-brush-stroke, at our leisure and for our delight, each and every night? In this way, what is bought and what is *owned* when we exchange money for a concert ticket? My mistake at

Wembley was Keith Butler's mistake in Manchester — what we expected was what we had been encouraged to expect by Dylan himself: where the express purpose of his project, or a decisive aspect of it, is continuously to disrupt his myth and so disrupt the complacency in the viewer or listener. Where his work becomes art is that, unlike the rock acts that drag themselves around stadia playing their greatest hits every time they need a cash boost, his own practice of dismantling and reassembling his material demonstrates the importance of acting on the world rather than simply *in* the world.

That Bob Dylan's changes can be abrupt and untelegraphed comes with the territory. Keith Butler, John Cordwell, Pete Seeger and thousands of others were not to know this in the mid-1960s and their response that Dylan had 'betrayed' them is understandable. What it took me far too long to discover was that Dylan might appear to betray his inventions but he has never betrayed his determination to be *inventive*. No one could ask more of a 'pop star' than that.

## References

Brocken, M. (2003) *The British Folk Revival 1944–2002*. Aldershot: Ashgate.

Butler, Keith quoted at http://www.expectingrain.eom/dok/who/b/butlerkeith.html [Accessed 10 January 2004].

Cantwell, R. (1996) *When We Were Good: The Folk Revival*. Cambridge, Mass.: Harvard University Press.

Denselow, R. (1990) *When the Music's Over: The Story of Political Pop*. London: Faber and Faber.

Hoggart, R. (1957) *The Uses of Literacy*. London: Penguin.

MacDonald, I. (2003) *The People's Musk*. London: Pimlico.

Marcus, G. (1997) *Invisible Republic: Bob Dylan's Basement Tapes*. London: Picador.

Miles, B. (1978) *Bob Dylan in His Own Words*. London: Omnibus.

Shelton, R. (1986) *No Direction Home: The Life and Music of Bob Dylan*. New York, Beech Tree Books/William Morrow.

Silber, I. (1990) 'Topical Song: Polarization Sets In', in C. McGregor, *Bob Dylan:The Early Years*, New York: Da Capo.

Spitz, B (1989) *Dylan: a Biography*, London: Michael Joseph.

Williams, P. (1990) *Performing Artist: The Music of Bob Dylan. Volume One, 1960–1973*, Novato-California: Underwood-Miller.

Lawrence Wilde

# The Cry of Humanity: Dylan's Expressionist Period

> The heritage of Expressionism has not yet ceased to exist,
> because we have not yet even started to consider it (Bloch,
> 1994).

On Dylan's first 'electric' tour of England in 1966, a young
man in the audience cried out 'Judas' just before the first
raunchy bars of 'Like a Rolling Stone' were to be played,
drawing an angry response from that quintessential angry
young man of the mid-1960s. The allegation of betrayal
clearly rankled, but what was he being accused of betraying? The folk revival to which he had contributed so richly
had become highly politicised, and the simplicity of the
acoustic form was an intrinsic part of that radicalism. The
pure and direct expression of 'wooden' music carried a serious intent, in contrast to the diversionary drivel churned
out by the entertainment industry. Indeed on *The Freewheelin' Bob Dylan*, the album which brought him to instant
fame, Dylan had parodied the idiocy of much of the
rock-and-roll of his day when he tells of 'Rock-a-Day
Johnny' singing 'Tell your Ma, Tell your Pa/Our Loves Are
Gonna Grow, Ooo-wah, Ooh-wah'. Now, apparently, the
singer who had written so many brilliant ballads about the
injustices of his day was turning into a Rock-a-Day Johnny,
and his fans were appalled. Dylan did nothing to dispel the
idea that he had turned his back on politics. In 'My Back
Pages' on the *Another Side Of Bob Dylan* album which

appeared towards the end of 1964, he declares his embarrassment at his former posturing as the poet of the protest movement, and laments that in the act of 'preaching' he had turned himself into the kind of judgemental figure that he had set out to oppose. He scorns the seriousness of his passion for equality and the self-righteousness of his judgement of right and wrong, concluding that he had moved beyond such immature 'oldness' to become 'much younger than that now'. However, while Dylan clearly refuses the mantle of troubadour of the radical opposition (Heylin 2001: 160), the 'political' phase of his songwriting career does not end in the summer of 1964. The political ballad form is left behind, but what follows is a cluster of coruscating songs which take 'protest' to another level and reveal a stunning and original political aesthetic.

In order to grasp the revolutionary nature of this achievement I turn to a rather unlikely source, the aesthetic theory of Theodor Adorno. 'Unlikely', because Adorno disdained popular music as a 'somatic stimulant' incapable of expressing an autonomous challenge to the status quo (Adorno 1997: 116). Nevertheless, his work on commitment in art can be applied as a valuable framework for appreciating the revolutionary artistic power of Dylan's long, image-laden songs which stand as a total protest against the prevailing greed, corruption and hypocrisy. These songs, I argue, fulfil Adorno's severe criteria for an autonomous aesthetics of protest, and in doing so they constitute an art of resistance which resolutely refuses to be assimilated by the social forces which it condemns. Adorno considered the original German Expressionist Movement of the early twentieth century to be the epitome of revolutionary art, and Dylan's critical work of this period revives that idiom in a new and widely popular form.

The songs concerned are largely on two albums which appeared in 1965, *Bringing it All Back Home* and *Highway 61 Revisited*. The most notable are 'Gates of Eden' and 'It's Alright Ma' from the former, and 'Ballad of a Thin Man' and 'Desolation Row' from the latter. However, these songs do not come unannounced, and two important precursors need to be considered as part of his 'social expressionist' body of work. The first is 'A Hard Rain's A-Gonna Fall', which dates back to the Cuban missile crisis of October 1962 and which first appears on *The Freewheelin' Bob Dylan* the following year. The second is 'Chimes of Freedom', from *Another Side Of Bob Dylan* (1964). The album as a whole may have been expressly non-political, but 'Chimes' is an unashamed profession of solidarity with the powerless and oppressed. Taken as a whole body of committed work, these songs constitute the most powerful and enduring political art. Casting away traditional narrative form and popular song conventions, they combine modernist poetic technique with withering social criticism, at the same time evoking a real alternative, a subversive ethical community, the 'underdog soldiers in the night' mentioned in 'Chimes of Freedom'. They can be understood as a new form of social expressionism which transcends conventional boundaries of popular culture and offers a profound challenge to pre-vailing values. There is a strong affinity between the spirit of Dylan's work during this period and the spirit of the German expressionist movement of the early twentieth century, with intriguing similarities in the ways in which the relationship between form and content is constructed in order to jolt the receiver into an emotional confrontation with the dominant conservative values. Dylan gives a clue as to the origins of this affinity in his autobiographical book *Chronicles*, in which he acknowledges the enormous impact of hearing the songs of Bertolt Brecht and Kurt Weill in New York in the early 1960s, particularly 'Pirate Jenny' (Dylan, 2004: 272-276 and 287). Struck by the 'raw intensity' of these heirs to the German expressionist tradition, Dylan's eyes were opened to the possibility of breaking popular song conventions with radical effect. Dylan's expressionist songs of the mid-sixties retain the anger at injustice evident in the ballads on *Times They Are A-Changin'* (1964), but raise it to a lacerating intensity when freed from the task of addressing specific social issues. Through sustained emotional empa-thy or confrontation they startle the listener into a profound reconsideration of values, an effect much deeper and more radical than that achieved through the overtly political songs.

The musically sparse jeremiads which catapulted Dylan to fame are brilliant commentaries on the injustices of the time, but they are, inevitably, very much tied to the specific issues of the day and directed towards a specific, already sympathetic audience. They galvanised a massive and mainly young audience with the force and eloquence of their exposure of the injustices of the time, but in cataloguing the wrongs of the world they tended to exhaust the medium. To continue in the same vein would be preaching to the converted, a problem inherent to overtly political art, as Adorno points out (Adorno 1997: 242). As Dylan developed as a songwriter and a thinker, he sought new forms of expression which could not be contained within the limitations of the simple folk-song form. His fans, however, wanted more of the same. The development which caused the greatest furore was his decision to 'go electric', adding electric guitars, drums and organ to his backing. All around the world fans who had adored him during his 1965 acoustic tours screamed their disapproval at the amplified noise that hit them in 1965–6. Dylan stood accused of 'selling out' the cause. The doyen of American folk, Pete Seeger, who had his passport revoked during the fierce anti-communist witch-hunts of the 1950s, helped to promote Dylan but was appalled at his abandonment of 'folk'. He tried to take an axe to the microphone cable when Dylan performed his first electric set at the Newport Folk Festival in 1965 (Heylin 2001: 212). However, the acoustic versus electric controversy masked important developments in his songwriting, which proved to be of greater artistic significance. The emergence of a more free-flowing form in which the succession of rich, often extreme, images challenges intelligibility, marks a period of expressionist song-writing of incomparable power. Until the end of 1965 many of these songs had a strong social dimension, yet its expression proved difficult to adapt to the new format of 'electric' music. Of the social expressionist songs discussed in this chapter, only 'Ballad of a Thin Man' has electric backing; it was tried on 'Desolation Row' but rejected in favour of a more simple accompaniment. These songs, therefore, are the products of a brief transition, although their artistic strength is enduring.

The next section deals with the problem of commitment in art as theorised by Adorno, in order to grasp how Dylan's rejection of 'official' politics enables him to develop a more complex songwriting style which is more powerful as a radical rejection of the prevailing structures and values of late capitalist society. There then follows a section dealing with the development of the form and content of the social expressionist songs, from 'A Hard Rain's A-Gonna Fall' to 'It's Alright Ma'. The third section deals with two of the most extreme and hard-hitting social expressionist songs, 'Ballad of a Thin Man' and 'Desolation Row'. In conclusion, I argue that during this brief period Dylan creates a revolutionary aesthetic of immense dramatic force, radical scope and lyrical panache. It constitutes a searing denunciation of the acquiescence to money and power, of the conservative worship of order and the fear of freedom. As long as the world continues to be profane, the power of the resolute opposition of these songs will endure. His achievement in breathing new life into old art forms by the radical modification of form and content has inspired millions of people throughout the world and reminds us that art can still awaken a sense of resistance to the fatalistic surrender to the idea that there is no alternative to a 'World Gone Wrong'.

## Commitment in Art

Adorno, in an essay on 'Commitment' written in 1962, considers the dilemma of politically engaged literature. On the one hand, art that is committed exposes non-committed work as little more than a fetish, an 'idle pastime' for those content to sleep through the major social problems of our times in an 'apoliticism that is in fact deeply political'. On the other hand, when art subordinates itself to the interests of a political cause it surrenders its autonomy and becomes part of the 'spiritual catastrophe' which its commitment originally set out to oppose (Adorno 1994: 177). Artless preaching subverts its goal of being deeply subversive. Lacking self-critical awareness, such works of art 'assimilate' themselves to the brute existence against which they protest, in forms so ephemeral that, according to Adorno, from their first day 'they belong in the seminars in which they inevitably end' (Adorno 1994: 177–8). Adorno is convinced that the prevailing culture is overwhelmingly alienated and that to try to protest against it in its own language necessarily misfires. Ostensibly revolutionary art fails to penetrate the alienated reality in which it operates, and merely serves to affirm the capacity of the established world of meaning to neutralise its opposition. Extreme though this position may be, it comes very close to Dylan's critical comments on his overtly political phase as set down in 'My Back Pages'. It would be a harsh judgement to write off Dylan's early protest ballads as mere propaganda pieces, for they are surely the finest expressions of that genre and provided a source of radical inspiration for millions. To persist with that type of song would be to exhaust its potential and to constrict his creative urge. He refused to become a prisoner of the expectations of his followers among the political activists.

The dilemma of committed art is well stated by Adorno, even if his proscriptions seem excessive. After all, there is a wide range of committed art which is not 'official' and which presumably offers some nourishment to humanistic consciousness even if, as he suggests, its impact is ephemeral and its transcendent quality is limited. But what is interesting is the way in which Adorno sees art as still capable of producing a resolute and transcendent opposition to the status quo. In his view, true revolutionary art has to effect a rupture with existing artistic form, even to the extent of rejecting intelligibility and coherence (Adorno 1994: 180). This is not a defence of meaninglessness or nihilism but rather a requirement that the terms on which art is produced and received need to be radically interrogated in the works of art themselves. In Adorno's first love, classical music, he prizes the revolutionary innovations of Arnold

Schoenberg, first in smashing orthodox tonality and then in introducing the twelve-tone compositional technique (Adorno 1981: 147–72). In the article on 'Commitment' in which the focus is on literature, Adorno's exemplars of the ability to produce autonomous revolutionary work are Franz Kafka and Samuel Beckett. Their writings, in Adorno's view, make 'officially' committed art look like pantomimes (Adorno 1994: 191). There is, in their work, a totally discomfiting protest against the alienation of which we are involved, and at the same time a deep, barely audible appeal to a sense of humanity still present despite its suppression. To protest the social system radically, art cannot be overtly political, as political processes are utterly compromised. Adorno considered the German Expressionist Movement of the years prior to the First World War to be the high point of autonomous, revolutionary art. He regards Schoenberg's music of this period as an extreme example of musical expressionism (Adorno 1992: 234), and the works of Kafka and Beckett can also be understood as developments of the Expressionist art form.

It may appear inappropriate to place Dylan's work of the mid-1960s in the company of Kafka or Beckett, or to think that it might qualify as autonomous revolutionary art under Adorno's severe strictures. Adorno made it clear that he saw no genuinely radical potential in popular music or jazz (Adorno 1981: 119–32), but then he had not heard Dylan when he made that judgement. It is not known whether he ever did before his death in 1969, but his likes and dislikes were well entrenched. In his Aesthetic Theory, published in 1970, he complains that the idea that jazz and popular music represent a resistance to affirmative culture was a subterfuge for the profit interest of the culture industry, and that these products are truly corrupt (Adorno 1997: 320–1). This conclusion about the inevitable sedation and incorporation of popular music has been well researched and to a great extent confirmed, as, for example, in Fred Goodman's book *The Mansion on the Hill*, in which he quotes Dylan saying in 1985 that the radical potential of popular music has probably passed forever (Goodman 1997: 351–2). But this argument does not apply to Dylan's work of this period. On the contrary, Dylan antagonised his first-generation supporters and fans in pursuit of his artistic freedom. Adorno's strictures about truly autonomous art are so severe and inherently elitist that we can assume that he would have considered it impossible for such an art to emerge in a popular form. How can the alienated masses reawaken to a truly revolutionary art? Nevertheless, we do not have to share his pessimism, and it is possible to apply his aesthetic theory to grasp the essence of Dylan's unique, if short-lived, achievement. It is no exaggeration to say that Dylan's songs of this period constitute a clear break with existing forms of song, using modernist poetic techniques and an ethical content which bears close similarities to that of German Expressionism.

Expressionism sought the most direct expression of intense human feelings through the use of condensed and intense imagery, delivered in order to shock the recipient into a strong emotional reaction. Syntactical compression, symbolic picture-sequences and a fervent declamatory tone were key features (Kellner 1983: 4). Expressionists subscribed to a clear social ethic which involved an intense commitment to individual freedom, the love of others (*nicht ich, sondern du*) and the brotherhood of all humanity (Bithell 1959: 361; Long 1993: part two). Their journals strove for a new ethics of humanity, rejecting not only art for art's sake but also politics for polities' sake, redefining true politics and true art as aspects of the philosophical ideal of 'the ethical' (Wright 1983: 83). Although its rebelliousness was clear for all to see, the specific forms of the 'new man' and the new society remained unclear, but it was also resolutely opposed to the prevailing conservatism, particularly to the strong authoritarianism and militarism displayed in Wilhelmite Germany. These central features of Expressionism are all salient in Dylan's work of this period, and there are more specific similarities in the content of the images. In Expressionist imagery these conservative forces were often related to torpor, decay or death. Adorno, citing lines from the Expressionist poets George Trakl and Theodor Daübler to the effect that the mass of people seem to be walking dead, comments that the unity of Expressionism consists in 'expressing that people wholly estranged from one another, life having receded within them, have thereby become, precisely, dead' (Adorno 1984: 191). Dylan assets in 'It's Alright, Ma' that 'he not busy being born is busy dying', while in 'Desolation Row' Casanova is being killed with self-confidence and Ophelia's great sin is her 'lifelessness'. On the liner notes to the *Highway 61* album Dylan talks of 'Lifelessness' as the 'Great Enemy' and depicts the Wipe-Out Gang as buying, owning and operating the Insanity Factory; anyone who does not know where the Insanity Factory is 'should hereby take two steps to the right, paint your teeth and go to sleep'. The more positive alternative to death and dying in expressionist imagery was ecstasy. As the painter Ludwig Meidner wrote in his manifesto of solidarity with the poor, 'ecstasy, rapture-passion is our daily work ... let us make common cause with our intimidated, brothers, for the sake of the spirit' (Meidner 1993: 175). Again, this is very much the spirit of 'Chimes of Freedom' with its flashing images of a transformed vision of the world. In Dylan's expressionist art the images are used to jolt, disturb and alarm the listener, and also occasionally to conjure liberation — they compel wonderment.

Most commentators, when considering Dylan's image-laden language of the mid-1960s, describe it as surrealistic. The boundaries between Expressionism and surrealism are often blurred, but I suggest that the intensity of the appeal for 'wholeness' is always present in expressionist art and not necessarily so in surrealism. The fragmented images of surrealism do not necessarily suggest that there is a wholeness that needs to be recovered, while those of expressionism portray a distorted humanity which begs to be put back together again, or an ideal which needs to be realised. As Bloch says, expressionism 'directed attention to human beings and their substance, in their quest for the most authentic expression possible' (Bloch 1994: 23). Expressionism has a harder edge than surrealism; it is more resolute and less susceptible to becoming regarded as a 'sophisticated' reflection of social unease (Adorno 1997: 229). The pacifism of the Expressionists, the recurring references to the human liberation and the willingness to renew folk art and other downgraded artistic resources, all apply to Dylan's songs of this period. Kokoschka's statement that 'Expressionism does not live in an ivory tower, it calls upon a fellow human being whom it awakens' is apposite (in Selz 1974: vi) and brings to mind Dylan's dismissive remarks about the ivory tower in 'Desolation Row' and his scorn for the professors in 'Ballad of a Thin Man'. It should be added that the original Expressionists were noted for lifestyles which displayed contempt for conventionality and middle- class values (Pachter 1983: 44), as indeed were the Abstract Expressionist American painters who were at the height of their popularity in Dylan's youth. Dylan in the period in question is an edgy, often aggressive figure, at war with the establishment, treating interviewers with contempt and making little attempt to please anyone, as we can see from Donn Pennebaker's film of the 1965 tour of Britain, *Don't Look Back*.

## Anguish and Defiance

Adorno's solution to the dilemma of committed art requires a radical reappraisal of the nature of politics itself. Conventional, politically committed art will miss the mark because it fails to stimulate a truly revolutionary consciousness. Yet there are works of art whose ruptured content and form can convey a fundamental rejection of the structures and values of our social life while retaining at least a glimmer of hope in the irrepressible urge for human freedom. Such art may not be political in the sense of supporting specific causes or subscribing to identifiable ideologies, but it is political in so far as it emits a visceral protest against the taken-for-granted conduct of alienated social life. It is not the politics of political parties and pressure groups working through established constitutional processes but rather politics in its original Greek sense in which it is inextricably tied to ethics and in which the central question is how we can achieve social justice. This is the sense of politics which I think is maintained by Dylan in his social expressionist songs, following his explicit rejection of politics in its narrower, modern sense. In one of the poems on the sleeve notes of the album *Another Side Of Bob Dylan* (1964), Dylan recounts an argument with a friend who speaks constantly of politics and complains that Dylan has changed and turned his back on the causes he once supported. On three occasions Dylan insists, 'I tell you there are no politics'. Note that he does not *reject* 'politics' as such but denies that there is any longer anything that can properly be termed 'politics'. In his own way he has arrived at the conclusion reached by Herbert Marcuse in *One Dimensional Man,* also published in 1964, that protest through established forms is doomed to replicate the oppressive totalising tendencies which it started out opposing (Marcuse 1991: chapters 2 and 10).

What turned Dylan away from the politics of the Left, which, in the US, was focused at that time on the Civil Rights Movement? There is no simple answer to this. In retrospect it seems obvious that for such a volcanic talent the restrictions of the orthodox folk-song format would have been intolerable, and the need to write in a less constrained fashion caused him to experiment with free-verse poetry and the prose-poem *Tarantula,* which was written in 1964. These unsuccessful experiments may have helped him to develop a new writing style which emerged in the form of songs quite unlike any that had been written before. In terms of the social context, it appears that the assassination of President Kennedy had a major impact on Dylan, suggesting that the formal political sphere was tightly controlled and that the dark forces who really controlled power could effectively exercise the ultimate veto (Heylin 2001: 136–43). With greater certainty we can say that Dylan gradually became irked by the conduct of those on the Left who sought to use him for their causes. The poem mentioned above and 'My Back Pages' convey his conviction that the propagandists for worthy causes were setting themselves up as figures of power, just like the figures of power they were ostensibly rejecting. In the poem he responds to his partner's political diatribe by complaining that someone has been tampering with her head, and when she understandably gets angry he depicts her raising her arm 'to the tone of principles'. His refusal to talk politics incenses her, and she shouts about the 'wasteland' that exists in television and proceeds to 'rant an' rave' about poverty. He hints at the deceitfulness of the political persona by describing how she berates him out of the corner of her mouth while talking on the telephone to a contact in a completely different manner. The poem expresses deep scepticism that this supercharged politics of protest can escape falling into dogmatism, reproducing in its actions the authoritarianism that was its original target. The image of the aggressive raised arm of the politically righteous recurs in 'My Back Pages', where he likens it to a soldier's stance and confesses that it had never occurred to him that in adopting the role of the preacher he would become his own enemy. This auto-critique reveals a young man convinced that he had been immature and naive in his previous acceptance of 'lies that life is black and white'. The poem and the song reveal a deep aversion to dogmatic sloganising, without in any way suggesting that the injustices with which they were concerned are any less real. Although at one stage Dylan adopted a cynical pose and claimed that he had written the protest songs for material gain (Gill 1998: 61), in an interview for *The New Yorker* magazine he declared that he still stood behind his 'finger-pointing' songs, even though he had now turned his back on being a spokesman (Heylin 2001: 160).

'A Hard Rain's A-Gonna Fall' stands out from the others on the *Free-wheelin'* album for its startling experimentation in content and form. It is not as though the life-or-death seriousness of the song comes as a complete surprise to the listener, for earlier tracks carried clear political messages. The first track, 'Blowin' in the Wind', is a simple humanistic appeal for peace and justice, and the third, 'Masters of War', is an excoriating diatribe against those who make their fortunes by supplying the weapons of war and encouraging their use. But the lines of these songs are quite clear and the listener is not required to puzzle over their meaning. By contrast, 'A Hard Rain's A-Gonna Fall' is more demanding. It starts out in traditional folk fashion, taking its musical form from an old ballad, 'Lord Randal', opening each verse with a repeated and closely related question (cf. Ricks 2003: 329–44). However, that is where the orthodoxy ends. In each of the ten verses of Lord Randal the question is met with a two-line answer, a repetitional device typical of many traditional folk songs. In Dylan's song the answers are much lengthier and their content is entirely given over to a concatenation of images, many of which, when taken in isolation, stretch the limits of intelligibility. The first four verses have five, seven, seven and six lines, respectively, in response to the questions where have you been?/what did you see?/ what did you hear?/who did you meet? 'my blue-eyed son' and 'my darling young one'. The final verse, answering the question 'what'll you do now?', has twelve lines of images, the length adding to the build-up of tension in a song of almost unbearable urgency. Faced with cataclysm, all the contradictions and the pain of humanity must be expressed. Each verse ends with four repeats of 'it's a hard' before the final 'it's a hard rain's a gonna fall', drumming home its dire warning in juxtaposition to the bewildering intensity of the disturbing images.

The condensed images convey a sense of global crisis that has led to the possibility of obliteration by nuclear war. Daxibler once commented that Expressionism could be characterised by the saying that when somebody is hanged his whole life flashes before him in the last moment (Daxibler, 1993: 85). In this case it is not the individual's life that is registered in the flashing images, but the life of the world. Faced with the threat of oblivion, the narrator rolls out a string of images which capture an intense impression of the wrongs that had brought the world to this plight. The first verse establishes the global nature of the subject, the universal being who has traversed highways, mountains, oceans and forests and who has been 'ten thousand miles in the mouth of a graveyard'. The use of numbers helps to establish this universality, from the low numbers specifying the mountains and other places to the use of 'ten thousand' to convey the vastness of the vision. He uses the same figure in the second and third verses to convey multitude, pared down to 100 to establish the assonant strength of 'one hundred drummers whose hands were a-blazin'. The middle three verses offer images of a largely calamitous nature. Although the image of the 'black branch with blood that kept dripping' appears to comment on the continuing violence against black people in the struggle for civil rights in his own country, for the most part the images are at a level of abstraction which lends them an enduring relevance. For example, listening now to the reference to 'guns and sharp swords in the hands of young children' triggers images of the child-soldiers involved in the atrocities in the recent civil war in Sierra Leone. A chronic failure to communicate is an important theme in the song, first flagged up in the second verse in the reference to the 'ten thousand talkers whose tongues were all broken' and then developed in the third verse which addresses what the singer hears. We have images of sheer volume drowning out everything, but also a sense of deep helplessness in the face of incessant rumours when he hears 'ten thousand whisperin' and nobody listening'. Once again, these images remain apposite when thinking of the false rhetoric which presaged the recent war against Iraq. There is also the hideous juxtaposition of the suddenly very specific sound of one person starving while many people are laughing. Not until the fourth verse do we see a ray of light in the shape of innocence, nature and colour when he recounts that he had 'met a young girl, she gave a rainbow'.

The final verse expresses a committed solidarity with the powerless. The narrator declares that he is going out to revisit the world before the apocalypse, or rather the world which lives with poverty, pollution ('the pellets of poison are flooding their waters'), ruthless injustice, starvation and neglect: 'Where the executioner's face is always well hidden Where hunger is ugly, where souls are forgotten'. Finally, the singer declares that these truths about the world must be announced to the world, 'so all souls can see it'. Reflectively, he claims that this time, even when faced with finality, he will know his song well before he starts singing. This is not a rehearsal and there is no time for carelessness; we must express our truths as best we can. Had there ever been a song like this? It sounds like modernist poetry set to music, and indeed Dylan wrote it first as a poem, but the adoption of an amended ballad form lends it a discipline and thematic development which bring the wild and sometimes unfathomable images into coherence. This is a new type of song, the earliest example of his social expressionism, a declaration of horror at the depths to which humanity had sunk. Technically, the focus on subjective judgement is reminiscent of the *Ich-Dramatik* device used in expressionist theatre. The song announces a unique talent, showing the ability to turn traditional verse forms into a vehicle for intense emotional expression, much as the original expressionist poets had attempted to do (Bithell 1959: 419–20). *Another Side Of Bob Dylan* disappointed many who had been excited by the political radicalism of his previous album, *The Times They Are A-Changin'*. It contained little 'real' political material and its sales were disappointing. However, standing in contrast to the rest of the songs is another experiment in social expressionism, 'Chimes of Freedom'. It has the all-encompassing embrace of 'A Hard Rain's A-Gonna Fall' but this time the tone is ecstatic rather than cataclysmic. Again, it is an expression of solidarity with the powerless, and he uses the literary device of catalogue verse in order to give them identity and, through that, substance. So, in each of the six verses a scene is set with the vivid, euphoric imagery of the journeyers in the city carried away with the spectacle of the thunder and lightning which produces the chimes. For example, the third verse opens by telling us that 'through the mad mystic hammering of the wild ripping hail/The sky cracked its poems in naked wonder', while the final verse confirms the epiphanic transcendence of the experience, describing themselves as 'starry-eyed and laughing as I recall when we were caught/Trapped by no track of hours for they hanged suspended'. The power of the stormy elements summons the majesty of the solidarity extended. The second part of each verse lists the groups of people for whom the chimes of freedom are flashing. The first of those are 'the warriors whose strength is not to fight' and the second are the 'refugees on the unarmed road of flight', both raising the spectre of the US's deeper involvement in the Vietnam War. The catalogue recounts society's many underdogs, as the chimes call out for the outcast burning constantly at the stake, for the deaf, mute and blind, for the single mother branded as a prostitute, for those who have been unjustly imprisoned, and even for the rejected lovers 'with too personal a tale'.

The embrace extends beyond victims to the gentle and the kind and also for the 'guardians and protectors of the mind'. It is for all who can find no peace in a world of unnecessary woe:

> Tolling for the aching ones who wounds cannot be nursed
> For the countless confused, accused, misused, strung-out
> ones an' worse
> An' for every hung-up person in the whole wide universe
> An' we gazed upon the chimes of freedom flashing.

Andy Gill rightly points to the song as a pivotal moment in Dylan's songwriting development, with the focus moving away from specific issues and towards the creation of a 'parallel universe in which the underlying forces were more subtly revealed' (Gill 1998: 58). Clearly, it announces a departure from the issue-based protest song without any loss of critical force, for the intensity of the images couched in the simple form of a folk song amounts to a genuine cry for humanity, and in this single instance it is an uplifting, ecstatic cry. 'A Hard Rain's A-Gonna Fall' might have been a discrete response to an extraordinary situation, but 'Chimes' showed that Dylan was artistically at his best when writing this extended form of rich imagery around a sustained theme.

The next album, *Bringing It All Back Home,* appeared early in 1965 and long-standing radical folk-fans were appalled not only by the absence of conventional protest ballads, but also by the introduction of a backing group with electric guitars and drums on some tracks. However, the songs which obviously fall into the category of social expressionism,

'Gates of Eden' and 'It's Alright, Ma (I'm Only Bleedin')',
are both performed with simple acoustic backing. Like
'Hard Rain' and 'Chimes', which are about seven minutes
long, they are exceptionally long by the conventions of popular music and, while abandoning conventional narrative,
deliver a fusillade of images laden with biting social criticism. There is, however, a marked contrast between the two
songs, with the dreary bleakness of 'Gates of Eden' conveying a resigned weariness while 'It's Alright, Ma' is a
razor-sharp, defiant masterpiece. The doleful melody of
'Gates of Eden' carries the song through its barren land-
scape. In contrast to the ideal of innocent perfection that is
Eden, we hear nine verses of elusive images which convey a
deep sense of alienation but otherwise lack the thematic
unity of the other social expressionist songs. The abundance
of negative verbs—twists, wail, complains, scream, weeps,
rot, squints—conveys distortion and desolation, but there
are few clues as what has been distorted and how it might be
restored to wholeness. The image of the savage soldier
sticking his head in the sand and then complaining to the
shoeless hunter may well allude to the developing morass
in Vietnam, an early example of heavily armed military
complaining at the unfairness of opponents who lack the
decency to come out into the open and be shot. The reference to Aladdin sitting with Utopian hermit monks
'side-saddle on the Golden Calf seems to be an attack on the
idolatrous nature of organised religion. The reference to the
'grey flannel dwarf being shocked by the strident image of
the leather-clad woman on the motorcycle mocks the pas-
sionless conservatism of the bourgeoisie. The image of pau-
pers changing possessions 'each one wishing for what the
other has got' laments the stultifying effect of consumerism.
The final verse offers little hope of resistance to the alienated reality; he sees in the unanalysed dreams of his lover at
least some hint of truth, but concludes that 'there are no
truths outside the Gates of Eden'. William Blake's poem
'Gates of Paradise' may well have inspired Dylan's composition, but this song lacks the dialectical subtlety of his other
expressionist efforts, particularly the song which follows it

on the album, 'It's Alright, Ma'. Nevertheless, 'Gates of Eden' reached a surprisingly large audience for it was placed on the 'B' side of the hit single 'Like A Rolling Stone'. In those days of massive sales for singles few people were aware in advance of what was on the 'B' side but always listened to it, so this was a ploy to encourage people to listen to this troubling song.

'It's Alright, Ma (I'm Only Bleedin')' marks a heightening in Dylan's artistic power, more effective as protest precisely because of the profound political pessimism that had set in (Gray 2000: 134). The phrase 'It's Alright, Ma' expresses a determination to stand fast in the face of a corrupt world, while at the same time the parenthetical qualification indicates the seriousness of the fight. The musical form adopted works beautifully with the lyrics. The 15 verses are organised in five groups of three, and each verse involves a repeated musical phrase imprisoned within a two-and-a-half tone pattern, going down in semi-tones. It lends an impression of the narrowness and restrictedness of its subject matter, a wholly corrupted world, and also its gradual decline. The verses are separated by a rapid succession of three major chords, adding to the tension and suggesting opposition, and then after each group of three verses the defiant retorts which lead up to the title line are played in a different chord sequence with a simple, uplifting melody.

The opening verse of the song establishes an eerie context, speaking of darkness at the break of noon and contrasting the violent, cutting image of 'the handmade blade' with the innocence and vulnerability of 'the child's balloon'. But there is also a comment on the difficulty of understanding the complexity and scale of the problems, a plea to listen rather than rush towards a rational comprehension which is not easily available—'to understand you know too soon/ There is no sense in trying'. The objects of his bitterness are more clearly drawn than in 'Gates of Eden'. The world is portrayed as an exploitative morass in which human relationships seem hopelessly perverted by the twin imperatives of making money and maintaining order. The 'human

Gods' are the manufacturers who manipulate needs and encourage a new idolatry, the worship of possessions:

> Disillusioned words like bullets bark
> As human Gods aim for their mark
> Make everything from toy guns that spark
> To flesh coloured Christs that glow in the dark
> It's easy to see without looking too far
> That not much is really sacred.

Not much at all. Preachers and teachers perform for money; reactionaries want not simply to kill people but to see them crawl as well. Corruption and manipulation are everywhere, 'money doesn't talk, it swears, obscenity who really cares, propaganda all is phoney'. Yet somehow their power and wealth cannot hide them from their true selves and they must stand exposed; even the President of the United States 'sometimes must have to stand naked'. When he sings that line in a sensational, frenetic live performance from his 1974 tour, recorded on *Before the Flood,* the audience go wild at the uncanny appropriateness of it to Richard Nixon's public disgrace. He also swipes at the indoctrination dispensed by the advertisers to fool their viewers into thinking that purchasing their goods can somehow turn them into achievers and winners, while the important issues of life are passed by unaddressed. This understanding of the manipulative power of the corporations and advertisers conforms with Marcuse's critique of 'repressive satisfaction' in *One Dimensional Man,* in which he writes that the chief feature of modern society is its 'effective suffocation of those needs which demand liberation' while sustaining 'the destructive power and repressive function of the affluent society' (Marcuse 1991: 7).

The fourth group of three verses is concerned with the would-be opposition to the world of the masters who make the rules. There is scorn for those who 'must obey authority' even when they do not respect it. They compromise themselves by holding on to jobs they despise, developing their talents only to place them at the disposal of a system which they don't like but which offers them a comfortable life. Then he turns his attention to those who identify with 'strict party platform ties' deriding them as 'social clubs in drag disguise' which do nothing except throw up leaders for us to idolise. Finally, he appears to engage in an auto-critique of his committed past, the one who once sang 'with his tongue on fire', memorably described as 'bent out of shape by society's pliers'. Now Dylan scorns the iconoclast, seeing no progress or hope of transcendence in that attitude, but rather a hopeless negativity dragging us 'down in the hole that's he's in'. Dylan forgives all of them who are imprisoned in their dogmatic 'vault' but he no longer cares 'if I can't please him'. The song offers no resolution to the hypocrisy it rages against, only a declaration of total opposition and defiance:

> And if my thought-dreams could be seen
> They'd probably put my head in a guillotine
> But it's alright, Ma, it's life, and life only.

The song is a withering critique of the values which sustain life in the affluent society, and, implicitly, an appeal to stand fast against the integrating power of the oppressive society.

## Revelling in Rebellion

Less than six months elapsed between the release of *Bringing it All Back Home* and the recording of the final studio takes of *Highway 61 Revisited* in August 1965, but it was a period of the highest intensity in American social and political life. In March President Johnson took the decision to commit combat troops to South Vietnam and to bomb North Vietnam, actions that triggered the first major protest meetings and demonstrations (Marwick 1998: 541–3). By the end of the year there were 180,000 US troops in Vietnam. Violent struggles continued to accompany attempts to enforce the Civil Rights Act of 1964 which outlawed racial discrimination in public places, and the disaffection of black Americans was not confined to the segregated South. The first of several urban riots exploded in the Los Angeles suburb of Watts in August 1965, claiming dozens of lives and causing immense destruction (Marwick 1998: 573–4). The riot slogan of 'Burn Baby Burn' symbolised the volatility of

American society at this time. The polarisation is aptly summarised by Dylan in 'Desolation Row', in which, as the *Titanic* sails out, 'everybody' is shouting 'Which Side Are You On?'.

The mood of *Highway 61 Revisited* is a confident expression of a counter-culture, a collective resistance to establishment values. If the oppositional voice of *Bringing It All Back Home* is an isolated one, crying in the wilderness, here Dylan is secure within the opposition. The songs no longer reflect the threat that society poses to him, but rather the threat that the new exponents of the great refusal — to use Marcuse's term — poses for society (Marcuse 1991: 63–4). The shift is even denoted by the photographs on the album sleeves. The mock cosiness of a domesticated Dylan with his little grey cat on the cover of *Bringing It All Back Home* is now succeeded by an unfettered image of him in a motorcycle T-shirt holding his shades, staring out calmly but uncompromisingly. The musical backing, too, takes a qualitative leap forward in the new album, dramatically announced in the first few bars of the opening track, 'Like A Rolling Stone', which makes the previous efforts at creating a new electric sound on *Bringing It All Back Home* sound rather feeble. Although there are elements of rebelliousness throughout the album, the two songs which come closest to giving us a complete expressionist rejection of conservative values are 'Ballad of a Thin Man' and 'Desolation Row'. In both songs Dylan effects a role-reversal between the 'respectable' and the outsiders. In these songs the underworld of the rebels or freaks is the liberated, sane place to be, and the world of the conservatives is shrivelled, hypocritical and in decay. If the Dylan of 'It's Alright, Ma' is a lonely voice, the Dylan of these songs has found a revolutionary band of those who refuse to play the game. Their presence is inherently oppositional, even if their consciousness is not political. They conform to Marcuse's invocation of the revolutionary potential of the 'outcasts and outsiders' (Marcuse 1991: 256–7), brought to life on their own territory, the world of the liberated imagination.

'Ballad of A Thin Man' directly challenges intelligibility in the manner prescribed by Adorno as a necessary feature of art that can claim to represent an autonomous challenge to the prevailing culture. It is not, of course, a ballad at all, and the irony of the title is brought home in the first few portentous bars of crashingly stated chords played on the piano, with a moaning organ and electric guitars producing a slow, heavy sound which conjures a menacing, claustrophobic atmosphere. The thin man may be a reference to T. S. Eliot's 'hollow man', a person of no substance, no integrity, and certainly this is how Mr. Jones, a reporter, is portrayed as he tries to find out what is going on in a party or a club populated by 'alternative' characters such as the geek, the sword swallower and the one-eyed midget. In the Pennebaker film *Don't Look Back* there are examples of Dylan's contempt for reporters who had no knowledge of or sympathy for their subject. One young middle-class reporter is treated mercilessly by Dylan as though he is some kind of voyeur trying to score social points by associating with people whose world was completely alien to him. Just as Dylan gave such characters a hard time in real life, so in the song the 'alternative' characters heap derision on these thoroughly bourgeois figures.

The ubiquity and blandness of the name 'Mr. Jones' suggests conformity and a respect for formality. In the first three verses there is simply no understanding between the reporter and the party people, and a picture is drawn of a total failure of communication. Jones watches the geek displaying his deformity but it is geek who asks Mr. Jones how it feels 'to be such a freak'. Appalled, Mr. Jones says 'Impossible' as the geek hands him a bone. The incongruity threatens to destroy the self-assurance of the establishment's representative. Each verse ends with a scathing mockery of the incapacity of the reporter to grasp this new discursive world — 'something is happening here but you don't know what it is, do you, Mister Jones?' The colourful assembly is the alternative society, confident and secure in its own values, scornful of the middle-of-the road reporter who has no interest in trying to understand or empathise.

The reporter, of course, has power. In the middle section of the song Dylan attacks the power of the press, referring to Jones's 'contacts among the lumberjacks', the ones who turn dead trees into newsprint to feed misinformation to the masses. They are readily able to summon up 'facts' to answer anything that attacks the limited imagination of Jones, hiding behind the positivist reliance on facts rather than understanding. 'Nobody has any respect', laments Dylan, reversing the meaning of this common conservative phrase, usually referring to respect for law, convention or position but now also meaning that there is no respect for the truth. Like everything else, it is bought off, and the conscience is soothed by handing over money to 'tax-deductible charity organizations'. Even charity must have its material advantages. The song accuses Mr. Jones of having 'your eyes in your pocket and your nose on the ground', that is to say being totally in thrall to the money interest and willing to sniff out anything that might be exploitable. In another use of radical ambiguity Dylan intones 'there ought to be a law against you coming around', mimicking a common conservative cry of the time that the authorities should come down hard on outward shows of rebelliousness. The coercive threat is now turned back against the establishment, and it is suggested that Mr. Jones be made to wear earphones so that he is forced to listen to sounds of the alternative society.

Dylan directs his anger at those who have power but who are too complacent to use it responsibly. The reporter is alerted to something strange, but the strangeness is not something to be understood, only something to be itemised and stereotyped, confirming to the prurient readers the freakish nature of these alternative lifestyles. The reporter is like a coloniser, mapping out a new territory for the Empire, renaming the places and pacifying its people. This time, however, there is a strange form of resistance; the natives simply dismiss him and carry on living. One of Dylan's targets here, repeated in 'Desolation Row', is the tendency to reduce learning and culture to affirmative apologias for the established order. Mr. Jones is a college man, admired by 'the professors' and associated with great lawyers with whom he has discussed 'lepers and crooks'. He is something of an expert on F. Scott Fitzgerald, that great illustrator of the American bourgeoisie, but for all the benefits of being 'very well read' he cannot grasp the meaning of the 'something' that is happening here, and he is being forced to confront that truth. The real world and its problems, the world of lepers and crooks, is nothing for him and his ilk but an abstract set of issues for intellectual contemplation. Knowledge itself has become reified, with real human relations transformed into topics for after-dinner conversation.

The radical impact of the song can be gauged from Bobby Scale's best-selling autobiographical book *Seize The Time: The Story of the Black Panther Party* (Seale 1970: 213–8). Seale tell us that 'Ballad of a Thin Man' was played repeatedly while the founding members of the Black Panther Party were laying out their first newspaper. Seale recounts the revolutionary 'reading' of the song presented to them by Huey Newton, leader of the Party. Newton explains the significance of the geek calling Jones a freak, for although the geek is a circus performer who has no option but to look and act in a hideous way, in Dylan's verse the geek exposes the real freaks, the people who pay money to be entertained by his deformity. The middle classes, he suggests, like to peek into the seamy world of the oppressed, and in this song they are exposed in the horror of their hypocrisy. Newton concludes:

> This song is hell. You've got to understand that this song is saying a hell of a lot about society (Seale 1970: 216).

Newton then extemporises on the theme by commenting on the way the alternative characters in the song reverse their relationship with Mr. Jones by casting him as the outsider. He likens it to the bragging of (the then) Cassius Clay in refusing the 'acceptable' role for a black athlete, that of the modest young man grateful for his chance to become heavyweight boxing champion of the world. Instead, he loudly claims 'I am the greatest' and declares himself to be 'so pretty', deliberately infuriating millions of racists. The song was played persistently by the Panthers, and Seale praises 'brother Bobby' for doing society a big favour. It is a remarkable feat for a young, lower-middle-class white man to command such respect from a party willing to take up arms against racist White America, and it is a testimony to the rich radical vein of the social expressionist songs. Dylan remained a staunch opponent of racism. In 1971, years after leaving the protest song form behind him, he released a single accusing the authorities of deliberately murdering Black Panther leader George Jackson. Four years later, he wrote a celebrated defence of the black boxer 'Hurricane' Carter who was wrongfully convicted of murder.

In 'Desolation Row' it is not immediately evident that the relationship between the mainstream and alternative worlds has been reversed. The opening line, 'They're selling postcards of the hanging', exposes the sadistic sickness of society and appears to be the first step in fleshing out the 'Desolation' of the title, but at the end of the verse it transpires that the shady world in which the riot police are itching for a riot is being watched *from* Desolation Row rather than *on* it. The Row in fact is a place of liberty adjacent to but wholly different in spirit from the 'real world' and its motley band of inadequate characters such as Romeo, Dr. Filth, Ophelia and the Phantom of the Opera. The separation is not total, for people pass between the two worlds, and this element of uncertainty and choice adds to the drama. Musically the song has a simple and pleasant melody with a beautiful guitar accompaniment by Charlie McCoy to what is otherwise a standard guitar and harmonica ballad form. The song was originally recorded with a full electric band behind him, but it was eventually decided to revert to a more simple format (Heylin 2001: 219–20). The addition of McCoy's ingenious improvisation gives the music a lightness of tone that belies the melodrama of the scenes depicted. The poetic form also conveys a sense of even, rhythmic inevitability; each of the ten verses has three quatrains, the rhyme scheme is rigid and each verse ends with something rhyming with Row.

The literary device used in 'Desolation Row' is collage, jumping from scene to scene through fragmented images over ten verses while managing to sustain coherence. We can detect here and elsewhere on the album the poetic influence of T. S. Eliot, except that Dylan is using Eliot's technique to subvert the latter's commitment to the idea of 'high art' accessible only to a gifted elite. Dylan not only constructs a masterpiece which commands the attention of millions of listeners, but he comments on the poetic sources of the song in the penultimate verse. Here he has the great exponents of collage technique, Ezra Pound and Eliot, 'fighting in the captain's tower' of the *Titanic* as it sails to its doom. They are mocked by the people's artists, the calypso singers, but the whole scene is a folly, a diversion which prevents all of them from thinking about Desolation Row. The diversion languishes 'between the windows of the sea/ Where lovely mermaids flow', hinting at Eliot's own images of 'mermaids singing' and the 'chambers of the sea' towards the end of 'The Love Song of J. Alfred Prufrock'. The verse rejects the feigned purity of the art-for-art's sake perspective and the song as a whole is clearly committed to making us confront the big questions about the overall direction in which society is travelling.

The images in 'Desolation Row' are confrontational — 'they need somewhere to go' as he says of the riot squad in the opening verse. The second verse contrasts the autonomy and confidence of the new woman, Cinderella, with the possessiveness of the moaning Romeo, who claims her for himself. Romeo is firmly reminded by an anonymous voice that he's in the wrong place 'my friend', and the nature of Romeo's expulsion from Desolation Row is hinted at by the sounds of departing ambulances and Cinderella sweeping up the damage, still firmly on Desolation Row. The stereotypical model lover is rejected. Casanova appears as one who is being killed with self-confidence after being poisoned with words as a punishment for going to Desolation Row. Love in Casanova's world is essentially about possession, contrived seduction and narcissism, in contrast to the open and reciprocal relationships on offer on the

Row. Free sexuality as repressive is contrasted with free sexuality as genuinely liberating. Repressed sexuality is lampooned in the fourth verse, where the young Ophelia is already 'an old maid'. Her chaste religiosity is mocked, for although her eyes are fixed upon 'Noah's great rainbow' she really spends her time 'peeking' into Desolation Row. Most bitingly, Dylan writes that 'her sin is her lifelessness'.

The mobility between the real world and Desolation lends an air of fascinating mystery to the song. In the third verse the Good Samaritan is getting ready to go to the carnival on Desolation Row, but it is not clear whether he and the other characters are already there or confined to the mundane world of 'making love or else expecting rain'. What is important is that it is the good guy who goes to the carnival. Similarly in the fifth verse we see Einstein passing by 'dressed as Robin Hood', rather dismissively described as bumming cigarettes, sniffing drainpipes 'and reciting the alphabet'. But then comes an unexpected compliment, that long ago Einstein used to play the electric violin on Desolation Row. The figure of Einstein clearly intrigues Dylan, perhaps because he left school poorly qualified and went on to achieve greatness. Einstein achieved a revolution in physics but continued to associate himself with radical causes—and play the violin—until his death in 1955. His last unfinished note declared that what he sought to accomplish was to serve truth and justice 'at the risk of pleasing no one', a sentiment which would have been shared by Dylan.

The fifth verse paints a dismissive picture of the lifeworld of Dr. Filth, his 'local loser' of a nurse and their 'sexless patients', and it is made very clear that they are far from Desolation Row, as you would need to lean your head far out to hear the sound of them playing on penny whistles. If there are still lingering doubts about Desolation Row being the refuge from the depredations of the 'real' world, they are dispelled with withering force in the eighth verse. Dylan conjures a Kafkaesque scene depicting the power of society to quell its dissidents and prevent them escaping into Desolation Row. If the listener has not grasped by now that the real desolation exists *outside* Desolation Row, then the message is quite unmistakable by the end of the verse:

> Now at midnight all the agents
> And the superhuman crew
> Come out and round up everyone
> That knows more than they do
> Then they bring them to the factory
> Where the heart-attack machine
> Is strapped across their shoulders
> And then the kerosene
> Is brought down from the castles
> By insurance men who go
> Check to see that nobody is escaping
> To Desolation Row

Those who oppose the values of mainstream society, who see through the dehumanising imperatives of the acquisitive society, are brought back into the world of work, forced there through economic necessity. The harsh competitive nature of that world is forced upon us, strapped as we are to the heart-attack machine. The reference to the castles brings to mind Kafka's use of the Castle as an impenetrable symbol of power in the novel of that name. The insurance men ensure that nobody will escape into the liberation of Desolation Row. They draw people back to the reality of life by warning them of the dire consequences of not having the right policies; they feed off insecurity in a totally insecure world.

In the final verse Dylan reintroduces himself for the first time since his romantic appearance with 'Lady' at the end of the first verse. Now we find him world-weary and contemptuous of his former acquaintances from the real world. He pleads for no further communication unless they are mailed from inside Desolation Row, the refuge of the human in an inhumane world. When asked what he would do if he were President of the US Dylan whimsically suggested that he would make schoolchildren memorise 'Desolation Row' instead of 'America the Beautiful' (Gill 1998: 89). Despite the apparent farewell to politics in 1964 the Dylan of 'Desolation Row' comes out with an outright and total rejection of the status quo, a vibrant, autonomous song which exposes and explodes hypocrisy without falling into the trap of dogmatic sermonising.

However, it is, more or less, his last word, an eleven-minute salvo at the established society and the values that sustain it. While the compositional style *of Blonde on Blonde* is similar, it is no longer *social* expressionism, while after that the serious motorcycle crash in the summer of 1966 signalled the end of a brief period of volcanic intensity in his writing. Even in 'Tears of Rage' on *The Basement Tapes* recording of 1967, a highly emotional reflection of America's Vietnam crisis, Dylan's depiction of the political leadership as the treacherous daughter of the country's founding father is ultimately a plea for reconciliation. When *John Wesley Harding* appeared in 1968 the songs are more wistful and meditative, and the bitterness of the social expressionist period has been left behind, despite the apocalyptic warning conveyed in 'All Along the Watchtower'. 'I Dreamed I Saw St. Augustine' can be seen as some sort of epitaph to the social engagement he had made over the previous five years. The opening of the song copies that of the great American labour ballad 'Joe Hill', made famous by Paul Robeson and later by Joan Baez. Joe Hill is a union leader murdered at the behest of the bosses, but in the song he denies he is dead, in the sense that every trade unionist who goes on to organise carries forward the essence of his life. In 'St. Augustine' Dylan has the saint lamenting from beyond the grave to his followers that they no longer have a 'martyr' to 'call your own', but he calls on the 'gifted Kings and Queens' to 'go on your way accordingly/And know you're not alone'. Dylan is letting his followers know that they need to find their own way rather than wait on the words of leaders, but there is no repudiation of the oppositional force of his early work involved here. He has said what he needed to say and moves on.

## Conclusion

Dylan's social expressionist songs rage against the injustices of the day in a completely different way from his early protest ballads. The emphasis switches to a biting critique of the everyday social practices and attitudes which sustain a society in thrall to the pursuit of wealth and the preservation of relations of domination and subordination. The device of the imaginary counter-culture used in 'Ballad of a Thin Man' and 'Desolation Row' sustains the aspiration to liberty and social harmony and shows that these ideals are not easily extinguished. In turning the popular song form into a musical poetry of protest he briefly captures the autonomous quality which for Adorno constitutes the peak of aesthetic achievement. I am sure that Adorno would have been loath to concede such exalted status to a popular art form, but within the framework he presents on his essay 'On Commitment' and in his *Aesthetic Theory*, Dylan's social expressionist songs resound with the ethical force and brilliance of the best of the original expressionism. The creation of a new form of song was not the result of long years of formal training and the refinement and transcendence of techniques, but it was a more spontaneous and utterly unique break with conventions driven to great heights of skill and energy. Not only was it an amazing feat to attract an audience of millions with such extraordinary work, but it should be remembered that this is a performance art in which he figures as part of the artistic production. This is particularly evident in the Pennebaker film, which shows Dylan relishing the role of the razor-sharp intellectual subversive. In this sense Dylan becomes an Expressionist character, rather like Baal, the eponymous hero of Bertolt Brecht's early Expressionist play, in which the anarchic wandering minstrel and poet seeks out all the extremes of life in order to squeeze out its essence (Speir 1982: 17–29). Like the Expressionist painter Ludwig Meidner, Dylan puts himself in the picture among the distorted, fragmented, and often tortured images (Selz 1974: 280–2). Indeed, what was once said of Meidner is uncannily appropriate to the Dylan of the social expressionist period:

> Everything he does is expression, eruption, explosion. This is the hottest crater of a volcanic epoch, spewing out the lava of its visions in unpredictable bursts with irresistible

power, in the relentless swell of the inner fire (Dube 1972: 176-7).

Meidner once commented that the bourgeois knows no love, only exploitation and fraud, and he appealed to compassionate people to 'arise to battle against the ugly beast of prey, the booty-hungry, thousand-headed emperor of tomorrow' (Meidner 1993: 175–6). Like Meidner, Dylan could not sustain that sort of righteous anger for long, preferring instead to search for spiritual reconciliation through religion. One of the strengths of early Expressionism was that its appeal for a new sensibility reached across the conventional divisions between the arts, an attack on all fronts to bring humanity to its senses. The Dylan songs in question defied convention and won a worldwide audience as he flayed the hypocrisy and complacency of the conservative forces of his day. His art, like the social expressionist paintings which expressed horror at the carnage of the First World War, portrays a world bled white, yet somehow clinging to the hope of a new humanism. This art, defying attempts to assimilate it, to dilute its rage or turn it into positive images, retains its revolutionary integrity.

## References

Adorno, Theodor (1981) *Prisms*. Cambridge, Mass.: MIT Press.

Adorno, Theodor (1984) *Minima Moralia: Reflections From Damaged Life*. London: Verso.

Adorno, Theodor (1992) *Quasi Una Fantasia: Essays on Modern Music*. London and New York: Verso.

Adorno, Theodor (1994) 'On Commitment', in Theodor Adorno, Walter Benjamin, Ernst Bloch, Bertolt Brecht and Georg Lukacs, *Aesthetics and Politics*. London: New Left Books.

Adorno, Theodor (1997) *Aesthetic Theory*. London: Athlone.

Bithell, Jethro (1959), *Modern German Literature, 1880-1950*. London: Methuen.

Bloch, Ernst (1994) 'Discussing Expressionism', in Theodor Adorno, Walter Benjamin, Ernst Bloch, Bertolt Brecht and Georg Lukacs, *Aesthetics and Politics*. London: New Left Books.

Deibler, Theodor (1993; originally 1916) 'Expressionism', in Rose-Carol Washton Long, ed. *German Expressionism*. New York: G. K. Hall.

Dube, Wolf-Dieter (1972) *The Expressionists*. London: Thames and Hudson.

Dylan, Bob (2004) *Chronicles, Volume One*. New York: Simon and Schuster.

Gill, Andy (1998) *Classic Bob Dylan, 1962-69: My Back Pages*. London: Carlton Books.

Gray, Michael (2000) *Song and Dance Man HI: The Art of Bob Dylan*. London and New York, Cassell.

Goodman, Fred (1997) *The Mansion on The Hill: Dylan, Young, Geffen, Springsteen and the Head-On Collision of Rock and Commerce*. London: Jonathan Cape.

Heylin, Clinton (2001) *Bob Dylan: Behind the Shades - Take Two*. London: Penguin.

Kellner, Douglas (1983) 'Expressionism and Rebellion', in Stephen Eric Bronner and Douglas Kellner (eds) *Passion and Rebellion: The Expressionist Heritage* .London: Croom Helm.

Long, Rose-Carol Washton (ed.) (1993) *German Expressionism: Documents from the End of the Wilhelmine Empire to the Rise of National Socialism*. New York: G. K. Hall.

Marcuse, Herbert (1991) *One Dimensional Man*. London: Routledge.

Marwick, Arthur (1998) *The Sixties*. London and New York: Oxford University Press.

Meidner, Ludwig (1993, originally published 1919). To All Artists, Musicians, Poets', in Rose-Carol Washton Long (ed.) *German Expressionism: Documents from the End of the Wilhelmine Empire to the Rise of National Socialism*. New York: G. K. Hall.

Pachter, Henry (1983) 'Expressionism and Cafe Culture', in Stephen Eric Bronner and Douglas Kellner (eds) *Passion and Rebellion: The Expressionist Heritage* .London: Groom Helm.

Ricks, Christopher (2003) *Dylan's Visions of Sin*. London: Penguin.

Seale, Bobby (1970) *Seize the Time: The Story of the Black Panther Party*. London: Arrow Books.

Selz, Peter (1974) *German Expressionist Painting*. Berkeley: University of California Press.

Speir, Ronald (1982) *Brecht's Early Plays*. London: Macmillan.

Wright, Barbara Dryulski (1983) 'Sublime Ambition: Art, Politics, and Ethical Idealism in the Cultural Journals of German Expressionism', in Stephen Eric Bronner and Douglas Kellner (eds) *Passion and Rebellion: The Expressionist Heritage*. London: Groom Helm.

Chris Brown[1]

# Bob Dylan, Live Aid, and the Politics of Popular Cosmopolitanism

## Introduction

I hope that some of the money that's raised for the people in
Africa, maybe they could just take a little bit of it— maybe
one or two million, maybe—and use it, say, to pay the ... er
... the mortgages on some of the farms ... the farmers here,
owe to the banks. (Bob Dylan at the *Live Aid* Concert in RFK
Stadium, NYC. 13 July 1985 (Sounes 2001: 367).

At least that's probably what he said—this section of the
concert was dropped from the subsequent Videos/DVDs
and can only be seen on *YouTube*, a reflection of the abysmal
nature of Dylan's performance on the day as well as the perceived political incorrectness of his comment. The one
Dylan number that can still be watched on DVD—a performance of 'Blowin' in the Wind' with Keith Richard and Ron
Wood—is ample evidence that all three of the performers
were very much the worse for wear. But two things about
Dylan's rambling statement are clear; first, this was a stimu-
lus for the formation of *Farm Aid* which was, and is,

---

[1]   I'm grateful to Kirsten Ainley, Stephanie Carvin, George Lawson and
      David Owen for comments on an earlier draft of this paper; the usual
      disclaimers apply.

designed to help American farmers, and second that Bob Geldof was furious with Dylan for going off message.

> He displayed a complete lack of understanding of the issues raised by Live Aid ... Live Aid was about people losing their lives. There is a radical difference between losing your livelihood and losing your life. It did instigate Farm Aid, which was a good thing in itself, but it was a crass, stupid, and nationalistic thing to say (Geldof 1986).[2]

The aim of this essay is to examine, and challenge, that final characterization; Dylan's comment may have been, in one sense, nationalistic, but it was neither crass nor stupid — rather, it can be taken to shed light on important debates in contemporary (international) political theory. To summarise what I hope to demonstrate at greater length below, what I take Dylan to be saying here is not that charity ought to begin and end at home, but that charity which does not begin at home ought not to be taken seriously — there is nothing in Dylan's comments that is designed to undermine a concern for the needs and interests of 'distant strangers'; rather, the import is that our concern for distant strangers ought not to displace our concern for those closer to home. Indeed we have greater obligations towards our fellow citizens than towards strangers, and the juxtaposition of 'loss of livelihood' and 'loss of life' leads to more complicated reflections than Geldof is prepared to allow.

The second half of this essay will address these portentous themes, but the first half will take the form of an exercise in Dylanology. Why did Dylan say what he did, when he did? Was his statement simply a reflection of 'Right Wing Bob' to quote the title of a hostile website, or of a general crankiness exhibited by Dylan in the early 1980s? [3] Or was it, as I want to suggest, very precisely targeted and thought-out — if not precisely expressed? And what of the event itself and Dylan's choice of songs? Again, I want to suggest that the apparently shambolic nature of Dylan's contribution to the concert can, in fact, be seen as far more calculated and thoughtful than appears on the face of it to be

[2]   Bob Geldof *Is That It* (1986)
[3]   http://www.rightwingbob.com/

the case — while most of the acts that performed that day simply did their stuff, mostly in a lacklustre manner, Dylan's contribution was deeply political, possibly the most political of the day, although, it should be said, worse than lacklustre in purely musical terms.

Before making this case, I should make also the usual disclaimer when it comes to interpreting Dylan. Although the man has become positively loquacious of late, with the first volume of his 'autobiography' *Chronicles* now available, and an 'authorised' documentary, *No Direction Home*, covering his early years, it is still the case that working out what Dylan's lyrics, behaviour or *obiter dicta* actually mean (if anything) is not a task to which he is prepared to contribute or to adjudicate the contributions of others (Dylan 2004).[4] To put it bluntly, I have no idea whether my interpretation of what Dylan was doing on 13 July 1985 bears any relationship to what he thought he was doing — all I can say is that I think my account makes sense in its own terms, and whether those terms were actually his is something we'll never know.

### Dylan at Live Aid

Right-Wing Bob? Well, Dylan's turn to evangelical Christianity in the later 1970s went down badly with those who still wanted to see him as a 'protest singer', and some of his songs from the early 1980s raised eyebrows in leftist circles. 'Neighbourhood Bully', for example, from the album *Infidels*, is a stirring defence of Israel which came out at just the point when progressive thought in the US was becoming anti-Zionist, and Dylan was taken to task by a *Rolling Stone* journalist for this transgression.[5] Still the idea of a right-wing 'turn' makes sense only if Dylan's previous

---

[4]   Bob Dylan *Chronicles: Volume One* NYC: Simon & Schuster, 2004; *No Direction Home* dir. Martin Scorsese, DVD, Paramount Home Entertainment, 2005.

[5]   For the lyrics of this, and other Dylan songs quoted here, see Bob Dylan *Lyrics: 1962 – 2001* NYC: Simon & Schuster, 2004. For the Rolling Stone Interview see *Dylan on Dylan: The Essential Interviews* ed. Jonathan Cott, London, Hodder and Stoughton, 2006, Interview with Kurt Loder, 21.6.1984, pp 290 ff.

position could be characterised as left-wing, and this, I think, would be wrong, or, at least, un-nuanced. In the 1960s Dylan was certainly part of the counter-culture, opposed the Vietnam War—indeed, in 'Masters of War', opposed war in general—and in the process tried out a number of roles including, briefly, that of protest singer, but it would be a mistake to think that he ever held to a consistent left-wing agenda. Other people, in the mainstream and alternative media, attempted to cast him as the 'voice of his generation' and for some contemporaries he probably was, but it was not a role he sought or accepted—in fact, it was one he consistently rejected, even when sometimes behaving in ways that provoked the sobriquet. His most famous 'protest song'—'Blowin' in the Wind'—is deeply ambiguous (what, if anything, does it mean that the answer is blowin' in the wind?) and his most effective songs in this genre are highly specific, focusing on cases of individual injustice, albeit making a general point thereby—for example, the cases of Hattie Carroll, Rubin Carter, and, on which see below, Hollis Brown. Even in the sixties, much less later on, there is no way in which Dylan can be described as plugging away at a consistently progressivist agenda, in the way that certainly was, and is, true of, for example, Joan Baez, and, of course, of older generation folk singers such as Pete Seeger or Woody Guthrie.

All this is, I think, highly relevant to Dylan's approach to *Live Aid 85*. Bob Geldof's self-appointed role here is very much the one Dylan rejected in the 1960s—the conscience of his generation. The emotional, simplistic appeals, the self-righteousness and self-satisfaction, the hectoring manner and frequent expletives all seemed ideally designed to encapsulate the notion of a representative, a young man speaking for the youth of the world, flaying the older generation for their neglect of a burning issue. The flaws in this persona are equally easy to identify; fabulously wealthy rock-stars giving their services for free to make a record or play in a charity concert sounds like a generous gesture, but the publicity value alone would have been worth more to the artists concerned than any fee could have generated, and, in any event, the notion of 'giving one's services for free' makes a lot more sense for those whose earnings are time-related—what exactly were these individuals giving up? The remedy for African starvation that Geldof incessantly plugged—in essence and in his words, 'give me your fucking money'[6]—was simplistic in the extreme, made no attempt to approach the causes of famines, and left a generation of young people with the quite false belief that transferring wealth to the poor is both easy to do and a solution to something. The money raised by these events was impressive—perhaps $250 million over an extended period—but even so much of the cash ended up directly or indirectly in the hands of the Ethiopian Government, which had created the famine in the first place.

Whether Dylan consciously articulated to himself such a critique is unknowable, but his behaviour is consistent with a critical approach to what was going on. His choice of numbers for his set is interesting in this context and may (one always stresses 'may') offer some clues to his thinking. Apart from the obligatory rendition of 'Blowin' in the Wind', Dylan chose two songs from his most protest-song packed album, *The Times They Are A-Changin'* which first appeared in 1963, namely 'The Ballad Of Hollis Brown' and 'When the Ship Comes In'. Neither song is amongst Dylan's most famous, or, for that matter, best; they don't appear in the standard 'Best of …' collections, and although they have been covered by other artists they aren't as immediately familiar to fans or musicians as many of the other tracks on that album—for example 'With God on our Side', 'The Lonesome Death of Hattie Carroll', and the title track itself. This unfamiliarity, and the apparent lack of rehearsal time, may account for the truly atrocious performance of Keith Richard and Ron Wood on the day, although this was

---

[6]    He probably didn't use these words on BBC TV , as legend has it, but the author heard him use them to make this 'request' when he received an Honorary Degree from the University of Kent in 1986. In fairness to Geldof, his book *Geldof in Africa* London: Arrow Books, 2006, presents a much more nuanced and intelligent picture of the causes of poverty.

probably overdetermined given the apparent substance abuse that was going on.

'Hollis Brown' is a savage, but not particularly well-crafted, song about a South Dakota sharecropper, starving as a result of the repossession of his farm, who kills his six children and commits suicide. The general appropriateness of the song is obvious, and is amplified by Dylan's obvious intent to draw the current plight of American farmers into the occasion. In some respects, 'When the Ship Comes In' is more interesting. This is a apocalyptic song in which it is prophesied that the ship of revolution will soon dock, and the foes of the people will be scattered. The nature of these foes — 'they' in the song — is never specified, and the imagery — fishes laughing and seagulls smiling when the ship comes in — is often strangely lighted-hearted (and pre-figures Dylan imagery of much later in the 1960s). According to the *Rough Guide to Bob Dylan* it is a song he had not played in concert for 22 years before 1985 (Williamson 2006: 152).[7] All told a weird choice of song for *Live Aid* — but there is one connection here that it is difficult to believe Dylan did not make.

Turn the clock back to a Dylan performance at another great international occasion devoted to a progressive cause. On 28 August 1963, a few weeks before the release of *The Times they Are A-Changin'*, the greatest of all the Civil Rights Marches ended in Washington DC at the Lincoln Memorial, and a crowd of hundreds of thousands heard Dr Martin Luther King give his greatest speech — 'I have a Dream ... '. It was a long day and between the speeches various sympathetic artists were brought forward to entertain the crowd, including Bob Dylan, and 'When the Ship Comes In' was one of the two songs he sang.[8] News footage of the occasion can be seen on *YouTube*, as can the indifference of the largely African-American crowd who were waiting for the next performer, Mahalia Jackson. Dylan may not have excited

[7]   Nigel Williamson *The Rough Guide to Bob Dylan* (2nd ed.) London: Rough Guides, 2006. p.152.

[8]   The other was 'Only a Pawn in Their Game' about the killer of the civil rights activist Medgar Evers.

the majority of his audience on this occasion—not really his demographic—but this was his true 'voice of my generation' moment. Surrounded, on the one hand, by African-American gospel, blues and variety artists, and on the other, by an older generation of leftist folk-singers, he was the one young, white man to perform.

Two years later things had changed, and it became clear that the role of voice of his generation, the successor to Woody Guthrie, Pete Seeger *et al.*, would be a path not taken. Dylan discovered drugs and rock n'roll. At the Newport Folk Festival in July 1965, he played a set with electric guitars, outraged the folkies in the process—you couldn't hear the words, was Seeger's explanation for trying to kill the amplification—and a year after that, the famous 'Judas' call at the Manchester Free Trade Hall Concert, and Dylan's response, to play 'Like A Rolling Stone' 'fucking loud', marked the end of whatever conscious attempt Dylan had made to occupy the 'voice of my generation' role.[9] Whereas for Seeger the music was always about politics, for Dylan music was his way of expressing himself and he had no intention of being trapped within any particular agenda. As the 'Judas' cry illustrated, some people wanted him to be the voice of his generation, but he made it clear that this was not something he wanted; instead he would accept no responsibility other than to his own great talent, and would allow it to take him wherever it pleased, occupying whichever persona made sense at the time. The sequence of albums that followed varied in quality—and in 1985 it had been some time since the last really great album—but they all represented his muse and his muse alone; if the public didn't like the Christian albums, or the support for Israel, so be it; there was no popularity contest here, or if there was, he hadn't entered so couldn't lose.

The contrast between this attitude and the *Live Aid* ethos is striking. For Geldof—and perhaps for his more recent avatar, Bono—what matters are precisely the things that Dylan isn't interested in. They fly around the world, meet important people, press the flesh, and try to trade their status as cultural icons for political influence, although it must be said that for Geldof his iconic status no longer has anything to do with the music produced by the Boomtown Rats a generation ago ('making Bono history' is a little more difficult since U2 still have some resonance with today's young, although personally I find it difficult to see why). Perhaps once, perhaps briefly, Dylan had been tempted to play the same kind of role, to go over to the dark side; if so, 28 August 1963 on the steps of the Lincoln Memorial must have been the time and place which most poignantly symbolised that temptation. Singing to such a crowd, and with a television audience that was enormous for its day, it would have been surprising if Dylan had not been tempted by the thought that he had the potential to make a political difference, should he be prepared to accept the artistic limitations involved in accepting a public role.

By singing at *Live Aid* the song he had sung on that August day Dylan was, perhaps, exorcising a ghost — reminding himself of something, confirming that he had been right to refuse representative status, that he had taken the right path — and by making his comment about American farmers he was making the point that he controlled his own agenda, that he wasn't there to fulfil Geldof's fantasy, but could instead push a cause of his own. And the thought that by going off message he would upset Geldof may have been an added attraction. The wider establishment pandered to the latter's crude, foul-mouthed populism — an honorary knighthood here, an honorary degree there — but Dylan was making it clear that he was not prepared to be overawed or to buy into the rather tawdry myth that Geldof was creating. He had had his own recognition. Geldof brought the Prince of Wales backstage to his concert, but Dylan had played in front of Dr King.

## The Critique of Popular Cosmopolitanism

Forty years ago a *Times* leader described the prosecution of Mick Jagger for a relatively minor drugs offence as 'breaking a butterfly on a wheel', and I suppose some might regard a close analysis of the international thought of Bob Geldof (or Bono) as the same kind of inappropriate over-reaction. Not so, I think—obviously figures such as Brian Barry, Charles Beitz, Simon Caney, David Held, Onora O'Neill, Thomas Pogge, Henry Shue and Peter Singer are the most significant modern cosmopolitan thinkers, but, like it or not, none of these august and distinguished figures have much impact on how ordinary people think about the world—the same is also true of their opponents, Michael Walzer, Michael Sandel and David Miller (Brown 2002 and 2006).[10] *The New York Review of Books*, the *Times Literary Supplement*, *Prospect*, the *London Review of Books* and so on—the places outside of academic publishing where writers of this quality appear—may influence a segment of the intellectu-ally-minded middle classes (in Britain, they seem to be largely written by and for Oxbridge arts graduates), but a Bono, a Geldof or a Dylan can reach an audience orders of magnitude larger. Moreover, the influence of the first two is negative as well as positive; by persuading people that 'making poverty history' is essentially pretty easy, simply a matter of willpower, they may actually generate apathy and cynicism. Making poverty history would be a massive achievement, if possible at all, which is doubtful; at best, only small steps along the way are achievable, but these small steps will be disappointing and disillusioning to those who have been conditioned to think that big steps are possible if only we, or our leaders, had the will to act. People who are disillusioned in this way either forget about politics altogether or become ensnared in extremism of one kind or another, both of which are undesirable reactions. In short, combating popular cosmopolitanism is a worthwhile task, and this particular butterfly is of the kind that, we are told, is capable, with a flap of its wings, of creating a tornado a con-tinent away—and, in any event, the Dylan/Geldof spat

[10]  I discuss these writers and others in, e.g. *Sovereignty, Rights and Justice* Cambridge, Polity Press, 2002, and 'From International to Global Justice?' in John Dryzek, Bonnie Honig & Anne Phillips, eds. *The Oxford Handbook of Political Theory* Oxford: OUP, 2006, Chapter 34.

does genuinely illuminate one or two quite important issues.

What are these issues? They are, I think, of two kinds, concerning the material and the psychological demands of cosmopolitanism. Consider first the material demands made by cosmopolitans. At the outset, we should dismiss Geldof's assertion that what is at stake is the difference between 'losing your livelihood and losing your life'. This stark alternative actually reflects a quite common rhetorical trick, sometimes used by actual political philosophers as well as pop stars. Consider the opening to Peter Singer's famous essay 'Famine, Affluence and Morality' in which he contrasts the amounts of money spent on Concorde and the Sydney Opera House, with the rather smaller sums devoted to relieving the then current (1971) famine in East Pakistan/ Bangladesh — the spur, as it happens, for the *Concert for Bangladesh* of August 1971 which was the most important precursor to *Live Aid 85* and at which Dylan played a longer, and far more impressive set, on that occasion with George Harrison and Leon Russell (Singer 1971). [11] Singer may be right to argue that famine-relief is a more important activity than opera-house-building, but the implicit suggestion is that if we — as individuals or collectively through our governments — recognise this to be the case, we should put all our efforts into the former rather than the latter. In other words, we should set down all our priorities, arrange them in order of importance, and put all our effort into the most important, thereafter working our way slowly down the list. This actually makes very little sense as a strategy, as will be immediately apparent once one thinks about it for more than a few seconds. Consider, for example, a new government coming into office and announcing, that the Health Service its his most important priority; this very obviously does not mean that all government expenditure next year will go on Health and none on Education, Defence, Pensions and so on — rather, the suggestion is a tilting of public expenditure in a particular direction. Similarly, the

[11]   Peter Singer 'Famine, Affluence and Morality' *Philosophy and Public Affairs* Vol 1. No. 1 1971.

importance we should attach to famine relief does not mean that we should abandon all opera house building until there is no more famine, or, to shift to the Dylan/Geldof spat, that we should not be concerned with unemployment amongst farmers anywhere until famine is abolished everywhere. Our aim surely should be to pursue policies that relieve both social problems, and the only practical question is, how much emphasis does each deserve, how steep should the tilt be?

Dylan's original remarks make it clear that he was not setting livelihood issues above life and death issues. He would like to see 'some of the money.....just a little bit of it....one or two million maybe..' devoted to this cause, in other words rather less than 1% of the eventual *Live Aid* take, which, even while the concert was ongoing, it was clear would be very large. This is a modest position which clearly does not involve prioritising livelihood over life, in fact, just the opposite—it acknowledges that the latter, famine relief, is the more important cause. The point is rather that the existence of an important cause should not preclude attention to other less-important causes. On the face of it, this is a very sensible position and hardly worthy to be seen as subversive of the overall project of *Live Aid*.

Does it matter that we are talking about *American* farmers losing their livelihoods while *African* farmers are losing their lives? Here we see a real difference of perspective, not simply a difference generated by loose rhetoric. It is here that the 'cosmopolitan-communitarian' debate comes to life in the mouths of the two icons. For Geldof, the fact that they are American farmers actually lessens the significance of their plight. America is a rich, democratic country with effective federal and state governments; it has the ability to help its own farmers and a political system that can turn that ability into reality if it chooses to do so. Africans live in poor countries which have neither effective nor democratic governments—indeed their governments frequently contribute to famine rather than to its solution. Geldof is famously Irish (although domiciled long-term in England) but it is, I think, clear that had he been an American citizen he would have taken the same view about the importance of the national dimension—he is a genuine, if sometimes confused (and confusing) cosmopolitan. Dylan, of course, is an American citizen but, more to the point I think, he sees the implications of citizenship differently. American farmers are his fellow citizens, and this creates a relationship that is qualitatively different from the relationship he believes himself to have with African farmers or other non-nationals. There are responsibilities in this case that do not arise in the other; there is a qualitative difference between the kind of obligation he has to American farmers, which is generated by common membership of a political community, and the rather generalised sense of benevolence that underpins the appeal of *Live Aid*.

This is an interesting connection that deserves to be investigated a little more closely. Community is sometimes based on shared experiences of a direct kind, but political community in this case simply rests on common citizenship. Some of the other artists who became the major promoters of *Farm Aid* in 1985, Willie Nelson, John Mellencamp, Johnny Cash, could claim a personal closeness to the American farming community, but neither Dylan's background and nor his contemporary lifestyle had much in common those he championed—at best, one might say that many of the songs that fascinated him in his early days as a performer, and to which he returned in two acoustic albums in the 1990s, *World Gone Wrong* and *Good As I Been To You*, came out of rural America, and perhaps one might add that the evangelical Christianity that he was just beginning to distance himself from in 1985 was similarly grounded. Still, it does seem that for Dylan it was the fact that the farmers were 'here' that was crucial, 'here' in America.

As an aside, in Dylan's lyrics one can perhaps see commitments to the American polity in other, rather unexpected places. Consider, for example, the song that many people regard as Dylan's best 'protest song', 'The Lonesome Death of Hattie Carroll'. As the sad story of her murder unfolds Dylan repeatedly tells us ('those who philosophize disgrace') that now is not the time for our tears. It is when we reach the courtroom, and the judge is given the opportunity to show the rule of law in action ('the ladder of law has no top and no bottom') but instead hands out a sentence of six-months—then we are told 'now's the time for your tears'. In other words, what is truly shocking is not the murder as such (although it is shocking) but the failure of the system to live up to its own ideals, something, of course, that is actually only shocking if one has some level of belief in the system in the first place.[12]

In any event, Geldof will have none of this—it is 'crass, stupid, nationalism'. Is this fair comment, if one is a cosmopolitan, as Geldof clearly is? Nationalism perhaps, but I suggest there is nothing crass or stupid about the variety of nationalism, which Dylan espouses. It rests on a concern for the underdog at home not on antagonism towards anyone abroad. It is a variant of the popular nationalism which can be traced back to the French Revolution and related to movements for national liberation in Europe in the nineteenth century and the rest of the world in the twentieth. Resisting the tendency to spread the discussion quite so widely, and retaining a focus in popular music, an obvious American reference point here would be Woody Guthrie, the mid-century folk-singer, troubadour and political activist who was Bob Dylan's earliest muse, and a figure for whom the latter always retained great respect, even after himself abandoning most of the political commitments of the older man. Guthrie was the poet of the dust-bowl, an itinerant political agitator who attempted to give voice to the victims of the great Depression in the US, perhaps in particular to those from rural communities. To illustrate his politics, when in 1938, Irving Berlin published the song that has since become almost a second, quasi-official, national anthem 'God Bless America', Guthrie reacted against what he saw as the lyric's political complacency, and in 1940 produced his response, an anthem of left-wing, progressive popular nationalism. 'This Land is Your Land' has ever since been a staple of left-inclined American performers,

[12] I owe this example and tentative analysis to David Owen.

from Pete Seeger to Bruce Springsteen.[13] It is an angry song, the lyrics of which ask many pointed questions;

> In the squares of the city,
> In the shadow of a steeple;
> By the relief office,
> I'd seen my people.
> As they stood there hungry,
> I stood there asking,
> Is this land made for you and me?

But the answer is always positive 'This land *is* made for you and me'. There is an assertion of popular sovereignty here that stands against the idea that the nation belongs to its rulers and invites pride in the beauty of the land.

> From California to the New York Island
> From the Redwood Forest to the Gulf Stream waters
> This land is made for you and me.
> For Guthrie it is my people and our land.

The website 'History in Song' (an invaluable source) gives an anarchist version which offers an interesting contrast:

> This land is their land, it isn't our land,
> From the Wall Street office, to the Cadillac car-land;
> From the plush apartments, to the Hollywood starland,
> This land is not for you and me. [14]

From this angle, Guthrie's anthem is as complacent as Berlin's—but for Guthrie (and for Dylan) progressive causes are not likely to be advanced by such a resounding 'no'. Rather, the progressive must identify with the aspirations of his or her fellow-citizens and stimulate pride in the nation. But this is not the pride of an inward-looking, America-first nationalist. Guthrie was a leading anti-fascist, a figure who did everything he could to promote America's entry into the Second World War;[15] he was also a communist party member—but these internationalist commitments did not lead him to water down the populism that

---

[13]  For performances and a discussion of the different lyrics to the song see Woody Guthrie *The Asch Recordings: Vols 1–4* A Smithsonian Folkways Box Set, 1999.

[14]  http://www.fortunecity.com/tinpan/parton/2/history.html

[15]  On his guitar was printed the optimistic and, sadly, implausible slogan 'This Machine Kills Fascists'.

made him such a quintessentially *American* figure, and whatever allegiance he gave to the international communist movement was on his own terms, rather than theirs. The internationalism emerged out of the nationalism. The same might be said for Pete Seeger (who left the Party in 1950), the Weavers, the Almanac Singers and the rest of the folk movement of the era. From their perspective, it was only possible to be an inter-nationalist if one was first a kind of nationalist. The commitment to the wretched of the earth flowed out of a prior commitment to the wretched *here*, the people who stood, hungry, by the relief office.

Bob Dylan reacted rather badly to the high seriousness of figures like Seeger, with their insistence that real folk-music was about advancing the worker's struggle—as Greil Marcus has argued with such eloquence, building on the work of pioneers such as Harry Smith, real folk-music is *weird* and doesn't advance any particular political agenda (Marcus 1998) [16]—but it seems to me the groundedness of Guthrie (who, most of the time, wasn't at all high-minded) stayed with Dylan, even when the political programme left. But what comes through most clearly to me from Dylan's *Live Aid* statements is his endorsement of the idea that nationalism and internationalism are not opposites, but rather complementary allegiances. This gets to the heart of the *psychology* of cosmopolitanism, the second issue illuminated by the Dylan/Geldof spat.

### The Psychological Failures of Popular Cosmopolitanism

There is no doubt but that *Live Aid 1985* struck a chord with a great many young people in Western Europe and the US, as have similar events ever since—as I write this, in early July 2007, *LiveEarth* is, perhaps, having a similar effect, amplified by saturation coverage on the BBC and other outlets (although, as noted below, concert-fatigue may be setting in). Probably most of the audience have tuned in to listen to

[16] Greil Marcus *Invisible Republic: Bob Dylan's Basement Tapes* London: Picador, 1998—the best single book on Bob Dylan I know.

particular favourite bands, or simply to be part of an 'event', but there is no reason to doubt that they pick up at least the general political message along with the music — and this is so even if the event itself actually contradicts that message, as is certainly the case with *Live Earth*, the carbon footprints of whose star performers do not bear thinking about. But the real question is, or ought to be, what is the longer term effect of such extravaganzas? Do people sustain an interest in the relief of famine in Africa once the last chords of music die away and the cheques have been put in the post? Will *Live Earth* actually change anyone's behaviour, as opposed to, at best, temporarily raising their consciousness? Make Poverty History was a good, albeit, as discussed above, a contentious slogan, but last year's ubiquitous white wrist-bands have disappeared already. Yesterday's good cause is recycled almost immediately.

Why do these events have so little effect, why is the attention span of those who seem genuinely impressed by the message so short? Obviously, material self-interest is part of the story here; pop stars don't want to give up their Chelsea Tractors and Lear jets, and you and I don't want to stop putting our TVs on stand-by or flushing our toilets — and, reverting to the focus of this paper, *Live Aid 85*, no-one actually wants to substantially reduce their own standard of living to finance transfers to the distant hungry. But even if this sort of selfishness is part of the human condition, so is a propensity to co-operate, and a willingness to help others as long as we don't hurt ourselves too much in the process. Altruism is as genuine a feature of our make-up as egoism — the important task is to try to identify the factors that cause altruism as opposed to egoism to kick-in in any particular case. In fact, it is pretty clear what the key factor actually is; co-operative and altruistic behaviours (which are not the same thing, but related I think) are in-group phenomena. We work with and for other people because we expect them to work with and for us, and we take note of their interests because we expect them to take note of ours; but, of course, this kind of notional, predicted reciprocity is only possible in cases where we have some reason to think that

we will experience regular social intercourse with the relevant others. Originally, such intercourse took place in
small, face-to-face groups, but gradually, over the last three
or four millennia, our 'circle of concern' has expanded, from
the kin-group to the village, to the city, to the nation, and
perhaps over the next millennia it will expand to all the
inhabitants of the planet—but we very clearly aren't there
yet. It simply isn't possible to argue plausibly that a directly
reciprocal relationship exists between the concert-goers of
the West and the starving farmers of Africa. Perhaps, as
Thomas Pogge and others have argued, the West created
the poverty of the rest of the world, but even if this were to
be true (and it seems to me to underestimate the importance
of other factors) it is difficult to see why it would generate
the kind of reciprocal relationship that underpins a concern
for the well-being of others within the circle of concern
(Pogge 2002).[17]Unable to rely on such a relationship, those
who desire to make poverty history have to rely on a general sense of benevolence—duty in Pogge's case, which
comes to much the same thing—and that, as suggested
above, fades pretty quickly when we are faced with the
implications of taking seriously our professed beliefs.

Assuming (as I do) that it would be good if those of us in
the affluent West did more to help the poor and disadvan-
taged of the world, how do we get round this problem?
How do we extend the circle of concern? It is clear that the
megaphone fund-raising of Geldof, Bono *et al.* doesn't do
the job; while the TV is on we might be convinced that we
really are concerned by the picture of misery painted for us
by these would-be moral entrepreneurs, but the effect soon
fades. It seems to me more plausible that the best way to
generate the moral environment that might lead us to
change our lives in the right direction is actually to show
concern for the poor and dispossessed in our midst. These
people are closer too us than the starving in Africa; they are
our fellow-citizens and we are in some sense, although a
very limited one, in a co-operative scheme with them. There

[17]  Thomas Pogge *World Poverty and Human Rights* Cambridge: Polity Press,
2002.

is something here for the altruistic impulse to get hold of; it is not totally fanciful to imagine that the homeless person on the streets of London could be you, or someone you know, or someone like you — we may not actually be engaged in a reciprocal relationship with man sleeping in the doorway of an Aldwych office block, but we can at least imagine what such a relationship would be like.

Charity begins at home — but does it have to end there? There are two relevant points to be made here, one positive, one negative. On the positive side, if we can extend our moral imagination so that our personal circle of concern is not confined to those with whom we have (or plausibly might have) actual reciprocal relations, but can encompass a wider group of our fellow citizens with whom we have very little in common other than common occupation of a particular patch of earth, then it is not impossible that we could come to extend this circle a little wider, and then a little wider again, until eventually, with luck, we reach those distant strangers that we are only ever likely to encounter in photographs or on TV. But also, and negatively, if we aren't prepared to reach out to those in need who are close to us, what likelihood is there that we will actually do anything for those who are far away? Subject to the moral blackmail of noisy pop stars we might put a cheque in the post for the *Live Aid* appeal, but if we step over and ignore a homeless person on the way to the post-box it doesn't seem very likely that we will sustain our concern for African poverty. Of course, there are some people who purport to love mankind, but seem not to be very fond of actual people, and they may prefer to focus on distant suffering — but most of us would be reluctant to describe their behaviour as reflecting a satisfactory moral position.

Bob Dylan, I hypothesise, instinctively got this point, the other Bob did not. Dylan could see that for millions of Americans to be gazing from a distance on, and trying to empathize with, African poverty — all the while averting their eyes from what was going on in the mid-West, the farms that were being sold, their owners, the fellow citizens of the concert-goers, being left destitute — was an act of (inadvertent) bad faith on their part which took the gloss off the whole event. By asking for some of the money to go to the cause of American farmers, Dylan was 'bringing it all back home', making the event real, even if Geldof didn't, perhaps couldn't, appreciate the service the older man was providing.

### Conclusion: Farm Aid and Live Aid Two Decades On

The idea that a suitable way to draw attention to a good cause is to organise a themed concert seems to have had a small revival recently, with the 2005 *Live 8* (unsurprisingly, no invitation for Dylan this time), the *LiveEarth* extravaganza, and even the rather bizarre *Concert for Diana* — although it is also noticeable that the level of sarcasm these events have generated is far higher than in 1985. In the case of *Live Earth*, it is, of course, difficult not to be sarcastic; hard to think of any activity less appropriate as a gesture of support for environmental awareness than a pop concert[18]– although the cause itself is easy to relate to the expanding circle of concern noted above, since this is an area where we actually are all in it together.

*Farm Aid* on the other hand, has not needed to be revived, because it has never gone away — nor does it attract sarcasm or charges of hypocrisy.[19]The first Farm Aid Concert took place in late 1985, and was organised by Willie Nelson, Neil Young and John Mellencamp. Concerts have taken place annually ever since, organised by the same team, with the addition of Dave Matthews in 2001. The three, later four, organisers perform and are joined by a mixture of other country, blues and rock artists — Dylan occasionally, Emmylou Harris, Gillian Welch, Steve Earle, Wilco, and others. *Farm Aid* doesn't simply organise the longest

[18]  Even Bob Geldof joined in the criticism, in an impressive example of irony failure. 'Live Earth? It's a Waste of Time, Geldof Tells Gore' *The Independent* 16 May 2007 at http://www.independent.co.uk/environment/climate_change/article2548756.ece. I'm grateful to Stephanie Carvin for the reference.

[19]  http://www.farmaid.org is the source for the statistics quoted below and for the work of *Farm Aid* more generally. See also Holly George Warren ed. *Farm Aid* Rodale Books, 2005.

running concert series in the US, it produces a newsletter, promotes organic and family-farm grown food, and runs advice phone lines to connect farmers to Family Farm organisations. Nelson and Mellencamp have led delegations of family farmers to Congress. *Farm Aid* has raised 30 million dollars, which is considerably less than *Live Aid 85*, brought in, but it spends the money on small grants to family farms and consumer groups—c. $750,000 to 59 family farm groups in 2006. I would hazard a guess that the amount of good done by this $30 million at least equals that generated by *Live Aid*'s $250 million, and certainly a much smaller percentage has ended up lining the pockets of corrupt governments.

*Farm Aid* survives because of the commitment of a small number of artists who are deeply engaged by the issues; they haven't given up their 'day jobs'—they still tour and make records. They don't go to Davos, and they don't pay patronising visits to the objects of their charity in the manner of Geldof and Bono. They do what they do because it reflects who they are; there is a groundedness here that is undeniable. Is this commitment at the expense of a commitment to the famine victims of Africa—is it actually the case that by focusing on livelihood issues in America these artists are neglecting life and death issues elsewhere in the world? It seems implausible that this should be so. The kind of political commitment shown by Nelson, Mellencamp *et al.* isn't of the sort that stops at the water's edge; I see no reason to doubt their internationalist convictions, or to think that we, or they, should regard the nationalism that makes them committed to American farmers precludes an internationalism that makes them aware of global problems, and indeed all of the main *Farm Aid* headliners have been engaged in most of the internationalist campaigns over the decades.

Bob Dylan's actual contribution to *Farm Aid* has been pretty minimal. He played the first two concerts, but hasn't been back since, and was never one of the organisers. Still, back in July 1985 he articulated a thought that was picked up by others and he deserves some credit for that. What lay behind that original thought, no-one knows and I suspect no one ever will know, unless later volumes of autobiography are less opaque than *Chronicles* Volume I. I have suggested here a possible account of why he did and said what he did and said that day but the accuracy of this reconstruction is unknowable. What we can know is that, behind the spat between Dylan and Geldof, serious issues in international political theory are at stake, and that remains the case whatever level of awareness they brought to the party. Popular cosmopolitanism has a hold on the consciousness if not the pockets of a great many young people, and my claim here is it would be good were this hold to be dislodged — and if that can be done through the words of Bob Dylan, so much the better.

Gary Browning

# Bob Dylan: (Post) Modern Times

Dylan has been labeled as postmodern. He has received many labels through his career, deflecting or subverting them in style. Perhaps labels don't matter much, but in considering Dylan's political art, the subject of this book, the label of postmodernism enables us to recognise Dylan's ambiguous and problematic relationship to politics. Todd Haynes' recent film on Dylan, *I'm Not There* highlights Dylan's multiplicity and his refusal to be owned by any simple identity. This many-sidedness is what critics such as Scobie and Rocheleau have in mind when alluding to Dylan's postmodernism (see Scobie, 1991 and Rocheleau, 2006). Postmodernism attends to ambiguities, refusing to see an essential meaning behind appearances and allowing for multiple perspectives to be brought to bear upon events. The ambiguities of Dylan's political art consist in part in his expression of differing perceptions of politics during the course of his career. A sympathy with the oppressed and victims of injustice animates the early songs of the 1960s, just as the albums of the mid 1960s show a more intense expressionist critique of social conformity whereas the later songs and albums from the 1970s onwards reflect a disenchanted preoccupation with personal and spiritual values.

Dylan, however, is more than what he does or performs. As his autobiographical *Chronicles Vol. 1* attests, a significant dimension of his life has been devoted to contending with the consequences of his own success (Dylan, 2004, 114–124). Dylan's reflexive relationship with his own celebrity surfaced at the outset of his career, but intensified in the mid 1960s as he rode the waves of his popularity, becoming an iconic figure for counter-cultural radicalism. Dylan reacted to the distorting mirrors of fame by reflecting back on to interviewers and devotees the political expectations that were projected on to him. His resistance to these expectations and his suspicion of celebrity politics underlie his scepticism over mainstream and dissident political projects and contribute to what may be termed a postmodern sense of the repressive possibilities of political power and ideological causes.

At the outset of his career Dylan touched a chord with young people and radicals by writing and performing songs highlighting injustice and supporting political emancipation, but he quickly became sensitive to the strains exerted upon his own distinct and sometimes contrary identity by the reactive absorption of his music and art within the orbit of sloganising political and counter-cultural movements. This encroachment on his identity was exacerbated by media stereotyping and by exposure to the commercial imperatives of the music industry and by the expectations of his audience on what and how he should perform. Dylan recognised, as perhaps only a reflective, contrary iconic figure might, that the expectations of even counter-cultural movements are liable to circumscribe the possibilities of personal and expressive development. In 'Subterranean Homesick Blues', Dylan warned in Woody Allen style, 'Don't follow leaders and watch your parking meters' (1965). In warning against leaders Dylan is also criticizing followers, who frame leaders in their own image. To critique the myopic conventionalism of leaders and led is to recognize the dangers to which politics is prone. It reflects Dylan's own burgeoning sense of how an individual who is pigeonholed and labelled rather than listened to, has to buck trends and confront conventions. This commitment to unconventionality has been accentuated by the peculiar pressures to which Dylan himself was subject, but it dramatizes a feature of late modern Western society, where what counts are the bottom line and political soundbites. Where appearances purport to be real, openness is a mask for social conformity.

Dylan's persisting insistence on controlling his own identity by continually transforming it, harmonises with postmodern notions of the self as a performative project, which is and should be free from regulatory and conventional images and constraints (see Butler, 1990). This sensitivity to social constraints, heightened by his awareness of the confining emptiness of cultural celebrity, is itself political insofar as it animates resistance to mainstream conventions *and* countervailing standardizing alternatives. If Dylan maintains a postmodern wariness about the normalizing pressures of social and political life, his life and art are also bound up with modernity and archetypical modern political post-2nd World War political movements and ideology. Lyotard, in his influential, *The Postmodern Condition* (1984), defined postmodernism by its antagonism to modernity and its grand solutions, identifying it by its scepticism towards modernity's grand narratives of progress and emancipation. Denying the possibility of political solutions if the questions to which they respond are impossibly general, he counselled a postmodern refusal to deliver a political consensus, arguing instead for disruptive and inventive dissensus. Dylan in the early 1960s was associated with modern movements such as the civil rights and anti-nuclear war movements that agitated for emancipatory goals. He was also implicated in the general resistance of young people to prevailing codes and conventions, which, despite its ethos of dissidence, itself constituted a movement of sorts by the mid 1960s, the counter-culture movement. Dylan's respective renunciations of expressly political songs consonant with a civil rights and an anti-war agenda and of counter-cultural iconoclasm are rejections of modern collective agendas of political and social change and signal adherence to a more individual, critical and postmodern exploration of art and spiritual self-development.

Dylan's album titles signify current themes of his art. *Another Side of Bob Dylan* in 1964 made the point that Dylan was not simply a political, finger-pointing singer and writer. *Nashville Skyline* announced he was looking towards country horizons not generally appreciated by counter-cultural progressive figures and *Self-Portrait* was an ironically combative easy-listening statement about Dylan's identity, drawing on bits and pieces from American popular music that sat uneasily with Dylan's hitherto dissident credo. The title of Dylan's recent album *Modern Times* is again suggestive about Dylan's current preoccupations. Its title is paradoxical given its content. The songs borrow titles, music and lines from traditional folk and blues songs and civil war poetry. *Modern Times* is troubling in its evocation of modern times, for the times they evoke are clearly neither contemporary nor recent. Dylan's perspective is again difficult to pin down, for he appears to adopt an expressly past persona. The style of the music comes from early to mid 20th century, its variations on blues, swing and folk, expressing a wistful empathy for former times and one of its major songs, 'Working Man's Blues#2' (2006) suggests a nostalgic sympathy for a protagonist, contending with social and economic changes of what seems to be the Depression era. Hence the modern times referred to in the album title reflect the passing of modern times or at least the passing of activist resistance to them. The title also evokes the Charlie Chaplin film of the same name. Chaplin's film was an ideological response to disturbing features of modern times, notably the injustice of capitalism and the dehumanizing effects of new technology. Automated production and the oppressiveness of capitalism are forces against which the tramp hero played by Chaplin himself offers bravado and anarchic resistance. The generally silent format of the film itself, save for an odd burst of song, offers symbolic resistance to the new technology of talking pictures In the final scene Chaplin and the gamine Paulette Goddard set off together along an open highway. The protagonist of the final track, 'Ain''t Talkin', on *Modern Times* revisits this road, but it is a lonesome and fugitive one. The protagonist is grimly silent, brooding as he walks, entering a garden where the gardener has gone. His silence is not the symbolic communicative and combative silence of

Chaplin's film, but a rueful grim reflection of the burden of an individual's solitary spiritual journey.

In the rest of this paper I want to explore Dylan's engagement with modernity and his suggestive postmodern withdrawal from collective political engagement. Modernity involves technological development, economic expansion and a political culture of competing ideologies offering solutions and political identities for the left and right. Late 20th Century modernity in the West combined economic progress with a withering of belief in ideological alternatives to capitalist democracy. Sophisticated technology and hyper-capitalism brought fluidity alongside a pervasive instrumentalism, intensifying consumerism and political alienation. Lyotard's postmodernism summarized all this as meaning the end of the grand promises of modernity, and as requiring radical perspectivalism on events and a pessimism over the possibilities of large-scale political change. Dylan's take on modernity and changing times runs with the grain of Lyotard's analysis. His early songs, highlighting the injustice and oppression suffered by blacks and poor whites and the timeliness of political change, accorded with the aspirations of the young and the disaffected in the aftermath of the 2nd World War. Dylan, appeared to be at one with a wider current of political expectation demanding the fulfillment of democracy and justice in Western societies, but his later more introspective artistic style reflects a subsequent trend in Western societies, where dreams of collective emancipation are succeeded by consumer acquisitiveness or introspective disenchantment. The claim that Dylan is a spokesman for a generation might well be true but in the subversive sense that Dylan's generation is one for which there can only be a self-denying spokesman, for in late modernity a disenchanted individualism haunts the spaces occupied formerly by collectivist organisations. At the same time, heightened by reflection upon his own personal circumstances, Dylan recognizes how experience itself is framed and contaminated by media hyperbole, global markets and a stultifying cultural conformity menacing individual autonomy.

Dylan can be seen as postmodern in a number of ways. His radical perspectivalism, expressed in love songs, exploring relationships from multiple vantage points, is evocative of Derrida's postmodern deconstructionism, which destabilizes apparently clear meanings. His self-awareness of the fragility and mobility of his own identity reflects a postmodern sensibility. The title of Scobie's book, *Alias Bob Dylan*, draws attention to Dylan's deconstruction of constructed identities, notably his own publicly constructed iconic identity. Scobie notes Dylan's scepticism about individuality, pointing to Dylan's recognition of 'the notion that we are not singular identities but variable and multiple personalities' (Scobie, 1991, p.18). Dylan's destabilizing of the self is evident throughout his career. From the early 'Mixed Up Confusion' that ends with the lines, 'Seein' my reflection 'I'm hung over, hung down, hung up'! to the reflexive interrogation of the ego in 'I and I' (1983), with the refrain, 'I and I, In creation where one's nature neither honours nor forgives, I and I, One says to the other, no man sees my face and lives'. Scobie is also alert to Dylan's suggestive and disconcerting way of addressing his songs to highly ambiguous figures. He recognises, for example, the multiple subjects that might be addressed in the song, 'What Was it You Wanted', where the 'you' addressed in the title might stand for a woman, God, Judas, Dylan himself or his audience (Scobie, 1991, p.26). This elasticity of a Dylan song, its capacity to address differing subjects and to suggest connections that complicate the ways in which the *private* self and a *public* political world are constructed, testifies to Dylan's disturbing and awareness of the opacity of meaning and self.

Dylan's imaginative and critical grasp of the interplay between the individual and the political world, in which the individual is susceptible to express and implicit pressures to conform to social expectations, makes him suspicious of ideological claims on the left and right. His continuing sympathy for outsiders, mavericks and minorities, reflecting a postmodern appreciation of marginal identities, jars with the unifying concerns of classic modern political ideologies.

Dylan's political art is best appreciated as a movement away from ideological causes towards a more critical wariness of the political sphere as a whole. This movement, reflecting wider currents of social and political change, can be seen as a turn from the modern to the postmodern and, in turn, can be evoked and demonstrated by relating his career and his commentary on modern times to the career of Lyotard. Lyotard's development of postmodernism shows a similar movement, from identifying with general ideological causes to sympathizing with marginal identities and oppressed groups.

## Dylan: The Early Years

Dylan emerged in the early 1960s, a seemingly central figure in the contemporary folk revival and in the civil rights movement. (Gonczy, 1990; Marqusee, 2003) A plain, unadorned style of singing and music that simulated the gruffness and weathered quality of blues singers authenticated his place in the folk movement (Turner, 1972). He was befriended by Pete Seeger and Joan Baez and was taken to be a voice of political activism. Dylan's political credentials were underlined by a stream of songs that became evocative rallying calls for the cause of civil rights. Hersch interprets these early political songs to be simple and straightforward anthems of the civic republicanism of the contemporary civil rights movement. He takes Dylan and this republicanism to prioritise political participation and straightforward authenticity of outlook, observing, 'Dylan's early songs depict a world of simple truths masked by deception and evil. The world and the self are not obscure; they do not need deciphering. Rather, Dylan seems to be say that if people only see what is in front of them, the truth will be revealed…' (Hersch, 1998, p.138). Certainly Dylan's 'The Times They Are A Changin'' (*The Times They are A Changin'*) expresses a clear-cut sense that there is a direction to history and political change, which favours the young and modern causes.

From the outset of his public career, though, Dylan's songs could not be subsumed so unequivocally to the service of a political cause. 'Blowin' in the Wind' (*The Free-wheelin' Bob Dylan*), for instance, does not affirm unambiguously the imminence of radical change. The answers to a series of questions such as, 'How many years can some people exist before they're allowed to be free?' are indirect in that they are blowing in a metaphorical wind. The ambiguity of the lyric, though, is compensated for by the insistent rhythm of the song, where the constancy of the music and refrain signal affirmative answers. The susceptibility of the song to differing interpretations, though, is evidenced by subsequent reworkings of the song, notably in recent live performances, where the music is taken at a slower, stately tempo and Dylan's singing is plaintive in its lament for what may not be achieved. The ambiguities involved in Dylan's political art in these early years are of a piece with Lyotard's qualified commitment to Marxism in his early writings of the 1950s. Lyotard's Marxism is evident in his writings on the Algerian question, in which he analysed and criticised French imperialism (Lyotard, 1993a). His commitment to orthodox Marxism, however, was qualified by his recognition of factors complicating the picture, such as the force of Arab nationalism and the redundancy of proletarian internationalism.

Dylan's credentials as a spokesperson for the civil rights and anti-nuclear war movements in the early 1960s were underlined by his prolific production of classic songs castigating war and empathising with black people. 'Let Me Die in My Footsteps', 'A Hard Rain's A-Gonna Fall', 'Talkin' World War 111 Blues', 'John Brown' and 'Masters of War' were hard-hitting songs denouncing war, and more particularly nuclear war. By the close of 1963, Dylan had also recorded 'Oxford Town', which narrated the story of the protest against exclusion of the black James Meredith from the University of Mississippi, 'The Lonesome Death of Hattie Carroll', 'The Death of Emmett Till' and 'Only a Pawn in Their Game', which dealt with the racist murders of Emmett Till, Hattie Carroll and the civil rights' leader,

Medgar Evers. The sheer quality of these songs and the force of Dylan's performances of them harmonized with the political aspirations of the time, the prospective realization of modern notions of political justice whereby black people could be included within the civic community. Alongside these political songs, however, Dylan recited more maverick stories that romanticised lawless outsiders, such as murderers, drifters and gamblers, notably in 'Rambling, Gambling Willie' and 'Dusty Old Fairgrounds'.

The individuality of all Dylan's songs, however, jars with the orthodoxy of the civil rights movement. This individuality is evident in 'Only a Pawn in their Game' (*The Times They Are A'Changin'*, 1963) which narrates the murder of Medgar Evers, the black civil rights leader. Dylan's lyric, unlike that of folk singer Phil Ochs in his song 'Ballad of Medgar Evers', sees the perpetrator of the crime to be a victim as well as an assassin. He is a victim of the poverty and propaganda to which 'southern white trash' were subject. While Dylan has always been reluctant to explain or even comment on his songs, his conversation with Studs Terkel at the latter's Wax Museum in Illinois, Chicago in May 1963 and broadcast by WMTF radio is open and engaging. In discussing 'A Hard Rain's A-Gonna Fall' Dylan insists that the rain to which the song refers is not nuclear war, but stands more generally for the lies in society against which individuals must struggle. The individuality of Dylan's early songs is matched by the singularity he brought to his singing, which did not fit neatly with the stereotype demanded by the contemporary folk revival. Dylan was prepared to mix things up in a way that compromised the vaunted purity of traditional folk music. Dylan in the sleeve notes to his production of a tribute album to Jimmie Rodgers, admires the idiosyncratic range of Rodgers' work, observing, 'His voice gives hope to the vanquished and humility to the mighty. Indeed, he sings not only among his bawdy, upbeat blues and railroading songs, but also tin pan alley trash and crooner lullabies as well' (Dylan, 1996). Similarly, Dylan, on his first album (*Bob Dylan*, 1962) sings the gospel song, 'Gospel Plow' at breakneck speed, and on his second (1963) he put the serious lyric of 'Oxford Town' to a jaunty old banjo tune while contemplating including an electronically backed 'Mixed-Up Confusion'.

If the ambiguities of Dylan's early songs show that he was never a mere propagandist, his uneasiness at his popular image as a 'political' protest singer is an express theme of his fourth album, *Another Side of Bob Dylan* (1964). The auto-biographical, 'My Back Pages', repudiates a stylized former political credo that could pronounce upon notions of good and bad, equality and liberty. Dylan is critical of those who would see liberty as being 'equality at school' and so he parts company with those in the civil rights movement, who would subordinate freedom and independence to its egalitarian demands. The songs on *Another Side of Bob Dylan* such as 'All I Really Want to Do' and 'It Ain't Me Babe' prize independence over commitments and warn fans, friends and all those who want to co-opt Dylan to a cause that his sense of himself is essentially negative, the pure independence of the self. He is also prepared to send up the liberal movement and its causes, thereby risking alienating his followers and audience. In 'I Shall Be Free No. 10', he observes, 'Now I'm liberal, but to a degree, I want ev'rybody to be free, But if you think that I'll let Barry Goldwater, Move in next door and marry my daughter, You must think I'm crazy I wouldn't do it for all the farms in Cuba'. Dylan's most overtly political song on the album, 'Chimes of Freedom' testifies to a desolate array of outcasts rather than signposting a political revolution.

### Dylan: The Mid 1960s and Electricity

On the mid 1960s electric albums, *Bringing it all Back Home*, *Highway 61 Revisited* and *Blonde on Blonde* Dylan turns his back on the folk revival and political movements, just as Lyotard broke from orthodox left politics during the course of the events of 1968. Lyotard was at the epicentre of these events, joining student radicals and advocating a disruptive rather than Marxist form of politics (see Lyotard, 1993a). Dylan in the mid 1960s assumes the identity of a rock star replete with Cuban heels, shades, a motor bike and an electric band. Political anthems and considered love songs give way to free form experimental songs exploring and dissecting notions of identity and a literally raucous rejection of authority and the system. The songs on these albums are not overtly political. They neither focus dissent on specific aspects of the political system, such as racial inequality, nor oppose specific policies such as the nuclear arms race. What they do is more insidious and yet, in a sense, equally political. They oppose an entire culture of lifeless conformity and hierarchy over which the political system presides, and promote a subversive freedom and experimentation.

Hersch has noted how the mid 1960s albums fuse form and content by observing, 'This (Dylan's) attack on social organization, standards and hierarchy is embodied in the form and structure of the songs as well as in their lyrics' (Hersch, 1998, p. 153). Certainly their electricity is emblematic of their expressive dissidence. 'Subterranean Homesick Blues' on the first electric album *Bringing It All Back Home* exploits a harder musical sound to make its point. It has a classic bluesy structure, and a machine gun rap-style vocal that is literally and figuratively disorienting, invoking an underground resistance to the dead-end world of culturally accepted values. The school system, work, the police, the law, conventional romance and even counterculture leaders are scorned in the name of subterranean freedom and authenticity. Again, 'It's Alright Ma (I'm Only Bleeding)' invokes Koestler's novel, *Darkness at Noon* at its outset and the guillotine of the French Revolution at its close, but it sees totalitarian cultural oppression in the so-called free societies of the West. This raw stripped down blues castigates capitalist materialism and the reduction of value to advertising copy. It takes religion, sex, and communication to be evacuated of meaning while political and social elites hypocritically enforce meaningless social values. The song offers no political resolution to the emptiness and alienation that the spareness of the musical structure symbolises. There is no exit from social hell, but a kind of release is offered by the unremitting honesty of the song's perspective. Towards its close, Dylan rasps, 'Say okay, I have had enough, What else can you show me?' (1965).

The album, *Highway 61 Revisited*, epitomises Dylan's turn away from a critique of specific forms of injustice, such as racism and towards a fundamental critique of mainstream culture. It is an album that is a wholesale critique of the USA, its culture and values. The title track is a case in point. Highway 61, a highway running from North to South, is an image for the dead hand of the system, stretching throughout the USA. It is a metaphor for the power of the system; its linking and framing of America in the values sustained by corporate power. As Brown has observed, 'The symbolic highway offers less potential for escape and more sense of cultural entrapment' (R. Brown, 2003, in N. Corcoran (ed), 2003, p.205). The opening lines of the song 'Highway 61 Revisited' replay Abraham's readiness to sacrifice his son at God's command, just as in contemporary America the political fathers were sacrificing their sons in the Vietnam war. This slaughter of America's sons is linked to an ineffectual welfare system, the straightjacket of family values, and the commodification of everything, including nuclear war. Dylan recognises the systemic nature of the corruption and desolation in contemporary America. He does not offer an alternative social vision. He satirises mainstream society and in so doing implies an alternative, but individual vision. By replaying the story of Isaac's sacrifice at electric breakneck speed, he registers both disgust at and dismissal of patriarchal American society. Dylan recognises the absurdity of mainstream social values, and in so doing goes beyond them. In 'Like a Rolling Stone' the woman who is addressed in the song is lost in a world of fashionable social connections, and her redemption is only possible when she touches bottom and realises that 'when you got nothing, you got nothing to lose' The reversal of values to which *Highway 61 Revisited* gives effect is emphasised by 'Desolation Row', where the acknowledged desolation of condemned men awaiting the death penalty is seen as positive whereas the unacknowledged desolation of mainstream society epitomised by establishment cultural icons such as

Ezra Pound and T.S. Eliot offers no prospect of redemption from lifelessness. Desolation is what characterises mainstream USA. As Corcoran observes 'I think we should understand by its actual title that, when you revisit Highway 61 — that literal, not fictional American highway... — what you find in 1965 is Desolation Row: a place of transformation and instability where identities are misplaced, replaced or forever lost in the ultimate loss that is death' (N. Corcoran, 2003, in N. Corcoran (ed), 2003, p.163).

In the songs on *Highway 61 Revisited* Dylan is not offering a political message separable from the dissident expressiveness of the songs themselves and from the free-wheeling atmosphere of the studio when they were created (see Kooper, 1998). Similarly, Lyotard in 1968 dropped orthodox Marxism in favour of dissident expressivism, which he would later elaborate as a postmodern exploration of creativity and difference (Lyotard, 1984). In *The Differend* (1983) he takes events to be indeterminate, resisting capture in any one set of descriptive terms and yet susceptible to repressive determination by dominant cultural and political forces. At the end of this book he poses an intractable question, 'Are you prejudging the Is it happening?' (Lyotard, 1988, p. 31). This rhetorical question is characteristic of Lyotard's postmodern sense of how the world should not be encapsulated in conventional terms. Events happen and what is happening, according to Lyotard is liable to be misjudged by being prejudged in stereotypical terms (see Browning, 2000). Lyotard's 'Is it Happening?' is redolent of Dylan's signature refrain in 'Ballad of a Thin Man' on *Highway 61 Revisited*. This refrain is pivotal to Todd Haynes' portrayal of Dylan in *I'm Not There* as a protean non-conformist who eschews mainstream identities and discourses. 'Ballad of a Thin Man' is a riposte to the normalizing pressures of the left and right to which Dylan has been subjected. For Dylan, like Lyotard, insight is not about the learning or social connections, which weigh down on the song's subject, Mr. Jones. Dylan anticipates Lyotard by critiquing the culturally sophisticated, socially conformist Mr. Jones, whose cultural baggage prevents him from

checking in to what is actually happening. Dylan sings ' …
there is something happening here but you don't know
what it is do you, Mr. Jones'. Throughout his career Dylan
rates a particular sensitivity to experience that is untainted
by social conformity and intellectual pretence. His rejection
of the generalities of the discourse of modernity goes along
with a postmodern sensitivity to experience. His sensitivity
to social pressures and search for personal expressiveness
appears on *Blonde on Blonde* as a desperate bid to find freedom from the congestion of complicated sexual relationships to which the album title refers. The burden of fame is
evident in 'Rainy Day Women 12 and 35', which satirises
the pressures on a star performer, who is target for critical
complaint as well as carping women.

### From the End of the 1960s to the End of the 1970s

The gathering pressures on Dylan as a cultural icon induced
his retreat from the limelight, a withdrawal occasioned and
sanctioned by a motorbike accident. With his backing
group, The Band, he drew back from the frenzied public
world of stardom and played music—old time blues, folk
and country songs and new compositions, invoked on the
humour and mystery of the old songs. Marcus in *Invisible
Republic- Bob Dylan's Basement Tapes* shows how the music
of *The Basement Tapes* draws on the rich but enigmatic songs
collected by Harry Smith on the Smithsonian album,
*Anthology of American Folk Music* (see G. Marcus, 1997).
Dylan recorded a new album at the end of 1967, *John Wesley
Harding*, which retreated from rock music. It was a sombre,
simple acoustic album, which resumed Dylan's critique of
America and its values. It reworked Biblical imagery and
scripture to effect a wholesale moral critique that was bleak
and unalloyed by a signposting of an alternative transformed society. 'I Pity the Poor Immigrant', 'Dear Landlord',
'As I Went Out One Morning' and 'The Ballad of Frankie Lee
and Judas Priest' critiqued America's constitutive myths of
the aspiring immigrant, prosperous materialism, the legacy
of Tom Paine and the wild west. In place of these myths, the

American landscape was revealed to be severe and unforgiving and its population alienated and despairing. There is no projected political resolution. The eponymous wicked messenger in the song of that name is told, 'If ye cannot bring good news, then don't bring any' (1967). And the listener is left only with the howling of the wind on 'All Along the Watchtower'.

In subsequent years Dylan, and Lyotard, explored multiple idioms of creativity. Lyotard broke finally and conclusively with erstwhile Marxist associates by publishing the incendiary *Libidinal Economy* (1993b), which valorized desire and depicted Marx as being in libidinous thrall to the very capitalist processes that he subjects to prolonged critique. Subsequently Lyotard went on to develop distinct linguistic, aesthetic ways of exploring postmodernism (see Lyotard, 1984, 1988 and 1999). Dylan's experimentation with country, blues and gospel idioms and his invocation of disparate figures and themes in his lyrics testify to his restless individuality that in its inventive exploration of multiple identities harmonises with the style of postmodernism. Dylan's songs invoke the fragility of the self itself, as he documents the pressures of celebrity, relationships and the political and social system. His autobiographical *Chronicles Vol. 1* reveals how, at the close of the 1960s he experimented with the presentation of his self and identity partly in response to the pressures exerted upon him to assume a fixed and counter-cultural identity (Dylan, 2004, pp. 107–141). Dylan's songs in the mid 1970s exhibit an uneasiness at public images of himself that fix his art and sense of self and he connects their oppressive identification with more general pressures on the self in the modern world. In 'Dirge' on *Planet Waves* (1974) Dylan opens with a verse that appears to be a denunciation of his rock idol persona:

> I hate myself for lovin' you and the weakness that it
> showed,
> You were just a painted face on a trip down Suicide Road,
> The stage was set, the lights went out all around the old

hotel,
I hate myself for loving you and I'm glad the curtain fell.

Dylan in this song, supported by the whining guitar of Robbie Robertson, appears to interweave critique of his own rock celebrity, of a lover, of himself and of the modernist sense of political progress. The 'you' who is addressed throughout the song fuses these objects and thereby conveys the overdetermination of social pressures. Social expectations and a sense of historical progress, like the demands of a lover, constrict an individual's freedom of manoeuvre. Dylan's own vulnerability to the specific pressures of celebrity is presented as being symptomatic of the pressures on the self in the contemporary world.

Dylan's most renowned songs after the 1960s are those on *Blood on the Tracks* (1975), which, in their plaintive lyrics and raw delivery express the anguish and bitterness of failed relationships. They attest to ineliminable differences between selves and the unravelling of deeply personal ties, perhaps engendered by Dylan's own personal life, or maybe, as Dylan himself seems to imply, by Chekhov's short stories (Dylan, 2004, p.122). Relationships are fraught, demanding decisions and responses that are both highly personal and yet inter-personal, demanding negotiation. Marcuse in a contemporary interview likened Dylan to Brecht in observing that Dylan's seemingly highly personal songs are at the same time his most revolutionary (Marcuse, 1984, p. 79). Certainly the songs on *Blood on the Tracks* in their raw expressiveness go beyond the commercialism of popular music, and the banality of most rock lyrics. They are suggestive in linking inter-personal dynamics to the enervating forces of political failure and media distortion, developing themes of his earlier love songs such as 'Don't Think Twice, It's Alright', 'It Ain't Me Babe' and 'Just Like A Woman'. In doing so they convey how a vulnerable and fragile self is touched by the intrusive corruption of the political world, and communicate the inter-connectedness of social and personal life in allusive postmodern suggestiveness. The songs encompass the pain of love, the disintegration of relationships, the unravelling of selves, the waywardness of social commentary, the unreliability of the media and the despair of a post-Watergate political culture. In 'Idiot Wind' the break up of a relationship is narrated against the background of a culture, in which stories are planted in the press and in which communication itself disturbs and distorts. It is likened to an 'Idiot wind, blowing like a circle around my skull, from the Grand Coulee Dam to the Capitol'. The narrator of the song, though, somehow becomes reconciled to his fate, the unreasonableness of critics, the unknowability of the other and the darkness of a corrupt public culture during the very singing of the song. The tone of the music and Dylan's voice on the version on *Blood on the Tracks*, rather than the unqualified sadness of the version on *The Bootleg Series volume 3* is fiery, defiant and yet sensitive. There is some kind of fusion of these elements by the last verse, suggesting the possibility of an experiential resolution of the discordance of social and personal life.

*Blood on the Tracks* was succeeded by *Desire*, where Dylan collaborated with the Off-Broadway stage director and lyricist Jacques Levy in writing distinct, particular songs that narrated stories of oppressed and maverick individuals. 'Hurricane' is a co-written song designed to press the case of Rubin 'Hurricane' Carter, a boxer serving a sentence for murder. The song is highly dramatic and narrates a compelling story, with lots of relevant and mostly authentic detail and driving musical accompaniment. The album contains further strong narrative songs about Joey Gallo, a hoodlum gunned down in New York, a Gipsy King, a Mexican bandit, an Egyptian goddess and a volcanic explosion. The stories swirl with the music and paint pictures of highly particular identities. The political cause of 'Hurricane' Carter is not espoused as part of a general political project but is determinedly singular in its evocation of political injustice. The following album, *Street Legal* (1978) is more personal and disturbed. The songs are difficult to pin down. 'Changing of the Guards' is a rambling metaphorical song that defies interpretation. The album expresses the confusion of interpreting and dealing with oneself. The gap between events and their conceptualization and the need to act in the interim is the specific theme of 'No Time to Think', the chorus of which rehearses the paralysis of the self that must act in time, but which also must negotiate the constraining abstractions that coagulate social action. 'Equality, liberty, humility, simplicity, You glance through the mirror and there's eyes staring clear, At the back of your head as you drink, And there's no time to think'. The album conveys the frustrations of the self. Its style and tenor are a long way from taking equality and liberty to be slogans for change. The allusive autobiographical song, 'Where Are You Tonight? (Journey Through Dark Heat)' declares, 'The truth was obscure, too profound and too pure, to live it you have to explode'. The explosion that Dylan was heading for was fundamentalist Christianity, to which his next and final album of the 1970s was devoted (see Shelton, 1996, Heylin, 2000 and Sounes, 2000).

### Dylan: From Slow Train Coming to Modern Times

Dylan's later songs, like Lyotard's later work disclose a deepening pessimism over the possibilities of joint social and political action. Dylan's disillusionment with the political is expressed most emphatically in the idiom of a religious condemnation of worldly politics. Politics is a realm of the ungodly, as well as of mass conformity. On his first fundamentalist album *Slow Train Coming* (1979) the title track denounces both Karl Marx and Henry Kissinger as being equally sources of confusion. On the title song of *Shot of Love* (1981) the protagonist confesses to a disillusion with the self and the world for which he needs a shot of love. Trouble is the subject of 'Trouble', which condemns the fabric of social, cultural and political life, in declaiming, 'Nightclubs of the broken-hearted, stadiums of the damned, legislature, perverted nature, doors that are rudely slammed, Look into infinity, all you see is trouble'. On *Oh Mercy* (1989) the political world appears as an actual and metaphorical sphere of corruption. Dylan moans that 'everything is broken'. On *Time Out of Mind* (1997) apocalyptic images of impending death and imminent darkness abound. In the rambling song 'Highlands' the prospect of death engenders a dream of idyllic peace offering an autonomy and tranquillity removed from the 'same old rat race, life in the same old cage'. Dylan laments, 'The party's over, and there's less and less to say, I've got new eyes, everything looks far away to me'. In the course of the song's critique of the present world, the narrator observes, 'Somebody asked me if I'd registered to vote'. The narrator doesn't reveal his response, but the listener is left in no doubt over the futility of voting, and indeed of politics in general.

Dylan's late pessimism is not merely a rejection of political activism. The political world looms as a threat to personal integrity, and if the individual is to survive then the political world must be circumvented. Like Lyotard, Dylan recognizes the repressiveness of contemporary public pressures. In 'Gloss on Resistance' in *The Postmodern explained to Children* Lyotard cites Orwell's *1984* as possessing a continuing relevance to contemporary society in its diagnosis of the neo-totalitarian, one-dimensional character of the contemporary social system, evident in the restricted linguistic currency produced by economic efficiency, cultural escapism and political regulation (Lyotard, 1992). In 'Political World' on *Oh Mercy* (1989) Dylan imagines, 'We live in a political world, turning and thrashing about, As soon as you're awake, you're trained to take, What looks like the easy way out'. In 'Clean-Cut Kid' on the album, *Empire Burlesque* (1985) Dylan rehearses the life and death of a clean-cut kid, who follows society's rules and conventions, and is brutalised and unhinged by Vietnam and the army. In 'Union Sundown' on *Infidels* (1983) he complains of how the processes of capitalist reproduction and global economic expansion circumscribe the 'private' space of individuals. In 'T.V. Talkin' Song' on *Under the Red Sky* (1990) he reports sympathetically on a speaker at Hyde Park ranting against the mind control exerted by T.V., observing, 'It's all been designed', he said, 'to make you lose your mind, And when you go back to find it, there's nothing there to find,

Every time you look at it, your situation's worse, If you feel it grabbing out for you, send for the nurse' (1990).

Lyotard, in identifying contemporary totalitarianism with the omnipresence of dominant discourses and the exclusion of expressive ways of thinking, sees art and the process of creative writing itself as framing a form of resistance to the prevailing system. In an essay on human rights, he offers another highly singular recipe of resistance in maintaining that an uncoerced silence can be of more value than a restricted but loquacious expressiveness (Lyotard, 1993c). Dylan, likewise, values artistic expression, creativity and singularity and is critical of standardizing, exclusionary processes at work in society. In 'Lenny Bruce' on *Shot of Love* (1981) he invokes the figure of Lenny Bruce to stand for the dissident, creative outsider, who is brought down by the forces of order. Dylan is only too aware of the difficulties facing an unorthodox celebrity, who is determined to play by his own rules. The last verse of the song highlights the value of a maverick figure like Bruce and the forces against which he must contend.

> They said that he was sick 'cause he didn't play by the rules
> He just showed the wise men of his day to be nothing more
> than fools
> They stamped him and they labeled him like they do with
> pants and shirts
> He fought on a battlefield where every victory hurts
> Lenny Bruce was bad, he was the brother that you never
> had

In a counterpoint to a de-humanising system, Dylan points to the allusive humanity of the singular nonconformist. Such a non-conformist is celebrated in the comic and unconventional poor boy whose story is recounted in the song, 'Po' Boy' on the album *Love and Theft* (2002). Dylan also acknowledges the value of traditional songs to serve as a counterpoint to the mindlessness of contemporary culture. His persisting sense of the expressive mystery and value of traditional songs, notwithstanding his uneasiness at conventional interpretations of them in the folk revival of the early 1960s, is evidenced in his continued singing of such songs and in the use he makes of them in his own lyrics (see Gray, 2000, pp. 268–390). In the 1990s Dylan released two albums of traditional songs and on the sleeve notes to the second, *World Gone Wrong* (1993) he counterposes their authenticity to a counterfeit present. He notes, 'technology to wipe out truth is now available. Not everybody can afford it but it's available. When the cost comes down look out there wont be songs like these anymore. Factually there aren't any now' (Dylan, 1993). Dylan's express recognition of the force of the art of traditional folk and blues songs is reflected in his continued drawing upon these songs for the tunes and lyrics of his own allusive compositions. The songs of his last three studio albums, *Time Out of Mind* (1997), *Love and Theft* (2002) and *Modern Times* (2004) draw heavily on themes and phrases of traditional blues and folk songs and celebrate a variety of traditional styles and idioms, for instance, in the express tribute to Charley Patton in 'Highwater' (for Charley Patton), (See M. Zuckerman, 1999 and M. Zuckerman, 1999/2000).

## Conclusion

Time and again in his songs and in interviews Dylan refuses to come up with answers; and this refusal is a refusal to answer to the public world and is itself a kind of statement on the public political world. The interest in Dylan's politics arises out of his early fame and the resonance of his early songs and their resonance with the civil rights and anti-war movements. Marqusee, in *The Chimes of Freedom: The Politics of Bob Dylan's Art* focuses upon Dylan's distinct contribution to the civil rights and anti-war movements of the early 1960s (Marqusee, 2003). But from the vantage point of the 21st century, the defining features of Dylan's politics are not his engagement with ideology but his disengagement from identification with political causes. Dylan's political art is about resisting the encroachment of politics. His songs do not reveal a set of core political beliefs, for there is a price to be paid for consorting with political casuses and allowing art to be shaped by public agendas. In *Chronicles Vol. 1*

Dylan recalls how he was hounded by the press and public to reflect and represent political and cultural values. He rehearses how, in the aftermath to the 1960s, 'Reporters would shoot questions at me and I would tell them repeatedly that I was not a spokesman for anything or anybody and that I was only a musician. ... I felt like a piece of meat that someone had thrown to the dogs' (Dylan, 2004, p. 119). Refusing to respond to this pressure is an aspect of Dylan's art; his singular development of his own art, with all its personal, evocative ambiguities, contrasts with and resists the sterotyping banality of politics and a media-saturated culture.

Dylan's artistry is as much a resistance to the demands of politics as is his refusal to play a role in the play of the politics of celebrity. Dylan's songs do not fit neatly with political agendas that ignore ambiguities and the elusiveness of individuals. The enduring appeal of Dylan's songs is paradoxically related to their insinuating allusiveness. Rocheleau observes, 'Dylan's protest music, which led to his being embraced as revolutionary spokesperson, exhibits Enlightenment social philosophy, while his work since this period provides an introduction to the political insights and ambiguities of postmodernism' (Rocheleau, 2006, 66). While Dylan's early songs do reflect modern political demands for justice and equality, all of his songs, from whatever era, tend to be suggestive rather than demonstrative in their evocation of scenes and themes. They invoke without determining a wind that is blowing, a slow train that is coming, a hard rain that will fall, skipping reels of rhyme that are not to be paid any mind, a blues that no-one can now sing and visions of Johanna that linger but resist decoding. Dylan's songs gesture at the elusiveness of the human condition rather than a programme for political action. The ambiguities of Dylan's songs are heightened by their performance, as Paul Williams observes in *Performing Artist: The Music of Bob Dylan* (P. Williams, 1990). In 'Like A Rolling Stone', the lyrical deconstruction of a former lover whose pride has preceded her fall is complicated by the sympathy that humanises the singing and intimates a possibility of redemption. Likewise the jauntiness of the music on 'Rainy Day Women: 12 and 35' fuses with its celebration of smoking cannabis and undercuts its complaint against the nagging carping of women and critics. Again, the plaintiveness of the singing and the tenderness of the accompaniment on 'Sad-eyed Lady of the Lowlands' (1966) are at odds with its lyrical coldness. The heroine is depicted as having a 'face like glass' and yet the words are delivered so seductively that listeners feel an ineffable sadness at her fate. Far from developing a set of political doctrines, Dylan recognizes the inscrutability of events and imagines a world that resists explanation. In 'Standing in the Doorway' on the album, *Time Out of Mind* (1997), Dylan characteristically maintains, 'I see nothing to be gained by any explanation, There's no words that need to be said'.

Dylan, like Lyotard and other postmoderns, questions the stability and knowability of the individual self. Lyotard's posthumous *The Confession of Augustine* sees the character of a confessing self as problematic, because the act of confession itself retards the process of explanation (Lyotard 2000). In Dylan's 'I Dreamed I saw St. Augustine' (1967) self-knowledge is secured via seeing a reflection in a glass, but it is in a dream, susceptible of multiple interpretations. Dylan and Lyotard contrast the fragility of the individual and the insecurity of knowledge with the banality and conformity of the social system. Both point to the creativity of art as counter-pointing the latter's one-dimensionality. Dylan's greatest songs and performances suggest what Lyotard in his late work terms the sublimity of art, its capacity to suggest what cannot be explained, notably the sense of 'something happening'. Lyotard admires what he took to be Malraux's sidestepping of nihilism and the political wreckage of modernity by recognising the sublime value of creative art, superseding its contexts. (Lyotard, 1999) Dylan's greatest songs can be understood as intimating the creative process of art itself, pointing to the inexplicability of creativity as resisting and superseding the repetitiveness of conventional society and the emptiness of political soundbites. Dylan's art, then, itself functions as a political critique of the orthodoxies and rigidities of the social and political world.

'Mr. Tambourine Man' can be interpreted on a number of levels, but Aidan Day is right to draw attention to its central paradox. He observes, 'As a lyric the work itself evidences an attainment of the creative moment which its speaker spends so much time invoking' (Day, 1987). The entire course of the song, with its repeated incantations and rhythms, appears to effect the creative release that is demanded insistently but never proclaimed or explained by the singer. In 'Visions of Johanna' Dylan imagines a liberating aesthetic beauty, shrouded by the asphyxiating paraphernalia of urban life. This image haunts the song's narrator, who disparages and scorns museums and art criticism that affect to explain and control images of beauty. The fourth verse goes,

> Inside the museums, infinity goes up on trial,
> Voices echo this is what salvation must be like after a while,
> But Mona Lisa must have had the highway blues,
> You can tell by the way she smiles,
> See the primitive wallflower freeze,
> When the jelly -faced women all sneeze,
> Hear the one with the moustache say,
> "Jeeze I can't find my knees",
> Oh jewels and binoculars hang from the mule,
> But these visions of Johanna, they make it all seem so cruel.

While there is no evident explanation of its lyric, the song's delivery is itself so haunting and plaintive that the listener is convinced of the visions of Johanna's beauty. Again, in his 1983 masterpiece, 'Blind Willie McTell', Dylan mourns his lack of powers to testify to the desolation of contemporary America. He confesses to a lack of authentic musical capacity to perform a blues like the late Blind Willie McTell. And yet, as the late John Bauldie observed, the listener is insistently aware that Dylan himself delivers an authentic performance so that the song achieves what its title pronounces as unrealisable (Bauldie, 1987). 'Blind Willie McTell' alludes to what in late modernity cannot be expressed, and yet by straining against what cannot be said, the fate of the present is suggested. The original blues was a lament and protest against the times, modern times, but as the album *Modern Times* suggests we are no longer able to react to modern times by protesting or organising resistance for we can barely testify to what we feel.

Dylan's political art is as disruptive as other aspects of his work and self. Most of all, perhaps, his art itself disrupts the clichéd sentiments of a culture limited by what fits the requirements of media reporting, commmercial imperatives and political calculations. Dylan's art, his mining of traditional music forms, blues, folk, country, gospel and jazz, to express individual dissident sentiments, out of joint with modern times if not leading a revolt against them, constitutes a critique of the political world. In recent interviews Dylan reaffirms his commitment to the traditions of popular music that he admires. He lauds the blues, folk, country and gospel masters. In an interview with John Pareles for the *New York Times* in 1997 Dylan rhapsodizes about the force of old songs, traditional and non-traditional, 'These old songs are my lexicon and my prayer book. ... All my beliefs come out of these old songs, literally anything from *Let Me Rest on that Peaceful Mountain* to *Keep on the Sunny Side*. You can find all my philosophy in those old songs. I believe in a God of time and space, but if people ask me about that, my impulse is to point them back toward those songs. I believe in Hank Williams singing 'I Saw the Light'. I've seen the light too' (*New York Times*, 1997, in Cott, 2006). In looking to the past and its traditions to disturb the bland ephemerality of the present, Dylan appears a traditionalist rather than the postmodern he was held to be at the outset of this essay. But Dylan's traditionalism recognizes that things have changed and that the world of the old blues and country singers isn't going to be revived. The meaning of this tradition of old songs changes in line with the times and the postmodern doesn't simply postdate the present, but can criticise or complicate it by invoking the past. Dylan's critique of the present draws on the past by showing its point is not exhausted by its place in a linear development of modern times and he works with a tradition of music and ballads that highlight a mystery that is not to be dissolved by the calculations of modern commerce and political strategy.

## References

Bauldie, John (1987) 'The Oppression of Knowledge: No-one Can Sing the Blues Like Blind Willie McTell', in M.Gray and J.Bauldie (eds.) *All across the Telegraph: A Bob Dylan Handbook*, London: Sidgwick and Jackson.

Butler, Judith (1990) *Gender Trouble: Feminism and the Subversion of Identity*, London: Routledge.

Brown, Richard (2003) 'Highway 61 and Other American States of Mind', in N. Corcoran (ed) *'Do You, Mr. Jones?' Bob Dylan with the Poets and Professors*, London: Pimlico.

Browning, Gary (2000) *Lyotard and the End of Grand Narratives*, Cardiff: University of Wales Press.

Corcoran, Neil. (2003), 'Death's Honesty', in N. Corcoran (ed) *'Do You Mr. Jones?' Bob Dylan With the Poets and the Professors*, London: Pimlico.

Corcoran, Neil. (ed), (2003) *'Do You, Mr. Jones?' Bob Dylan with the Poets and Professors*, London: Pimlico.

Cott, Jonathan (ed), (2006) *Dylan on Dylan*, London: Wenner Media, LLC.

Day, Aidan, (1987) 'Reels of Rhyme: Mr. Tambourine Man, in M.Gray and J.Bauldie (eds.) All Across the Telegraph: A Bob Dylan Handbook, London: Sidgwick and Jackson.

Dylan, Bob. (1993) *World Gone Wrong-Sleeve Notes*, New York: Sony Music Entertainment.

Dylan, Bob (1996) *Sleeve Notes to Jimmie Rodgers Tribute Album.*

Dylan, Bob (2004) *Chronicles: Volume 1* London: Simon and Schuster Ltd.

Gonczy, D.J. (1990) 'The folk music of the 1960s: its rise and Fall' in E. Thomson and D. Gutman (eds) *The Dylan Companion*, London: Macmillan.

Gray, Michael, (2000) *Song and Dance Man 111: The Art of Bob Dylan*, London and New York: Cassell.

Hersch, Charles. (1998) *Democratic Artworks – Politics and The Arts from Trilling to Dylan*, New York: State University of New York Press.

Heylin, Clinton, *Bob Dylan: Behind the Shades-Take Two* (2000) New York: Viking.

Kooper. Al *Back Stage Passes and Backstabbing Bastards* (1998) New York: Billboard Books.

Lyotard, Jean-Frabncois (1984) *The Postmodern Condition: A Report on Knowlege* trans. G. Bennington and B. Massumi, Manchester: Manchester University Press.

Lyotard, Jean-Francois. (1988) *The Differend*. Manchester: Manchester University Press.

Lyotard, Jean-Francois (1992) *The Postmodern Explained to Children: Correspondence 1982-1985*, London: Turnaround Books

Lyotard, Jean-Francois (1993a) *Political Writings* trans. B. Readings and K. Geiman, London: UCL Press.

Lyotard, Jean-Francois, (1993b) *Libidinal Economy*, trans. I. Hamilton Grant, London, Athlone.

Lyotard, Jean-Francois (1993c) 'The other's rights', in S. Shute and S. Hurley (eds) *On Huma Rights: The Oxford Amnesty Lectures 1993*, New York: Basic Books.

Lyotard, Jean-Francois (1999) *Signed Malraux*, Minneapolis: University Of Minnesota Press.

Lyotard, Jean-Francois., *The Confession of Augustine* (2000) Stanford, California: Stanford University Press.

Marcuse, Herbert (1984) 'Dialogue with Hebert Marcuse', in R. Kearney (ed.) *Dialogues With Contemporary Continental Thinkers* Manchester: Manchester University Press.

Marcus, Greil (1997) *Invisible Republic – The Basement Tapes* New York: Henry Holt

Marqusee, Michael (2003) *Chimes of Freedom - The Politics of Bob Dylan's Art*, The New Press: New York.

Rocheleau, Jordy (2006) ''Far Between Sundown's Finish An' Midnight's Broken Toll': Enlightenment and Postmodernism in Dylan's Social Criticism', in P. Vernezze and C.J. Porter (2006) *Bob Dylan and Philosophy – It's Alright Ma (I'm Only Thinking)* Open Court: Chicago and La Salle, Illinois.

Scobie, Stephen (1991) *Alias Bob Dylan* Red Deer, Alberta Canada: Red Deer Press.

Shelton, Robert (1986) *Dylan: A Biography* New York: McGraw Hill.

Sounes, Howard (2000) *Down the Highway – The Life of Bob Dylan* London and New York: Doubleday.

Turner, Gil (1972) 'Bob Dylan – A New Voice Singing New Songs' in Craig McGregor (ed) (1972) *Bob Dylan – The Early Years A Retrospective*, New York: De Capo Press (originally published in *Sing Out!* 1962).

Zuckerman, Matthew (1999) 'If There's An Original Thought Out There, I could Use it Right Now – The Folk Roots of Bob Dylan', *Isis* 87, Bedworth Warwickshire.

Zuckerman, Matthew (1999–2000) 'If There's An original Thought Out There, I could Use It Right Now – The Folk Roots of Bob Dylan', *Isis* 88, Bedworth, Warwickshire.

Elizabeth Brake

# 'You can always come back, but you can't come back all the way': Freedom and the Past in Dylan's Recent Work

Philosophical concepts of fate and freedom are at play in Dylan's recent work. In an earlier essay, I tried to show that Dylan's 1964–66 lyrics suggest a dialogue between something like Hegel's concept of negative freedom and an Emersonian ideal of self-realization (Brake, 2006). In this essay, I continue this investigation into what is meant by 'freedom' in Dylan's lyrics through exploring the recurrent image of comeback. The concepts of negative freedom and self-realization evolve in Dylan's latest work in response to the complications of age, memory, and the past. I suggest that the recent work is attentive to certain conditions, or complications, of freedom: is freedom possible when one is somehow caught up in the past?

The figure of comeback which runs through this work suggests a—possibly illusory—ideal of self-recovery. A central concept of freedom in Dylan's lyrics has been an idea of self-realization or self-creation. Comeback, or self-recovery, is thus linked to this concept of freedom: recovering oneself is a precondition for realizing or creating oneself. In part, comeback is a figure for escape from nostalgia and overcoming loss, a necessary condition for continuing self-creation. The film and the lyrics rightly pose the question of whether comeback is even possible.

Freedom and comeback link with the political in complex ways. The ideal of self-realization rejects the abstractions of political principles and the conformities which adherence to them may demand. Dylan called political thoughts 'trivial' in 1963,[1] and nothing here suggests a revised judgment. However, his art equally insists on the necessity of resistance, of not speaking the words power commands. In his recent work, a minor theme has been the infringement of liberties by the state. In this respect, the work is very much about political freedom: as Whitman wrote, 'In the make of the great masters the idea of political liberty is indispensable' (Whitman, 1855, 17–18). While Whitman's 'Song of Myself' is, like Dylan's work, not a political protest, it, also like Dylan's work, celebrates the human liberty for which political liberty is an inspiration and a precondition.

The beginning of this essay focuses on Dylan's last three albums — *Time Out of Mind* (1997), '*Love and Theft*' (2001), and *Modern Times* (2006) — and in particular, on their central preoccupation with how the past forecloses present options, and time steals away the space for new beginnings. Time conditions everything; the negative freedom flirted with in earlier lyrics ('it ain't me, babe') is no longer on the table. Negative freedom, as Hegel articulated this ideal (which he considered bankrupt) consists in the rejection of roles and self-definitions as limiting. But one who has acted and become someone over time can no longer refuse all definitions. These albums also suggest a limitation in the contrasting ideal of self-realization or self-creation. Secondarily, images of poverty, exploitation, war, and intimidation suggest different kinds of threats to freedom.

---

[1] In a speech made upon accepting an award from the National Emergency Civil Liberties Committee; excerpted in the documentary *No Direction Home*, directed by Martin Scorsese, 2005.

The latter part of this essay pursues these themes in the film *Masked and Anonymous* (2003), co-written by and starring Dylan. This film foregrounds the political: it is set in a dystopian state in which fascistic control does not prevent anarchic street violence. The film prompts the viewer to ask (among other things) how, in a world of political uncertainty, where the state threatens arbitrary imprisonment, where work is futile or degrading, where media misinform, one can live with some degree of freedom. Dylan plays a character called Fate, whose father is the President of this state; the film thus links the political and the personal. The theme of comeback (which the film shares with the recent albums) entwines with the theme of political freedom.

## I

*Time Out of Mind* is an album haunted with love and memory and foreshadowing removal from the world. The speaker of many of the songs is bound by his past, his only destination darkness, heaven, or the Highlands. The album's tone is stately, slow, elegiac. In contrast, *'Love and Theft'* (the title's quotation marks drawing attention to its own theft, or borrowing, or artistic reinvention[2]), is a restless tour through mythologized Americana, its personae engaged in, mortgaged to, the world. *Modern Times* (this time without quotation marks, though the title is also that of a 1936 Chaplin film critical of industrialized capitalism) is more attentive to injustice, and more overtly spiritual, beginning with a god's descent ('Thunder on the Mountain') and ending with his departure ('Ain't Talkin''). The experience of advancing age is a shared theme, and images of lost youth are echoed by images of a lost America. While

[2]    According to Dylan scholars, it is borrowed from Lott, 1995; see Scobie, 2003, 78. One example of the inventive and layered significance of Dylan's borrowings: verses in 'Thunder on the Mountain' (e.g. 'I'm wondering where in the world Alicia Keys could be/ I been looking for her even clear through Tennessee') rework Memphis Minnie's 'Ma Rainey' ('I was thinking about Ma Rainey, wonder where could Ma Rainey be/ I been looking for her, even been 'n old Tennessee'). A tribute from a younger to an older female singer becomes Dylan's homage to a younger female singer and creates a genealogy linking Ma Rainey to Alicia Keys.

nostalgia is a dominant register, that's not all: for just as the narrators of '*Love and Theft*' have seen, and done, some horrors in the past, the lost America was a world of war, poverty, and injustice. We—individually and collectively—cannot escape our mistakes simply by going away from them in time.

Nostalgia is a longing for the past, a homesickness (like some of Dylan's recent imagery, its meaning elides time and space).[3] It is, on one hand, a reasonable response to real losses accompanying age and change: 'When you think that you lost everything/You find out you can always lose a little more' ('Tryin' to get to heaven'). These may be losses of energy, resilience, emotional strength: 'Yesterday everything was going too fast/Today, it's moving too slow/I got no place left to turn/I got nothing left to burn' ('Standing in the Doorway'); 'Got nothing for you, I had nothing before/Don't even have anything for myself anymore' ('Mississippi'). They may also be losses of first-order desires to engage with the world:

> I don't want nothing from anyone, ain't that much to take
> Wouldn't know the difference between a real blonde and a
> fake
> Feel like a prisoner in a world of mystery
> I wish someone would come
> And push back the clock for me … ('Highlands')[4]

Here, the 'object of desire … is elusive, out of range, both before in time past and ahead in a heaven threatening to close its door before the speaker can get there'.[5] The speaker seems to desire to desire, but cannot find an object, as in 'Things Have Changed', with its refrain, 'I used to care, but things have changed': 'I'm in love with a woman who don't

---

[3]   Thanks to Rod McGillis for prompting me to think further on nostalgia and desire. My discussion of nostalgia, in particular the contrast between what may be called 'restorative' and 'rehabilitative' nostalgia, follows McGillis 2009, chapter 3, which draws in turn on the work of Debbora Battaglia and Sveltana Boym.

[4]   To the waitress who asks for a portrait, the speaker of 'Highlands' replies: 'I would if I could, but,/ I don't do sketches from memory.' There is a sense of the absurd associated with the political too: 'Somebody just asked me/If I registered to vote'.

[5]   Rod McGillis, private correspondence.

even appeal to me'.[6] Such nostalgia can be a trap. Longing for what one has lost—youth, strength, innocence, love—may turn into an obsession with the past itself, leading the nostalgist to invest it with false value or blocking him from engagement with the present. Perhaps this is why Dylan writes in his memoirs that neither he nor his friend Bono 'are nostalgic, and nostalgia doesn't enter into anything and we're gonna make damn sure about that' (Dylan, 2004, 175).

While age brings loss, it also brings, paradoxically, a lumbering accumulation of identities, leaving no room—or strength—to turn (to change), boxing us in as if in pigeonholes. Images of physical entrapment ('I got no place left to turn') recur: 'Junk is piling up; taking up space' ('Til I Fell in Love with You'), 'There's not even room enough to be anywhere', ('Not Dark Yet'); 'Time is pilin' up, we struggle and we scrape/We're all boxed in, nowhere to escape', 'tight as the corner that I painted myself in' ('Mississippi').[7] The consequences of the past are inescapable: 'I've still got the scars that the sun didn't heal' ('Not Dark Yet'). Lost loves and memory condition the present: 'I left my life with you somewhere back there along the line/I thought somehow that I would be spared this fate' ('Can't Wait'); 'the future for me is already a thing of the past' ('Bye and Bye'); 'Some of these memories you can learn to live with and some of them you can't' ('Sugar Baby'). The self is both depleted and burdened with painful memories—for example, a sense that something has gone wrong, needs to be revisited or changed. Tellingly, Dylan writes of such a sense in his memoirs: 'The previous ten years had left me pretty whitewashed and wasted out professionally .... Many times I'd ... catch myself thinking that I wasn't keeping my word with myself. ... There was a missing person inside of myself and I needed to find him' (Dylan, 2004, 147).

Feelings of loss and error explain the desire for 'comeback'—recovery of one's lost self. Of course, replacing these

---

[6]   On the *Wonder Boys* (dir. Curtis Hanson) soundtrack (2000). Compare: 'I'm not even acquainted with my own desires' ('Bye and Bye').

[7]   This song was recorded in sessions for *Time out of Mind* but published on 'Love and Theft'.

losses and erasing the past are impossible. The desire to be now just as one was before cannot be fulfilled: 'You can always come back, but you can't come back all the way' ('Mississippi'). If 'comeback' is to be meaningful, then, it must mean something else. With this in mind, *'Love and Theft'*'s repeated references to reanimation, even in an attenuated fashion, bear consideration. An exchange borrowed almost word-for-word from *The Great Gatsby* (itself a kind of revivification of Gatsby) underscores the potentially deceptive appeal of 'comeback': 'She says, 'You can't repeat the past'. I say, 'You can't? What do you mean, you can't? Of course you can' ('Summer Days').[8] In the novel, Gatsby hopes to repeat the past with his now-married sweetheart, as if she had never loved another, but his pursuit of this dream proves fatal. Directly following the exchange about repeating the past, the narrator tells us, Gatsby 'talked a lot about the past and I gathered that he wanted to recover something, some idea of himself perhaps, that had gone into loving Daisy. His life had been confused and disordered since then, but if he could once return to a certain starting place and go over it all slowly, he could find out what that thing was' (Fitzgerald, 1925, 117). But Gatsby has changed himself, reinventing himself as a wealthy socialite. Not only has he changed, but Daisy is not the Daisy he remembers (if she ever was, if his memories are not an idealization). The book's famous closing line emphasizes how the seductions of memory continually impede our attempts to move on: 'So we beat on, boats against the current, borne back ceaselessly into the past' (189).

It is *'Love and Theft'*'s second song, 'Mississippi', in which we find the line, 'You can always come back, but you can't come back all the way'. But in 'Sugar Baby', the album's last song, we hear: 'You can't turn back — you can't come back, sometimes we push too far'. Here, 'come back' might mean 'return home again' — prompting the question, what else might 'come back' mean, as in 'Mississippi'? There is perhaps sly reference to Dylan's artistic comeback. But the

---

[8]   See Fitzgerald, 1925, p. 116: '"You can't repeat the past". "Can't repeat the past?" he cried incredulously. "Why of course you can!"'

interesting meaning is that of a recovery of powers, of self — what Gatsby sought to recover by retrieving his past. This recovery is metaphorically connected to a larger recovery project: the speaker of 'Rollin and tumblin' (the song itself a controversially unacknowledged borrowing) has 'been conjuring up all these long dead souls from their crumblin' tombs'. Coming back — recovering an earlier self — may have something to do with what Dylan is doing artistically, the recovery and renewal of past forms; Dylan borrows old songs and phrases (just as one might use one's own past personae) but makes from them something new. (Such recovery also, under the name 'resurrection', has religious overtones).

This recovery process should be distinguished from Gatsby's. Gatsby looked for answers in the past; he thought his self had been lost there, and that the woman he loved then could be had again just as she was. Dylan's artistic reanimations are a form of moving on, of constructing new artworks, new objects of desire. Such reanimation does not aim to recreate what no longer exists and no longer can exist (Dylan is not just covering these old songs but remaking them). In this way it is a release from nostalgic desire. In life too, leaving the past, giving it up, may be a prologue to spiritual growth (alternatively, it may precede death): 'got no future, got no past/ But my heart is not weary, it's light and it's free' ('Mississippi'). Self-recovery apparently differs from an artistic process of reviving old forms. But if we are no longer the selves we once were, then conjuring up (imaginatively inhabiting, acting as if one were) Muddy Waters or Memphis Minnie is not so different from conjuring up one's own past self. Or, at least, contrasting these processes raises the interesting question of what the difference comes to.

A minor thread in *'Love and Theft'* and *Modern Times* — linking them to *Masked and Anonymous* — is injustice. Things are not just lost in time, but also stolen. What is stolen is taken unjustly,[9] and injustice is rampant in these lyrics, from epic destruction to bad employment practices.

> The buyin' power of the proletariat's gone down ...
> The place I love best is a sweet memory
> It's a new path that we trod
> They say low wages are a reality
> If we want to compete abroad
> Now they worry and they hurry and they fuss and they fret
> They waste your nights and days
> ('Workingman's Blues #2').

While these lyrics are nostalgic in suggesting that a 'place' (perhaps an ideal America) is lost in the past, other songs, set in past times of war and poverty, undercut such nostalgia. The lyrics of *Modern Times* are especially attuned to the loss of self which comes from social injustice, from parasitism — 'Some people never worked a day in their life/ Don't know what work even means' ('Workingman's Blues #2') — or the urge to dominate — 'They will crush you with wealth and power' ('Ain't Talkin') — or greed — 'Some of these people gonna strip you of all they can take/ Some people on the road carrying everything that they own' ('The Levee's Gonna Break'). These injustices prompt urges for revenge and resistance (as in 'Ain't Talkin' and 'Floater'). But revenge is not self-recovery, just as the negative freedom of rejecting social conformity does not amount to self-realization. Can we recover our selves, even if not all the way, and continue with our project of selfhood? I'll suggest that this question is taken up in *Masked and Anonymous*, where it is inserted into a context of overtly political concern.

## II

These themes of loss and theft, and the question of a comeback, or the overcoming of loss, are related to ethical and political questions, including the most fundamental ethical question of all: how should one live? (Notably, Dylan remarks in *No Direction Home* that when he first heard

---

[9]  Another kind of theft here is Dylan's artistic reworking of older material; thus the album title invites us to consider what distinguished legitimate use from theft.

Guthrie's songs he realized songs could be about how to live). If freedom is a process of self-realization or self-creation, the question of comeback, or recovery of self, becomes a question of freedom.

In an earlier essay, I used the concepts of negative freedom and self-realization to read Dylan's lyrics. Negative freedom is identified (and criticized) by Hegel as freedom understood as the rejection of roles and labels. The underlying thought is that the self has infinite potentiality, so that any definition limits the self by excluding some of those potentialities (Hegel, 1821, 37, par. 5). Such a thought appears in Dylan's early lyrics. However, negative freedom, Hegel pointed out, is itself an inadequate ideal: if one only rejects definition, one cannot become anything. One simply refuses (tending at the extreme, he says, to self-emptying or to the destructive terror of the French Revolution). But Dylan's lyrics are not liable to this critique, for they do not merely reject labels, but hint at a positive ideal which has some commonalities with Emerson's ideal of self-realization, or living according to one's nature.

Dylan's later work suggests new limitations inherent in the concept of negative freedom. The accumulations of age rule out the rejection of definition. For someone with these accumulations (junk pilin' up, all boxed in, no place to turn), negative freedom, freedom as rejection of definition, is no longer a thinkable ideal: one is defined already. 'I thought somehow that I would be spared this fate', but the past catches up with one; some memories cannot be forgotten. One is no longer capable of assuming any shape whatsoever, and hence rejecting them all. One has a past. Thus, Hegelian negative freedom is simply unrealizable; with age, the ethos of rejection loses any appeal it may have had.

Like Emerson's essay 'Self-Reliance', Dylan's lyrics suggest that independence of judgment from external threats or inducements is a condition of freedom. Certain thoughts, ideas, and feelings carry an internal authority which we recognize, but they are easily overwhelmed by external pressures. As Emerson writes: 'the voices which we hear in solitude, … grow faint and inaudible as we enter into the world' (Emerson, 1841, 133; see also Brake, 2006). Like Dylan, Emerson insisted on nonconformity to social convention, but he also suggested a law to which we should conform: 'No law can be sacred to me but that of my nature' (p. 134). However, this ideal of self-realization suggests a fixed and given nature which Dylan's lyrical emphasis on rejuvenating old forms, or the masks of *Masked and Anonymous*, somewhat undercut. The lyrics' presentation of what Scobie identifies as a 'trickster' with a 'fluid sense of self' is at odds with the idea of an authentic self to be realized (Scobie, 2003, 26). In his memoirs, Dylan remembers the poet Rimbaud's line 'je est un autre', 'I is someone else', as revelatory; the line suggests a gap between the thinking self and the constructed identity (Dylan, 2004, 288).

A scene in *Masked and Anonymous* suggests the paucity of the idea of a fixed and given nature. Val Kilmer plays an animal wrangler who prefers animals to humans: 'they're beautiful because they just are, they do what they do', and they do not try to be what they are not. Humans, the implication is, try to be what they are not: they 'are, along with their secrets, masked and anonymous — no-one truly knows them' (Compare Whitman, 1855, section 32). 'Amazing Grace' plays on the soundtrack as Kilmer voices an ideal of living in the moment according to the law of one's own nature, a juxtaposition ironized by Fate's wry comment: 'the guy's into animals, I guess'. This wryness may be a tip-off that the wrangler's idea of selfhood as immutable like species membership is primitive, inadequate. On the other hand, Dylan in his memoirs seems critical of the 'dominant myth ... that anybody could do anything, even go to the moon. ... It was almost like a war against the self' (Dylan, 2004, 90).

If self-creation is, like artistic creation, a matter of 'conjuring up ... long dead souls' (perhaps including one's own past selves), the self is not all one's own, self-created *ex nihilo*, but created from borrowed materials. Alternatively, perhaps the past guises are just masks the self wears. There is a contrast between the notion of an authentic self, whose law self-creation must respect, and that of a self undergoing continual construction from borrowed materials. If the process of self-creation is open-ended — if its results are not determined already — and if it involves borrowing, then the self is not fixed or already given. Moreover, if self-creation is a continual process — not something to be achieved once and finished — such a fixed self will never be available.[10]

Like the notion of an authentic self, the notion of a self in continual open-ended process faces tough philosophical questions: for example, who is doing the creating? Perhaps it is creativity (whatever that is), in which case creative artistry is linked with selfhood, and hence freedom (a suggestion we see in *Masked and Anonymous*, in which singing is a metaphor for freedom). I leave these metaphysical questions regarding the nature of the self to one side, because settling them can be done independently of exploring two aspects of freedom shared in *Masked and Anonymous* and the early lyrics: the resistance to external pressures to conform and the insistence on acting according to one's inner voice. Besides, the lyrics raise many more philosophical questions than they promise to answer.

Just as age complicates the ideal of negative freedom, it poses problems for an ideal of self-creation. If one's powers have diminished ('Don't even have anything for myself anymore'), how can one realize or create a self? Further, as time passes, one has to recognize as one's past what has happened to one as well as what one chose. Time fixes one with a history only partly of one's own making. This interplay between external events and one's own choices will recur, with political overtones, in *Masked and Anonymous*. These problems are related to the issue of comeback, of overcoming loss and one's past.

To anticipate: I take *Masked and Anonymous* to explore what it means to be free in conditions of limitation and loss, including past mistakes and political dictatorship. We are told that Fate, the character Dylan plays, is 'virtually free'. But as the film opens, he is in prison, and his first words are:

[10] Thanks to Rod McGillis for prodding me on these issues. Dylan's comments on artistic creation in *No Direction Home* suggest he sees being an artist as a continual, never-finished, process.

'I ain't felt free in a long time'. (The phrase 'feeling free' suggests freedom is merely a sensation, an illusion[11]). As the
film ends, Fate is heading back to prison — or death. The film
explores the effect of lack of basic civil liberties — of the
press, of movement, of due process. And it flirts with fatal-
ism, as in an exchange in which an old man sitting at a bus
station ('Prospero'[12]) asks Fate 'Leaving town? ... By choice
this time?' He replies: 'Not really'. Prospero's response:
'Nothing ever really is'.[13] The film suggests the futility of
struggling against fate as well as political injustice: three of
the film's main characters are unable to evade the consequences of their actions. What fate itself is is left open-
ended: the film seems to me to leave open the possibility
that one's fate may be self-made, the consequence of earlier freely chosen actions, rather than determined by
causes outside the agent.

This inability to escape the consequences of the past I link
to the theme of 'comeback'. The film exploits this word's
ambiguities, between coming home again, reclaiming
celebrity or success, and self-recovery (which Gatsby
sought) or recovery of the powers of self-creation. It links
coming back to oneself with freedom, and it explores different approaches to comeback — through political struggle,
pursuing success, recognition.

One sense of comeback is of coming home again, of
retrieving a lost self through returning to past places and
people, winning the recognition of those who knew the
younger self. This theme of recognition recalls the Hegelian
idea that recognition is necessary for self-consciousness. In
Hegel's famous parable of the master and slave, two men
each recognize themselves as persons through the other's
recognition of him; their subsequent struggle to secure this

---

[11] A similar locution is found in James' *The Ambassadors* and is made much of
in Robert Pippin's philosophical reading of that work: 'Still, one has the
illusion of freedom'. See Pippin, 2000, 159.

[12] Prospero lays down his powers at the end of Shakespeare's *Tempest* in a
famous abdication from creation.

[13] The fatalistic dialogue continues: 'Which way you headin?' 'That way'.
'That's a good way, one of my favorites. I've done that a lot. Know what
else is good — that way'. The traveler ends up in the same place either way.

recognition raises the issue of how it is possible to secure such recognition. This struggle concludes when one man yields and is enslaved. Ironically, the master can no longer receive recognition from the slave, as the slave is no longer his equal; whereas the slave is able to find self-recognition in his work (Hegel, 1807, pars. 178–196). Hegel's answer to the problem of securing equal mutual recognition, in part, is that we secure it by adopting the publicly recognized roles of ethical life, especially through equal citizenship in the state. In Hegel's view, we come to know ourselves and to be particular selves through the reactions of others and through public recognition. This view has a certain resemblance to Dylan's project of creating identities from cultural icons such as the outlaw or the blues singer. However, Dylan's personae usually reshape rather than simply replicating socially recognized forms. Indeed, *Masked and Anonymous* seems to reject the notion that freedom and selfhood depends on recognition. Fate knows better than to seek self-knowledge from his fans, but his quest to achieve his dying father's recognition suggests a temptation to seek himself in recognition by former intimates. However, this quest is unfulfilled; he remains anonymous.

In its strange and indefinite way, the film suggests that only Fate can accord recognition to himself; freedom does not depend on the attitudes of others. If, in my earlier essay, I argued that the lyrics seem to reach an Emersonian ideal by overcoming Hegelian negative freedom, here I suggest that *Masked and Anonymous* reaches towards an Emersonian ideal of responsibility to oneself by overcoming the Hegelian dialectic of recognition. Ultimately, Fate seems to abandon the search for external recognition or a past self; the 'comeback' is not to be a comeback in the eyes of others – 'I ain't looking for nothing in anyone's eyes' ('Not Dark Yet') – but to be oneself again, or to continue to be oneself, by recognizing oneself, in the face of threats and temptations of all kinds. To recognize oneself is at least (and this is the Emersonian theme) to recognize the authority of one's own inner promptings and to deny the legitimacy of claims not made by that voice. It may also be to see oneself in what one does (whether artistic performance or work of another kind) and in this way to take responsibility for, as in ownership of, one's actions.

## III

*Masked and Anonymous* is, at one level, the story of a failed comeback.[14] A singer who has lost everything is falsely promised another chance to make it big. He knows this promise is false and refuses to play along with his producer's demands. The big chance never materializes, and as the film ends, he has lost a little more.

Issues of political liberty and security recur throughout the film. A fascistic government wages a partly staged civil war. The film opens with images of bombs, floods, and fighting. Outside barricaded buildings, disorder goes unpoliced. Violence is universal and reasonless: as a character says, 'Everybody's doing the killing now, everybody's doing the dying'. Trucks full of armed men roll through the streets. Homeless people line the sidewalks. Paper money has lost its value. But the government, which fails to provide security or end the bloody war of all against all, is also omni-present and omni-punitive. Posters of the President in military dress hang in the streets, the interiors, even Fate's hotel room. Passports are legally required. Freedom of speech and of the press are fragile. As the film begins, the President is dying.

In this setting, an unsavory promoter, Uncle Sweetheart, is threatened with death by his creditors. He decides to save himself by organizing a benefit concert for the victims of the war, with the majority of funds to be siphoned, he says, to 'the kitty of the fattest cat of all—me'. Because the country is so dangerous, only one singer will agree to perform. The network executives are unimpressed: 'Jack Nobody', they call him. The promoter, on the other hand, calls him a 'legend' and compares him to Christ. The singer, Jack Fate,

---

[14] Other predominant themes are spirituality and religion, theatricality, the media, art, and criticism—as well as the psychoanalytic interest of the film's family drama.

is played by Dylan, and he sings Dylan's songs. Fate is also, as it happens, the son of the President — a fact to which only three other characters, one a ghost, allude.

Sweetheart arranges Fate's release from prison — why he is there, we are not told — and Fate journeys to the capital. There he checks into a faded hotel (the Whitman[15]) where he says he stayed before (possibly during a tryst with his father's mistress). In the lead-up to the concert, Fate is sweet-talked by Sweetheart, harangued by TV producer Nina Veronica, and goaded by music critic Tom Friend. He visits his father's mistress, his mother's grave, and his father's deathbed. He spends time with an old friend, Bobby Cupid. He also encounters the President-in-waiting, Edmund, a usurper or upstart, who reminisces that his parents were immigrants, 'formerly illegal, now in charge'.[16]

The benefit concert begins just as the President dies. Fate's performance of 'Cold Irons Bound' is intercut with Edmund's inaugural address. Edmund promises to rewrite history, erase the collective memory, and seek peace — through bombing. Meanwhile, Fate sings:

> I'm beginning to hear voices and there's no one around …
> It's almost like, almost like I don't exist …
> The walls of pride are high and wide
> Can't see over to the other side …

Edmund's speech usurps Fate's performance on the air-waves, and his troops brutally end the concert, taking over the network. Earlier, Fate met the ghost of a blackface minstrel, Oscar Vogel, who spoke out against the President on stage — committing suicide by opening his mouth. If we are to take Fate's own performance as an inheritance, we must

[15]  Surely it is not an accident that the hotel is named the Whitman. There are echoes of Whitman in the film as well as of the preface to *Leaves of Grass* in Dylan's *Chronicles* — for example, Dylan, like Whitman, claims to have had to invent his own art form or way of writing because what he needed to express himself did not yet exist.

[16]  Is the name a reference to the usurping bastard in *Lear*, whose deception forces his half-brother Edgar to flee in exile, then feign madness? (The film also features an Edgar, a featureless aide to Edmund.) If the dying President is Lear, is Fate the truly loving, yet unrecognized, Cordelia? Both plots, too, end in sacrifices which may be redemptive or meaningless. On *Lear*, responsibility, recognition, and renunciation, see Cavell, 1987.

take 'Cold Irons Bound' as a protest song (recalling Dylan's famous reply to a crowd calling on him to sing protest songs, 'these are all protest songs' — just before launching into 'Ballad of a Thin Man'; see Marqusee, 2003, 199).

This comeback performance fails, at least in terms of regaining celebrity and recognition. Fate seems in need of a comeback: he has lost a musical career, a woman, the time spent in prison, and his father's affection and power. Characters repeatedly ask whether he still has songs in him. Prospero asks, 'You ever comin' back?' and Fate replies: 'I did come back'. Perhaps this response refers to leaving prison; more surely and significantly, it means that Fate is not looking to come back — it has already happened. He is uninterested in the kind of celebrity comeback to which Prospero likely refers: when Sweetheart promises a 'big chance', Fate's reaction is cynical: 'Yet another big chance'. While Fate says he has songs left in him, he also accepts that his so-called 'last chance' is meaningless; he knows Sweetheart's promises are empty, and says to Prospero that he does not expect to have a 'next time'. Fame and money, like political power, do not matter to him.

Fate does express one hope for a comeback, a hope superficially linking him to Gatsby. His father's mistress asks him, 'What you coming back for?' and he answers, 'I got to see him [my father] .... I want him to see me'. Fate wants not so much to relive relationships with past intimates (as Gatsby wished to do) as to have them recognize him. But this poses a problem: what are they to recognize? The man they knew twenty years before? But he is changed, so this is impossible. Rather, he seems to seek recognition as the individual that he is. But when Fate sits at his father's deathbed, his father seems not to recognize him at all. Nor do other characters recognize him as this man's son. Moreover, Fate suggests that those around him were always incapable of recognizing him. He says of his mother: 'I think she was trying to kill me — she couldn't recognize me as her son'. The mistress says that he gave the best of himself away, and he replies: 'I gave it all to sons of bitches either unwilling or unable to accept it'. Fate's homesickness takes the form of seeking recognition from his father, but this quest will go unfulfilled, as it must. Fate's apparent acceptance of this distinguishes him from Gatsby.

Other comeback attempts contrast with Fate's. Both Sweetheart and Friend attempt comebacks. Both have fallen from success; for each, the concert is a last chance — in Sweetheart's case, to repay money and save his life, in Friend's, to save his career. Both fail, and both fail to be (or at least feel) free. Sweetheart lacks self-control, and, as he admits, 'Freedom's only for those who practice self-control — ain't that what you're thinking?' As the film ends, he will pay the price for his earlier lack of control. Friend, the journalist, has won awards, but his career is in unspecified trouble: the assignment to cover the benefit concert is his last chance. Friend is blinded by bitterness. His girlfriend warns that he is in danger of making the world tragic because he sees it as tragic.[17] He forgets to live his own life: he recognizes the 'absurdity of a lifetime of futile labor', of being 'condemned to some pointless task' — unlike Camus' Sisyphus, he is unable to rise above this fate.[18] His demise too is a consequence of his earlier actions, his mistreatment of musicians. (This suggests a different sense of 'comeback': a hostile response).

Unlike Sweetheart and Friend, Fate calmly accepts his fate — yet in doing so manifests a kind of personal freedom. Uncle Sweetheart says of him: 'He's virtually free — who else can you say that about?' To which Veronica replies: 'Virtually free? No-one is virtually free. Either you're free or you're not free .... If he's gonna play this concert, he's gonna play exactly what we tell him'. When Fate leaves to play with his band, she worries about his priorities: 'Have you explained the restrictions, the boundaries, the limitations, the rules?' Fate, of course, ignores these rules.

---

[17]  'You're making everything so tragic', she says. 'I'm not *making* it tragic', he replies (the implication being that that is how he finds it). But their dialogue and his actions, as well as Fate's comments on beauty lying in the eye of the beholder, suggest that she is right after all.

[18]  On existentialism in Dylan's recent work, see Furtak, 2006.

If the performance of 'Cold Irons Bound' is a protest, it is in the cause of personal freedom. The TV network has dictated a play-list of 'protest' songs: the Beatles' 'Revolution', the Rolling Stones' 'Street fighting man', 'The Who's 'Won't get fooled again', 'Cell block #9', 'Neil Young's 'Ohio', 'Eve of Destruction' and 'Kick out the jams'.[19] (Later they add 'Jailhouse Rock', because it sounds egalitarian and may 'plant the seeds of hope'). Singing, in the film, is a kind of protest, a metaphor for freedom. Vogel spoke out from the stage. The opening line of 'Cold Irons Bound' — which plays as Edmund begins his Presidential address — recalls Emerson's inner voice: 'I'm beginning to hear voices and there's no one around'. Fate's protest, in this light, is singing as his inner voice prompts — and not for friendship, fame, or money. Later, a guitar becomes a weapon, and one remembers Guthrie's instrument, emblazoned 'this guitar kills fascists'.

The film is imprecise and open to interpretation, as a character within the film says of Fate's songs; but it is clearly a meditation on human freedom, among other things. Fate is systematically stripped of the material conditions of freedom, yet continues in some way to be free. In his foils, we see different ways to fail at being free — through lack of control, or negativity. In the young Bobby Cupid, we see Fate's inheritor, perhaps a young Fate, who is associated, to a greater extent than Fate, with negative freedom and hostile reactivity: Cupid walks away from his job, repudiates passports, and dismisses an offer of money as meaningless. Yet Cupid also echoes Emerson. To Uncle Sweetheart (whose office is in the 'Midas Judas Building') he says: 'You would commit treason against your own self'. When Sweetheart responds 'Who's talking to you?' the answer is Emersonian: 'Common sense, the voice inside my head'.

The revolution itself can be seen as an attempt for the country to come back, to return to its prelapsarian freedom.

---

[19] Of the list, the first two songs endorse revolution, but reject violence, the third is about a revolution which leaves things unchanged, the fifth and sixth straight forward protest songs. The Satire seems to be more about the idea of a protest song than these particular songs.

The theme of usurpation reflects the sense (shared by Gatsby) that something has gone wrong (as in 'Highlands': 'Well, I'm lost somewhere/I must have made a few bad turns'). The odd idea of America being resurrected appears in Dylan's memoirs too (Dylan, 2004, 86). But this, like other comeback attempts, will fail. Political attempts to recover some ideal state are shown to be futile. A soldier next to Fate on the bus tells his story:

> I joined the rebels. ... I didn't know what the answers were, I just knew you had to take sides. ... The rebel movement was corrupt ... they wanted to replace the old government with a new government which was just as bad. ... [There was a] small movement of counter-revolutionaries. ... I changed sides—no-one noticed. ... Then I realized this new movement was being funded by the very government I wanted to topple—then I realized I didn't want the government to fall—it would only be replaced with anarchy. ... I joined the government forces ... then one day we wiped out a small village ... it was my village.

Immediately after this, counter-revolutionaries stop the bus; the soldier rushes out and is shot, apparently meaninglessly. (On the other hand, the bus escapes while the soldier distracts the armed men; perhaps this is a heroic act of self-sacrifice. This is one of many deliberate ambiguities).

One point here is the deluding nature of abstractions and political parties. Later in the film, Fate sings 'Dixieland' like a national anthem. The lyrics endorse action ('I'll take my stand/ to live and die in Dixie'), but action of a highly personal kind, given that it is also a love song to Dixieland. This perhaps provides an insight into what Fate takes to be the correct motivator—love for a particular land, not abstract principles.[20] Fate insists on the value of the particular, as opposed to the abstract: 'The sacred is in the ordinary, the common things of life'. This is precisely the love from which politics distracted the soldier who helped to massacre his

---

[20] Another deflation of abstraction: Crew Guy #1 says, 'You know what really gets my goat–all this talk about race this, race that, ethnic this, ethnic that. When you come right down to it there's only two races—workers and bosses'. Crew Guy #2 says, 'You said the same thing last week'.

village. ('Dixieland' is also, of course, a song of great home-sickness: 'I wish I was in Dixie').

Protesting and politicking are shown to interfere with personal freedom in less lethal ways. Demands to join the party of 'freedom' (or to sing protest songs) can threaten freedom as much as the government being rebelled against. Struggle for political change is at best a distraction. Friend, a reporter for an anti-government paper, wears an ankle cuff to which his editor holds the key. Uncle Sweetheart's bene-fit concert—to help the 'real victims of this revolution'—is only a cash grab. The hotelier-cum-pimp, after offering Fate a woman, says: 'I do not belong to any political party, sir—I guess you could call me a feminist'—implying a kinship between politics and pimping, the selling of persons. The President, in Fate's words, has 'sacrificed everything to rule', and Edmund's claim to be 'the man your [Fate's] father always wanted you to be' suggests that he is not his own man. Personal freedom comes in spite of the political, if at all.

The film does emphasize the value of political liberties, especially freedom of speech. A radio show intones: 'the only power the government has is to crack down on crimi-nals—when they're aren't enough criminals you make them—you make so many things a crime that it becomes impossible to live without breaking laws ... you create a nation of lawbreakers and then cash in on guilt—that's the system ... Once you understand that you'll sleep a lot eas-ier'. Governments can do nothing more than prohibit, imprison, and kill. They can not directly control wills. How-ever, by criminalizing (or moralizing against) basic human desires and needs, governments (or media, or corporations) can exploit and manipulate the resultant guilt. Law is a subtle control mechanism, necessitating resistance.

Fate, we are told, exemplifies personal freedom (virtu-ally). His past conditions his present choices; he has been rejected by his father, exiled, imprisoned, become a com-plete unknown, and this 'fall from grace' which began with his transgression of sleeping with his father's mistress. How does he manage freedom within these conditions? He doesn't. He is only 'virtually' free. As we first see him emerging from an underground cell, he says: 'I ain't felt free in a long time'.[21] This suggests he only feels free, is not actually free. Luck determines our achievement: 'Some of us pursue perfection and virtue and if we're lucky we catch up to it'. But happiness can't even be pursued (rendering that part of the Declaration of Independence nonsensical): 'it either comes to you or it doesn't'.

The film concludes with a murder; in a scene of swiftly escalating violence, Cupid kills a man with Blind Lemon's guitar. Fate tells Cupid to leave, giving him his own guitar, handing on the torch. Armed men appear, and at their behest Veronica fingers Fate as the murderer, saying: 'You can put his whole life on trial'. Fate walks out handcuffed into brightness. The closing shot is of Fate being taken away in the back of a police bus; the camera lingers on his face, its expression serene, even half-smiling. It is difficult not to see intimations of a Christ-like sacrifice. But the accompanying voice-over suggests, as with the soldier's earlier 'sacrifice', the danger of assigning meaning:

> Sometimes it's not enough to know the meaning of things, sometimes we have to know what things don't mean as well. Like what does it mean to not know what the person you love is capable of? Things fall apart, especially all the neat order of rules and laws. The way we look at the world is the way we really are. See it from a fair garden and everything looks cheerful. Climb to a higher plateau and you'll see plunder and murder. Truth and beauty are in the eye of the beholder. I stopped trying to figure everything out a long time ago.

Of the many philosophical themes at play here, let me select only one for comment—Fate's admission that he did not know what Cupid (whom he loved) could do. This links to the theme of recognition. Individuals remain unknown to one another.

Initially, Fate sought his father's recognition and was bitter that his best had gone unrecognized. Latterly, though, Fate—unlike Sweetheart and Friend—accepts his fate. In

---

[21]   The jailor responds: 'Keeping people from being free is big business'.

doing so, he accepts himself ('Fate'). Fate is able to recognize himself, though unrecognized by others. In a voice-over, Fate intones: 'They tell you that everything is nonsense, that the laws of nature are nonsense ... everything's up for grabs and there's no cause of anything; that's what they'd have you believe'. His rejection of this view implies, among other things, that things do have causes, that people are responsible. Fate's taking responsibility for his own actions—his acceptance of their consequences, his fate—distinguishes him from the others. What it means to recognize oneself, I suggest, is to act in ways responsible to one's inner promptings—to recognize one's own authority. When one has done so, one can recognize oneself in one's works or deeds, like the slave in Hegel's parable. Unlike the slave, of course, Fate is able to choose what work to do—that is, which songs to sing. But he knowingly faces penalties in doing so.

As the film ends, although Fate is to be imprisoned, he is free because he has acted according to his inner promptings, protecting the person he loves, and, by choosing not to fear the state, deprived it of power over him. He is thus in his own power. The state and media, which prohibit and manipulate, threaten this power, but they can only do so if the self is attached to the threats and inducements on offer—just as nostalgia only threatens freedom if one becomes attached to the past. To come back is to cease to desire the past and the objects of past desires and leave the past behind (as Fate seems to make peace with his past, as Gatsby was unable to). When no attachment and no penalty deter one from acting as one's inner self requires, the film implies, one is 'virtually free'.

## References

Brake, Elizabeth (2006) '"To live outside the law, you must be honest": freedom in Dylan's lyrics', in Peter Vernezze and Carl J. Porter (eds) *Dylan and Philosophy*, Chicago: Open Court, pp. 78–89.

Cavell, Stanley (1987) 'The Avoidance of Love: A Reading of *King Lear*', in Stanley Cavell, *Disowning Knowledge in Six Plays of Shakespeare*, Cambridge: Cambridge University Press, pp. 39–123.

Dylan, Bob (2004) *Chronicles: Volume One*, New York: Simon and Schuster.

Emerson, Ralph Waldo (1841) 'Self-Reliance', in Richard Poirier (ed) *Ralph Waldo Emerson*, Oxford: Oxford University Press, 1990, pp. 131–151.

Fitzgerald, F. Scott (1925) *The Great Gatsby*, New York: Scribner Paperback Edition, Simon and Schuster, 1995.

Furtak, Rick (2006) '"I Used to Care, But Things Have Changed": Passion and the Absurd in Dylan's Later Work', in Peter Vernezze and Carl J. Porter (eds) *Dylan and Philosophy*, Chicago: Open Court, pp. 16–28.

Hegel, G.W.F. (1821) *Elements of the Philosophy of Right*, ed. Allen Wood, trans. H. B. Nisbet, Cambridge: Cambridge University Press, 1995.

Hegel, G.W.F. (1807) *Phenomenology of Spirit*, trans. Arnold V. Miller, Oxford: Clarendon Press, 1977.

Lott, Eric (1995) *Love & Theft: Blackface Minstrelsy and the American Working Class*, Oxford: Oxford University Press.

McGills, Rod (forthcoming, 2009) *He Was Some Kind of Man: Masculinities in the B Western*, Waterloo, Ont.: Wilfred Laurier University Press.

Marqusee, Mike (2003) *Chimes of Freedom: The Politics of Bob Dylan's Art*, New York: The New Press, W.W. Norton & Co.

Pippin, Robert (2000) *Henry James and Modern Moral Life*, Cambridge: Cambridge University Press.

Scobie, Stephen (2003) *Alias Bob Dylan Revisited*, Calgary: Red Deer Press.

Whitman, Walt (1855) *Leaves of Grass*, intro. by Harold Bloom, New York: Penguin, 2005.

David Boucher[1]

# Images and Distorted Facts Politics, Poetry and Protest in the Songs of Bob Dylan

Robert Shelton, the folk music critic of *The New York Times*, described the young Dylan as 'one of the musical-poetic geniuses of our time' (Shelton n.d.). Elsewhere, he suggested that 'Some of Mr Dylan's lyrics are obviously "camp fantasies" while others are poetically profound' (Shelton 1990: 79). Paul Williams describes Dylan's work as 'great art', and Leonard Cohen suggested in 1985 that Dylan 'is the Piccasso of song' (Williams 1994: xii; Devlin 1998: 82). The literary critics Frank Kermode and Christopher Ricks were thought perverse when they compared Dylan with Keats and Wordsworth (Glaister 1997: 3). Kermode, in discussing the transition from folk through rock to country, argued: 'And Dylan remains a poet, as he has remained a virtuoso of

---

[1] Versions of this paper were presented at the Political Studies Association Annual Conference LSE and UCL, 10–13 April 2000; The Third Robert Shelton Memorial Day, 19 May 2001 at the Bluecoat Arts Centre, Liverpool; and the ECPR annual Conference, University of Kent, September 2001. Here I elaborate one of the theses of my book *Dylan and Cohen: Poets of Rock and Roll* (2004). I am grateful to Continuum Press for allowing me to use some of the material.

the voice—snarling, pushing words and tunes askew, endlessly inventive' (Kermode and Spender 2001: 159).

These views were contested by many academics who rejected the claim and accused Dylan of being a self-conscious second-rate imitator of Jack Kerouac, and who had managed to seduce and fool feebleminded youth who were ignorant of poetry. Whatever the merits of the counter-claims, it cannot be denied that Dylan made poetry popular, elevated from its secluded shade in a corner of academia into the horizon of a new and inquisitive audience, hitherto not renowned for its cultural and artistic discernment. In 1968, Henrietta Yurchenco contended that 'if Dylan has done nothing else, he is responsible for the present widespread interest in poetry'. She went on to claim that: 'He has given poetry a significance and stature which it has never had in American life. Furthermore, he is a bard—a singing poet in an ancient but thoroughly neglected tradition' (Yurchenco, in Benson 1998: 67 and 69). Adrian Rawlings, commenting on Dylan's 1996 Australian tour, proclaimed that he had rescued poetry from obscurity 'in a way that neither Eliot nor Pound nor the American poetry and jazz movement ever could' (Rawlings, in Benson 1998: 73).

There are those, of course, who acknowledge the poetic element in Dylan but refuse to ignore the centrality of music to his art.[2] Christopher Butler, for example, suggests that Dylan's songs are not poems meant to be read without musical accompaniment, 'they carry rhythms and rhymes and emphases which are designed for musical performance' (Butler 2002: 68). Allen Ginsberg, in the sleeve notes to Desire, comments that the songs of Dylan are 'the culmination of Poetry-music as dreamt of in the '50s and early '60s'. Gerard Malanga similarly asserts that 'Music is the soul of Bob Dylan's poems' (Malanga 1978). Paul Williams takes this relationship seriously in analysing Dylan as a

---

[2]   See, for example, the collection of essays edited by Neil Corcoran, 'Do You Mr. Jones?': Bob Dylan with the Poets and Professors (Londons: Chatto and Windus, 2002). The editor, for example, suggests that: 'So, recognising the centrality of the music, these essayists understand that Dylan cannot be viewed without reserve as a poet' ('Introduction', 12).

performing artist, showing how Dylan transformed the import or point of a song by altering its accompaniment and changing the intonation and style of delivery (Williams 1994). This was always evident in live performances, but is even more perceptible with the much wider availability of alternative versions of his songs, as for example on vol. 8 of the bootleg series.

Christopher Ricks, nevertheless, wants to maintain that 'It ought to be possible, then, to attend to Dylan's words without forgetting that they are one element only, one medium, of his art' (Ricks 2003: 13). Andrew Motion goes even further in separating the lyrics from the music when he dissents from Robert Lowell's view that Dylan needs to 'lean on the crutch of his guitar' (Motion 1999: 78). Given that the melody, the music, the intonation and even the context in which the songs are sung undergo complete transformations in the performance, all we are left with that are relatively stable (but not necessarily in their meaning) are the words.

The curiosity of the live performance is not that Dylan revives songs from the whole of his career, but that he invariably changes the arrangement, rhythm, melody and timbre. Often the songs are almost unrecognisable, except for the words. Dylan is ambiguous and even contradictory in explaining the relationship between the music and the words. He has at different time given primacy to the words and to the tune, and at others suggested that they are equally significant. In practice, however, he is far less reticent to take liberties with the music than he is with the words, and on this basis we can give more weight to his emphasis on the primacy of the words. In an interview with Richard Farina, Joan Baez's brother-in-law, Dylan contended that: 'It ain't the melodies that're important, man, it's the words. I don't give a damn 'bout melodies'.[3] To Robert Shelton Dylan confessed, I consider myself a poet first and a musician second' (cited in Ricks 2003: 11). The vast amount of commentary, when it is not obsessively

---

[3] For Dylan's relationship with Farina, see David Hajdu, *Positively 4th Street* (London: Bloomsbury, 2001).

biographical, concentrates, not upon the music as such, except to explain the different styles, but upon the words that, when at their best, for many commentators attain the level of poetry. Both Michael Gray and Christopher Ricks take Dylan's words very seriously, analysing them as works of poetry in themselves, or as having broader biographical, historical or literary/poetic referents. Gray is much harsher on the later material, although the greater part of his book is devoted to it, than is Ricks, who extends a generosity of spirit to the whole of Dylan's *oeuvre* (Gray 2000; Ricks 2003). Generally, interpretation of Dylan's lyrics takes the form of decoding the apparent or hidden meaning embedded in the songs, as, for example, Mike Marqusee, who acknowledges Dylan's work as art and views it as a personal take on rather than a reflection of the times (Marqusee 2003).

I do not wish to engage in the interpretation of Dylan's lyric poetry as such in this chapter, but instead to engage in a discussion of how to interpret. I want to look first at how commentators have interpreted Dylan and highlight what seems to me some obvious flaws in their methods. I go on to suggest that commentators lack a vocabulary to distinguish what might appropriately be asked of different songs. Different questions may be pertinent to different songs, and therefore the way to interpret them may hinge upon asking the right sort of questions. As R. G. Collingwood long ago recognised, asking the right questions is a prerequisite to arriving at the right answers.[4] I want to provide some theoretical basis to the appropriateness of particular questions to particular types of lyric or poetry.

Such an exercise is not self-evidently justifiable. Indeed pop music is often banal in the extreme, and the extremes of banality may rescue it from the pretence, or pretentiousness, of aspiring to art, as almost all singer-songwriters of the last 40 years do. Stephen Trousse, for instance, suggests that the 'splendid banality' of Marc Bolan's lines 'I drive a Rolls Royce/Cos it's good for my voice' is a more profound

[4]   The classic formulation is to be found in R. G. Collingwood, *An Autobiography* (Oxford: Oxford University Press, 1970: first published 1939), chapter V.

gift to the history of pop than the contributions of all of the sad-eyed singer-songwriters of the 1970s (Trousse 1999: 44). He calls it the aesthetic of the artful artlessness. Although Dylan is one such sad-eyed singer-songwriter, he can certainly match Bolan in banality. Without even having to resort to 'Wiggle Wiggle', such 'classics' as 'Peggy Day' come to mind:

> Peggy Day stole my poor heart away,
> By golly, what more can I say,
> Love to spend the night with Peggy Day

If banality typifies pop music, then such singer-songwriters as Jacques Brel, Bob Dylan, Leonard Cohen and Tom Waits, at least in certain moods, constitute the exceptions that prove the rule. Bob Dylan, in particular, was hailed as the great poet and spokesman of his generation and accepted by many of the Beat poets and artists as the culmination of what they aspired to achieve.

# I

When faced with different views, implicit and explicit, about the appropriate way to 'read' Dylan's lyric poetry, how do we differentiate between the validity of the claims? How should we read Dylan? And if we are to read different types of poem differently, in what ways are the types to be distinguished? Christopher Ricks, for example, distinguishes between songs that are about matters of historical fact, what Leonard Cohen called *reportage,* such as 'The Lonesome Death of Hattie Carroll', and songs that inhabit the world of myth and consequently whose 'Truth is to be tested and manifested otherwise than in history' (Ricks 2003: 234). Variations and modifications and refusals to acknowledge this distinction abound in the commentaries on Dylan.

The first claim I want to distinguish is prevalent in the literature and internet discussions of Dylan. A whole website is devoted to it — Dylan Lyric Commentaries (www.geocites. com). Its distinguishing characteristic is the search for referents in places, people and objects. The second interpretative approach is the search for referents in influences, whether they are musical or poetic. James Abbott McNeill Whistler dismisses such preoccupations, describing them as 'collect-ing-comparing-compiling-classifying-contradicting' and he suggests that these are the people for whom 'a date is an accomplishment — a hall-mark, success'. In fact, they reduce 'art to statistics, they 'file' the fifteenth century, and 'pi-geon-hole' the antique' (Whistler 1998: 532). The third approach to interpreting Dylan's lyrics may be called the Emotional response. What is important is not establishing the meaning, the historical or literary context, but the power of the images to evoke and invoke emotions.

The first approach, finding referents in people, places and objects, assumes that the more you know about the refer-ents, the better appreciation you have of the song/poem. Take, for example, 'Positively 4th Street', the single that immediately followed 'Like a Rolling Stone', and was recorded four days after the 1965 Newport Folk Festival. It has widely been interpreted as a bitter attack by Dylan on his former friends and critics in the folk world and the title refers to where he was living on West 4th Street in Green-wich Village at the time. The fact that Dylan denies that this was the subject-matter of the song seems to make no differ-ence (booklet accompanying *Biograph,* 52). Alternatively, Minneapolis has been identified at the location because Dylan went to university there and dropped out, and there-fore the vitriol is directed at a different target. For example, something like the following story illuminates or gives meaning to 'Just like a Woman'. Edie Sedgwick was both a fashion model and the star of many of Andy Warhol's films, a fixture of the Factory crowd and resident at the Chelsea Hotel. Sedgwick dated Dylan for a while in early 1966, at a time, Jonathan Taplin suggests, when 'his transition from folk purity to the rock insanity was overwhelming him' (Stein 1983: 228). Sedgwick overindulged in various cock-tails of drugs and lived life on the edge, subject to extreme highs and lows induced by a vicious circle of uppers and downers to keep pace with her frenetic life-style. She was in fact self-destructive. Her flamboyant and confident exterior disguised a deep inner fragility. Understood in this way the lines in the song are propositions about an identifiable women, and it is legitimate to ask of them whether they are true or false:

> Ah, you fake just like a woman, yes, you do.
> You make love just like a woman, yes, you do.
> Then you ache just like a woman.
> But you break just like a little girl.

Such an approach has a tendency to prioritise the detail over the song and the danger is that we won't see the wood for the trees — the referents of the song become more important than the song itself. The imagery, for example, of Leonard Cohen's famous lines, 'She feeds you tea and oranges that come all the way from China' ('Suzanne') is destroyed by too literal attachment to its referents. The tea in question is Bigalow's Constant Comment tea flavoured with the rind of oranges and sweet spice. But does the gathering of new facts about a subject lead to cumulative understanding? Mark Twain provides a good answer. In his *Life on the Mississippi* he tells how he immersed himself in every detail of the great river. He knew it, he said, as well as he knew the letters of the alphabet. Twain maintained that far from being a wholly positive achievement, 'I had lost something, too. I had lost something which could never be restored to me while I lived. All the grace, the beauty, the poetry had gone out of the majestic river' (*New Oxford Book of English Prose* 1998: 533–4).

The author may appear to invite us to make the link with outside referents, but the referents may serve intentionally to obscure rather than illuminate, and complicate rather than elucidate. Let's take two examples: first, the title song to the album that made Dylan a star, 'Highway 61 Revisited'. 'Highway 61' is, of course, an old blues song recorded in various versions and under various titles by many of Dylan's early exemplars, in which the route and towns through which it winds are not always faithfully rendered. Both Michael Gray and John Gibbens trace the blues and geographical associations of Highway 61. The term 'revisited' is seen to refer to both the bluesmen and the music that influenced Dylan's youth and to the highway that passed through his home towns of Duluth and Hibbing, Minnesota. Gibbens, for example, spends 26 pages discussing the route of the highway, and the places where famous bluesmen were born or lived (Gibbens 2001: 66–92). This information says nothing about the song itself, nor the fact that the song mentions no places or blues singers, but instead capitalises on the symbolism of the road as the site of discrete and unconnected narrative sketches, ranging from the biblical story of Abraham relocated to Highway 61, to the possible location of the Third World War. In other words, Highway 61 is an image on which other images are placed, and connected to each by the common site of their occurrence. Nothing we know about the real Highway 61 adds to our understanding of the lyrics of the song. Had the subject matter been 'Route 66' doing something of a travel guide might have been relevant. The song actually recommends a route for those planning to travel West, on the grounds that you can get your kicks on Route 66. On Highway 61 you get more than you bargain for, 1,000 useless telephones, a man whose application for clothing was turned down by the welfare department, a second mother with a seventh son, and cheap seating in a temporary grandstand for viewing the next world war.

Second, take the following lines: 'Situations have ended sad/Relationships have all been bad/Mine've been like Verlaine's and Rimbeau' ('You're Gonna Make Me Lonesome When You Go'). At the surface level the lines are self-explanatory and self-referential. They indicate that Verlaine and Rimbaud had a relationship that was certainly less than happy. At the level of particulars, when we try to anchor the poem to the specifics of the actual relationship between Verlaine and Rimbaud the simple allusion becomes complicated. Questions arise such as: Who in this relation does Dylan identify with—the older Verlaine or the younger dominant Rimbaud? Although neither admitted that their relationship was homosexual, and in fact denied it in print, it is generally believed that they were lovers throughout their tempestuous intermittent periods together.

The relationship was characterised by drunkeness, violent quarrels and Rimbeau's quest for power and its exercise through experiencing every type of debauchery. The relationship in Paris, London and Brussels was sporadic between 1871 and 1873, at which time Verlaine was imprisoned for attempted manslaughter after shooting Rimbaud in the wrist and trying to prevent him from leaving Brussels (Fowlie 1994: 43–4).

What then is the sense of meaning sought here? It is, in fact, similar to Frege's correlation of the sense and reference of a sentence in the use of language. Frege added an additional distinction which he deemed irrelevant to the meaning of an expression, what he called its colour. Thus the use of guy, chap or man as synonyms in a sentence is a matter of coloration rather than offering propositions. The sense of a sentence has to do with the dictionary definition of the words in the context of the sentence, or at least those that are relevant to the truth value of an expression, and those things to which they refer, the referents of the words. Basically, by identifying Edie Sedgwick as the subject of 'Just Like a Woman', we are able to determine the truth value of the statements in the song. In this respect we understand poetry just as we would understand any other sentence, as a statement about the world. In this approach relating to the search for referents meaning is equated with the psychology of the author, that is with authorial intention, and building up the context assists us in retrieving the intention. In philosophical hermeneutics it has a long and distinguished heritage in Wilhelm Dilthey, and more recently with E. D. Hirsch Jr. As Hirsch suggests, 'a text cannot be interpreted from a perspective different from the original author's. Meaning is understood from the perspective that lends existence to meaning. Any other procedure is not interpretation but authorship' (Hirsch 1976: 49). A more radical version of the attachment of meaning to the psychology of the author is that of Emilio Betti who contended that in order to understand another person's work the interpreter has to be of equal intelligence to the author (Betti, 1980).

The second approach is similarly a search for referents, but instead of in places and people, or events, in the identification of influences in poetic and musical sources. This approach is exemplified by Michael Gray and Christopher Ricks (both with strong leanings towards F. R. Leavis) and Greil Marcus. The assumption is that if we can discover that someone wrote or sang something similar elsewhere, this adds to our understanding of what Dylan has wrote and sung. All three are dismissive of what Gray calls 'superficial message hunting' (Gray 2000: I).[5]

So the question remains, is this alternative nothing more than superficial influence hunting, something that the clever use of a concordance of poetry, or of blues lyrics, could match words and phrases with similar words and phrases in Dylan's songs. Such resemblances are almost invariably linked not by evidence, but by subjective intuitions. The connections are impressionistic and tenuous and expressed in deliberately imprecise language. Hence, for example, when linking Dylan's work with other poets Gray uses such connecting lines as, 'it seems to me to contain many recollections of major English poets'; it 'sometimes calls John Donne to mind'; 'the techniques resemble each other'; 'seems to remind one vaguely'; 'there is a keen correspondence'; a 'minor correspondence'; and even 'an exact echo'. We are also told that 'Dylan inherits ideas from Patchen too, I think — or again, perhaps just from the milieu that Patchen was a creative part of. (See Gray 2000: 54, 65, 70, 76 and 77).

Ricks is largely sympathetic to Gray's manner of interpretation, but nevertheless disagrees on the substance of some of the interpretations themselves.[6] Ricks is equally, if not more, imaginative in the links that he makes between the lyrics of Dylan and the poems of the great canon of poets, using equally as impressionistic, imprecise and deliberatively

---

[5]  Christopher Ricks in distinguishing songs with their basis in historical fact and those that have their basis in myth, often talks of the latter category in terms of poetic influences particularly in Keats, Andrew Marvell, Shakespeare, Tennyson and more recently Philip Larkin.

[6]  While acknowledging the bracing discipline of Leavis's approach, Ricks nevertheless finds it too constraining. *Dylan's Visions of Sin*, 103.

vague words and phrases to make the connections. Take, for example, Ricks' discussion of 'Sad Eyed Lady of the Lowlands' as an instance of the sin of covetousness, and the comparison made with Algernon Charles Swinburne. He maintains that Swinburne's *Dolores* need not be the source of 'Sad Eyed Lady for the Lowlands', nor would Dylan have to be alluding to the poem for it to 'illuminate' the song's art. Ricks suggests that Dylan's use of the word 'outguess' in 'Sad Eyed Lady of the Lowlands' 'is in *tune* [my emphasis] with Swinburne's "outsizing", "outlove", "outface and outlove us"' (Ricks 2003: 100). Ricks goes on to make the claim that *Dolores 'may* be heard as a prophecy of the Dylan song, a song that has been sensed, in its turn, as blandishingly hypnotic' (Ricks 2003: 100). In discussing Dylan's 'Day of the Locusts' Ricks asserts, to give another example of his style, that the use of the word 'birdies' Dylan is 'calling up the songs of Robert Burns' (Ricks 2003: 195). Elsewhere Ricks tells us the 'Desolation Row' is 'terrifically like *The Waste Land*, which is terrifically like Pope's *Dunciad'* (Ricks, 2008: 2).

Marcus's approach is much more subtle, sophisticated, authentically appropriate and evocative of the American horizon with which Dylan fused. In exploring the breadth and depth of the 'Basement Tapes' he tries to capture what Dylan and the Band 'took out of the air' and what they put back into it. They captured not abstractions, but the ghosts of the real sons and daughters of American history, manifest for a moment on the *Anthology of American Folk Music,* 'the founding document of the American folk revival' compiled and produced by Harry Smith (Marcus 1998: 87). The Basement tapes were in fact a 'shambling' version of this anthology.

The problem with the search for influence and origins is that of infinite regress. To say 'Dylan shares with Eliot the use of urban imagery and the expression of urban disillusionment' (Gray 2000: 72) is to invite the process of infinite regress. Dylan shares this with a whole range of other poets, including Baudelaire, Rimbaud and Lorca. It should come as no surprise that poets, artists and philosophers share things with others of their kind. Indeed, Picasso made no apology for his pillaging of past art, which he nevertheless transformed and made his own.

The use of Browning by Michael Gray serves to illustrate the point that I am trying to make. Gray spends a great deal of time detailing what he sees as the resemblances between Dylan and Browning. In this concordance approach what Gray misses entirely is the scientific and philosophical world-views that converge in Browning, and which are completely absent from Dylan, and without which any resemblances are superficial. What is called the metaphysical element, the underlying philosophy which gives unity to all of Browning's works, is an important factor in understanding him and the work that he produced. Browning tries to explain all things, even good and evil, as manifestions of the principle of love. Browning relies in his poetry upon the underlying assumptions of the day. He assumes, for example, the principle of evolution at work in human experience, and also subscribes to philosophical Idealism, the view that the mind constitutes reality, the idea that nature and spirit are inseparable, not that nature is intelligent, but that it is intelligible to mind, and is therefore mind-dependent. Ultimately, however, and pace Dylan, Browning's whole outlook expressed in his poems rests upon agnosticism and the idea that truth is unattainable (Jones 1892: 321-2).

The third approach to appreciating the lyrical poetry of a song is what we may call, for want of a better word, the emotional response, and it implicitly rejects this narrow conception of language. In this respect the words are not taken as statements. The words are indeed colours on the poet's palette that are used to conjure powerful images which have the capacity to move us emotionally without having a determinate meaning or prepositional value. This is what Neill Tennant of the Pet Shop Boys meant when he said that the lyrics of REM's 'Losing my Religion' were brilliant, despite the fact that he didn't have a clue what they meant (cited in Lumsden 1999: 95). This is also what Paul Williams meant when he wrote that asking who the real Bob Dylan is and what he is really trying to say are not strictly speaking answerable questions. Williams argues that he can listen to 'Sad Eyed Lady of the Lowlands' and empathise with the song, feel what it is about, because the words successfully communicate an emotion despite the fact that the line 'My warehouse eyes and my Arabian drum' have no clear meaning to him, but nevertheless have a clear relevance to him in his understanding of the song. In his view, art is not interpreted but experienced (Williams 1996: 19). For Williams the *Basement Tapes* signify the point at which Dylan purposely goes beyond the conscious statement. More recently after quoting the first four lines of 'I Want You', John Harris asks: 'What is all that about? It probably doesn't matter. It sounds beautiful ...' (Harris 2000: 12). While not wanting to banish analysis from art Henry Jones warns that it destroys the very thing that it analyses: 'The beauty of form and the music of speech which criticism destroys, and to which philosophy is, at best, indifferent, are elements essential to poetry' (Jones, 1892: 3).

Here the text distances itself from the author in a process Gadamer and Ricoeur call distanciation. The text is gradually severed from the intention of the author, its contextual referents, and joins the company of a quasi-world of texts. It represents the move away from epistemological hermeneutics which links the meaning of a text to the author's intentions. Instead, Gadamer puts forward an ontological hermeneutics which is suggested to him by Martin Heidegger's notion of 'being there in the world'. The question for Gadamer becomes not 'how should we interpret texts?' which is an epistemological question relating to the acquistion of knowledge, but instead 'what happens to us every time we interpret a text?' which is an ontological question about the nature of our being. The answer is that a text is articulated within a tradition, even if it is reacting to that tradition, and projects in front of itself a horizon. The person trying to understand such a text also stands at a point in this tradition, and has a fore-structure of meanings with which to encounter the text, what Gadamer calls prejudice in a non-pejorative sense. Any understanding or experiencing of texts constitutes a 'fusion of horizons' (Gadamer 1985).

I want to focus now on those early works which belong to the genre of 'protest' or 'topical' song, what Dylan called 'finger-pointing' songs, and those that represent his more abstract expressionist phase up to the release of *John Wesley Harding*, including *The Basement Tapes* recorded around the same time. This encompasses the period in 1965–6 when Dylan, in the words of Michael Gray, 'reached the absolute peak of divine inspiration' (Gray 2000: 16). I want to analyse the work in terms of the aesthetic theories of the philosophers R. G. Collingwood, Michael Oakeshott and of the Spanish poet and playwright Federico Garcia Lorca. The purpose of referring to these theories is not to establish whether one is better than another, but to invoke a vocabulary in terms of which to discuss Dylan's lyric poetry, or indeed anyone else's, and how we might make some distinctions, and appreciate it better.

## II

In this section I will briefly discuss R. G. Collingwood's widely read and influential theory of art, which covers not only fine art, but all forms of artistic expression. I want to contrast this with the less well-known theory of Michael Oakeshott, who denies that art is the expression of emotion, and with Lorca's distinction between imaginative and inspirational poetry, which in turn is linked to his notion of *duende* which has so deeply influenced Nick Cave and Leonard Cohen. The purpose is not to deny or confirm the theories, but to use them as a way of understanding and distinguishing between the different phases in Dylan's development. As I intimated earlier, I do not wish to suggest that these phases are distinct or discrete, and it is most certainly the case that examples of each may be found throughout his career, and therefore may be said to overlap.

Collingwood's *The Principles of Art is* a book that distinguishes art from craft, and pseudo-art from art proper.[7] Craft is essentially utilitarian, having a value not in itself, but for the use to which it is put. Through acquiring and developing certain technical skills the craftsman can conceive of an object and produce it according to that plan. Take, for example, the various statues and paintings found inside the tombs of Egyptian Pharaohs. The craftsman produces the artifacts according to the religious conventions of the time designed to assist the body of the pharaoh into the afterlife. Although they may be beautifully executed they are not meant to be viewed or displayed. They are objects conceived on a means end relation. The objects are the means to an end, in this case to ward off evil spirits and to assist the Pharaoh on his journey. Here the objects do not express the emotion of the craftsman. It is undoubtedly the case that they may incidentally do this, and border on something like art.

Art proper, Collingwood argues, is different from craft, but is often confused with art as magic and art as amusement. Art as magic shares with craft a utilitarian function, but in addition it is designed to arouse emotions in the community to which it is addressed. It has a practical purpose in that the emotions that are aroused are channelled into an activity for some perceived social benefit. A fertility dance, for example, is designed to arouse emotions of love and desire, to be channelled into socially beneficial and institutionally sanctioned relationships between men and women. In so far as art as emotion also suppresses some emotions that are not socially beneficial, art as magic is a denial and perversion of art. A war dance, for example, is meant to

[7]    In an earlier work, *Speculum Mentis, or the Map of Knowledge* (1924) Collingwood had equated art with imagination. In *The Principles of Art* emotion and imagination are linked. The Italian philosopher Benedetto Croce had developed a theory of art as imagination, but it is also found in Percy Bysshe Shelley, who argued in *A Defence of Poetry* that: 'Poetry, in a general sense, may be defined to be the expression of the imagination; and poetry is connate with the origin of man' (cited in Michael McClure (1974), 'The Poet's Poet', in Rolling Stone, *Knocking on Dylan's Door*, London: Michael Dempsey in Association with Cassell).

arouse emotions of fearfulness, and suppress those of fear, channeling the positive emotions into the activity of war. Art proper, in Collingwood's view, is the expression of emotion. The emotion that is expressed is not preconceived. It is not first formulated and then expressed. It exists in a confused and unarticulated form in the mind of the artist. The emotion formulated, defined and expressed in the artistic act itself and is inseparable from it. Stephen Mulhall captures the theory precisely and succinctly when he says of the artist: 'He begins in an emotional state whose chaotic indeterminacy perturbs him, and leads him to search for a clearer conception of it; and his search ends when he has succeeded in giving concrete expression to that state in a work of art. Artistic creation is thus a process of self-exploration, and the enhanced self-understanding which results is embodied in the work of art itself (Mulhall 1992: 144). Nor does the production of the work of art have an ulterior purpose, but its success depends on evoking that same emotion in the audience and thus contributes to the viewer's own self understanding of his or her emotional life (Collingwood 1937).

Although many of the details of Collingwood's theory may be challenged by aestheticians, the idea that art is the expression of emotion has widespread support. Paul Williams in his book on Dylan talks of artistic performance as the expression of emotion, or of what the performer is feeling at that particular time (Williams 1994: 3). In contrast with this view Michael Oakeshott takes poetry to be a certain way of imagining, distinct from practical, scientific or historical images. What distinguishes the voice of poetry in the conversation of mankind from the other voices is its manner of being active. This activity is contemplating or delighting in the making of images. They are, as opposed to the images in other idioms of discourse, 'mere' images. They are not facts about the world because they are not propositions, and here truth and falsity are inappropriate terms in which to appreciate them.

You do not ask of the images: Could this have happened? Is it possible or probable or just an illusion or make-believe?

because to ask these questions assumes the distinction between fact and not fact which is out of place in poetic contemplative imagining. Furthermore, they are present images, they have no past nor future. They are delighted in for what they are, rather than for what they are related to, that is, the occasions that may have inspired them. A photograph may lie if it purports to be a true likeness of its subject, but a poetic image cannot lie because it affirms nothing. It is irrelevant to the work of art that it does not faithfully represent the subject. Paul Cezanne's 'Rocky Scenery of Provence' is a composition of irregular shapes of colour comprising an image whose aesthetic quality has nothing to do with whether it looks like Provence or not, and the appeal of Vincent van Gogh's cornfields does not require that the corn and the clouds really swirl in harmony in the South of France. His starry sky is of no practical use to the traveller wanting to get from one place to another without the aid of a map, and scientifically it is a travesty, but to judge its practical or scientific value is to misunderstand it. Van Gogh's starry sky exists only in the poetic image that he has created. The arrangement and diction of the contemplative images are what distinguishes one poet from another, the symbols are not interchangeable; to substitute one as a synonym for another destroys the image. Take for example, the following lines: 'In this room the heat pipes just cough' ('Visions of Johanna'). To substitue: 'the central heating in this room is inadequate' is practically to say the same thing, but the poetic image is destroyed.

Why, then, are poetic images mere images? It is because the relation between symbol (language) and meaning (thought) is different in poetry from the relation in other modes of experience. This is a view Michael Oakeshott shares with Collingwood who, in *Speculum Mentis* (1924), distinguishes, art, religion, science, history and philosophy with reference to their different relations between symbol and meaning. In our everyday practical lives, for example, each symbol or word has a determinate referent or signification. The more determinate, the better the communication. If I ask for a pint of beer, I am using a symbol to evoke an image, not to create one. I am not trying to give a novel nuance to the symbol, merely to be understood in a settled language. In other words, meaning and symbol are distinct, but not radically separable because in this mode 'every word has its proper reference or signification' (Oakeshott 1991: 503). The symbol is separable from and the means by which we convey meaning. The reason why art or poetry is different is because there is no separation of symbol and meaning: A poetic image is its meaning: it symbolises nothing outside of itself (Oakeshott 1991: 527). This view is confirmed by a fellow Idealist Henry Jones in his study of Browning. He contends that the worth of a work of art 'must be recognised as lying wholly within itself, and that in it 'thought and expression are inseparable' (Jones 1892: 3).

Oakeshott explicitly denies that poetry is the expression of emotion designed to evoke the same emotion in the audience. If he intended his target to be Collingwood, then he misses it. Collingwood is unequivocal in ruling out a means-ends relationship in art, which the idea of design and execution posits. Emotion is discovered only in its expression. The ability to evoke that same emotion in others is the criterion of good art. Oakeshott argues that although the idea that art is the expression of emotion is commonly held, it rests on the mistaken view that poetry must be in some way informative and instructive. The poet must have undergone the emotion from which the poetic image derives. This, Oakeshott argues, 'makes a necessity of what is no more than an unlikely possibility' (Oakeshott 1991: 524). It is important to emphasise that Oakeshott is trying to establish what makes the poetic utterance unique; he is not suggesting that poets only contemplate or delight in images, but instead that when they do anything else it is not poetry.

Lorca enables us to refine this understanding of poetry a little further. Lorca's New York poems reflect his unease with the landscape of a vast impersonal city, with its poverty, degradation, segregation and violence—a suffering which seems to defy explanation. These poems mark a significant development in Lorca's style, from the poetry of imagination to the poetry of inspiration. This distinction is elaborated in a number of lectures variously reported in the press and collected under the title 'Imagination, Inspiration, Evasion'. The distinction is further refined with the introduction of the concept of *duende* which Lorca presented in his 'Theory and Play of the *Duende*'. Imagination is synonymous with the aptitude we have for discovery. It enables us to illuminate what is hidden and breathe life into fragments of reality to which humankind is blind. Imaginative poetry, however, has horizons and is constrained by reality. Imaginative poetry is limited by the laws of logic and reason, it makes connections with the world, discovering unexpected relations between objects and ideas, and in doing so abates mystery. It is the poetry that explores and describes the universe. As Lorca suggests: 'One's imagination needs objects, landscapes, numbers and planets and the relationship between them within the purest form of logic is vital'.[8]

Lorca argues that imagination is located within human logic and controlled by reason. It is a special way of creating that requires order and boundaries. Imagination is the starting point in poetry, and the poet constructs a tower against the elements and against mystery. His voice is listened to because he creates order, but he finds it difficult to inspire intense emotions free from constraints. Imagination is ultimately impoverished, and poetic imagination even more so. Visible reality is far more nuanced than we imagine and far more poetic than imagination can comprehend, as is often evidenced in the conflict between scientific reality and imaginary myths. For example, imagination has attributed to giants the construction of huge grottoes and cities of enchantment. We have subsequently realised that they were created by continuous patient and eternal drops of water, the triumph of reality over imagination. Or more correctly, imagination becomes conscious of its shortcomings. Lorca argues that:

[8] Federico Garcia Lorca (1997). The text of the quotation comes from 'El Defensor de Grenada' Granada, 11 October, 1928. I am indebted to Lisa Davies for translating the text.

> Imagination seemed to be operating in a logical manner
> when it attributed to giants that which did, indeed, seem to
> be the work of giants. However, scientific reality, poetic to
> the extreme and beyond the logical field, showed us that
> the truth was to be found in eternal, crystal-clear water
> droplets. It is a great deal more beautiful to think that a
> grotto is the result of the mysterious caprice of water bound
> and governed by eternal laws, than the caprices of some
> giants which have no more meaning than that of an expla-
> nation (Lorca 1997).

The poetry of inspiration, on the other hand, acknowledges
mystery and moves in a world of poetic harmony and order
that avoids imaginative reality with its currently perceived
norms of beauty and ugliness, and enters instead into a
poetic reality far more astonishing, sometimes characterised by tenderness and sometimes by immense depth of
cruelty: 'Poetry surrounds itself with brambles and fragments of broken glass so that the hands that reach out for it
are cut and injured with love' (Lorca 1997).[9] It is elusive and
evades reality by tracing the pathway of dreams that leads
in the subconscious to an unsuspected fact. The traditional
metaphor in poetry gives way to the poetic fact which is tied
to poetic logic. The order and balance of imagination often
gives way to the incongruity of inspiration. In this respect
the poem is a 'self-sufficient entity without reference to any
reality outside itself (Derek Harris, cited in Maurer 1990:
xiv). Poetry of inspiration breaks free from logical control
and passionately rejects the temptation to be understood. In
Lorca's view, poetry cannot be understood; it is received,
not analysed. It is counter to intelligence and the received
order of things. The poet of inspiration has to look at the
world with the eyes of a child, and when asking for the
moon truly believe that someone will reach out and place it
in his hands.[10] In sum, then, the poet of imagination is constrained by human logic, abates mystery by explaining the
inexplicable, while the poet of inspiration is set free by poet
logic, acknowledging that not everything has a cause and
effect, and that pure reality evades explanation. The

---

[9]   The text comes from 'El Sol', Madrid, 16 February 1929.
[10]  The text comes from 'El Sol', Madrid, 16 February 1929.

implication seems to be that imaginative poetry craves to be understood, makes propositions about reality which can be explored and refuted. Inspirational poetry delights in mystery, rejects the temptation to be understood and presents images to which truth and falsity are inapplicable. In a 1930 lecture Lorca talks about and personifies the Spanish term '*duende*' (doo-end-day). It expresses the dark inexpressible sinister and unsettling undercurrents of all traditional societies. It is not something that comes from outside of the artist, it surges up from the inside in torrents of blood pumping through one's veins. It is an ineffable sadness or sorrow, a terrible deep harrowing question that has no answer: 'it burns the blood like powdered glass, that exhausts, rejects all sweet geometry we understand' Lorca 2004: 5). In other words, together, 'inspiration' and '*duende*' intimate a challenge to the settled reality we know, a deep, dark overthrow of certainty, replaced by a disturbing, frightening mystery. Quoting Goethe Lorca maintains that *duende* is 'a mysterious power that all may feel and no philosophy can explain' (Lorca 2004: 3).

Taken together these three theorists enable us to construct a view of poetry that is capable of characterising the overlapping forms of poetic expression found in Dylan's work. The first phase is pseudo-art, or art as magic, having a preconceived purpose and desired practical effect, represented by the 'topical' or 'finger-pointing' songs. Examples in this genre would include 'Let me Die in My Footsteps', 'Who Killed Davey More?', 'Lonesome Death of Hattie Carroll', 'Only a Pawn in Their Game', 'George Jackson', 'Hurricane' and 'Union Sundown'. Second, we have art as the expression of emotion, or imaginative art, which has no preconceived purpose or desired practical effect, but which nevertheless expresses what the artist is feeling. Here the logic of reality is explored, the unexpected connections exposed, and the imagery embedded in occasions or situations. In this category we can place such songs as 'My Back Pages', 'Ballad in Plain D', 'Chimes of Freedom' and 'Subterranean Homesick Blues', 'You're a Big Girl Now', 'If You See Her Say Hello', 'Shot of Love', 'Most of the Time' and

'Not Dark Yet'. Third, we have what Oakeshott refers to as a delighting in images, and what Lorca calls inspirational poetry or *duende* with no necessary external referents and with an internal logic of its own. This form of poetry is typically represented by such songs as 'Hard Rain's A-Gonna Fall', 'Tombstone Blues', 'Stuck Inside of Mobile with the Memphis Blues Again', 'Desolation Row', 'Sad Eyed Lady of the Lowlands' and 'Visions of Johanna'.

### III

What I want to suggest is that Bob Dylan's development in the formative years of his career falls into three overlapping and concurrent phases which correspond to the three types of poetry identified by Collingwood, Oakeshott and Lorca: pseudo-poetry or art, that is art as magic, art proper or art as the expression of emotion, and contemplative art or poetry —what Lorca called inspirational poetry or *duende*. Why should we want to understand Dylan's work in these terms? Besides providing a vocabulary to explore his work, it also allows us to identify and eliminate inappropriate questions.

   To misunderstand the inspirational poetic phase, for example, leads to absurd conclusions. Let me illustrate with an example from C. P. Lee's *Like the Night*. In interpreting Bob Dylan's 'Just Like a Woman' he cites the opening line: 'Nobody feels any pain'. In taking this statement to be a proposition, Lee offers a contorted and inappropriately literal analysis of the song: 'Is this one of the greatest ironic statements in the history of the universe? Everybody feels pain of some sort at some time or another' (Lee 2002: 124). When taken as an expression of emotion or as imaginative poetry, the question of whether the statement is right or wrong does not arise. 'Nobody feels any pain. Tonight as I stand inside the rain'. Taken as poetry of inspiration it conveys self-absorption, despondency, resignation—an obliviousness to the world and the feelings of other individuals because rain serves to isolate the self and its thoughts. As inspirational poetry the lyrics are a series of images: 'Nobody feels any pain. Tonight as I stand inside the rain.

Everybody knows that baby's got new clothes. But lately I see her ribbons and her bows, have fallen from her curls'. Each line is an image and it makes no difference to the appreciation of that imagery whether Edie Sedgwick is or is not the subject of the song. Indeed, if you take the song to be a series of statements about Edie Sedgwick, you would have to conclude that Dylan was wrong, because she had straight, metallic blonde hair. And this is the point that Bob Dylan is making when in talking of the film 'Renaldo and Clara' he says, 'when you go to a movie, do you ask what does that person do in real life?' (cited by Ginsberg).

What I want to suggest, then, is that there is a point at which Dylan ceases to be a craftsman, ceases to have a pre-conceived idea with a determinate purpose, ceases to express his emotion, which was largely anger, *by* writing songs, and came to express it instead *in* writing songs. This, I think, is what he was trying to say in October 1965 when he commented: 'I don't write now unless it just happens' (cited in Heylin 1992: 125). The process by which 'Like a Rolling Stone' became a song confirms this. His diversions into free-form prose and poetry, and even play-writing, were an expression of his frustration at the restrictions of the medium of the song in which to express himself. 'Like a Rolling Stone' was a spontaneous expression of the anger and frustration he felt at the sterility of his art. He was bored with what he was doing and dissatisfied with what he had produced. On the plane home from London after his short 1965 acoustic tour, he vented his anger in a flow of con-sciousness with no preconceived subject and at an abstract focal point. At this stage 'it was ten pages long, it wasn't called anything, just a rhythm thing on paper all about my steady hatred directed at some point that was honest' (cited in Heylin 1992: 129).

The absence of intention also characterises the film pro-ject of 1966. ABC commissioned a one-hour television spe-cial based upon the tour of 1966. Pennebaker, the specialist in cinema-verite, was hired once again after the successful collaboration on *Don't Look Back*. Harry Rasky, the serious film- and documentary-maker, was recruited to produce the special using Pennebaker's crew. After 35 years, Rasky has published his account of the unfortunate collaboration. He asked Dylan what he thought the film should say. Dylan answered: 'Say, man. It doesn't have to say anything'. Dylan goes on to suggest that the film has to be something, but when asked what, he answered: 'I don't know. How can I know now?' (Rasky 2001: 146). In other words, whatever was going to be expressed in that abortive film was not going to be formulated beforehand, but instead would be expressed in the making of it.

At this point I want to apply the theories to Bob Dylan's writings, but first I would like to deal with a possible objection. Given that Dylan is so unequivocally associated with the political activism of the civil rights movement, wouldn't it be more appropriate to explore his work through a theory directly applicable to social movements? Serge Denisoff, for example, has attempted to classify protest songs and their function in American left-wing social movements (Denisoff 1972). The first type of song he calls magnetic in that it serves the function of attracting new adherents to the cause or strengthens the resolve of those already committed. They are songs which encourage mobilisation by relying upon relatively simple and often well-known melodies, repetitive verses for audience participation and the message is uncomplicated and direct. The music itself is secondary and merely a vehicle for delivering the simple message. The second category of song is what he calls 'rhetorical', and its focus is on expressing indignation and dissent, a counter to the dominant images of the age, but bereft of solutions to the problems it highlights. They are, in general, much more of a vehicle for musical innovation and sophistication than the 'magnet' songs allow, but do, nevertheless give scope for lyrical expression. He argues that these are the types of protest song that became prevalent in the 1960s and had very little measurable political impact.

This functionalist approach has many limitations. First, it is utilitarian, equating means and ends, demanding justification in terms of utility or usefulness. The measure of the usefulness of the songs being political activism. However, political activism is not the only measure of the purpose of a song, and indeed, may be almost impossible to measure in any meaningful way. The expression of discomfort, dissatisfaction, disillusionment and despair may have a corrosive effect on the fundamental and unquestioned principles of society without having to incite direct action. Second, the songs may keep alive the continuity of the struggle against perceived injustice, and provide the necessary social cohesiveness in holding common-minded people together, by linking them with the past and with their fellow sufferers or protesters. In other words, they serve to forge and perpetuate identities, which are alternatives to the identities that the authorities seek to impose on them, and they can do this without a call to action. The songs demand that their identities be recognised, and implicitly realise that misrecognition, an imposed alien identity, is just as much a form of oppression as any other, and perhaps more insidious in that it deprives one of one's self respect, and the cultural and ideological roots to which one belongs. Third, it is not sensitive to the poetic element in song and indeed dismisses anything that is not overtly political or 'magnetic' as of questionable value. It is not a theory that allows us to explore the diversity of Dylan's songs and doesn't really enable us to distinguish the early Dylan from the later, or from the whole host of contemporaries such as Phil Ochs, Tom Paxton or P. F. Sloan, and in that the theory's criterion of worth is the song's utility, it is questionable whether the usefulness of the poetic is a legitimate avenue to explore, and even if it is, it cannot be taken to be exhaustive.

Dylan wrote many overtly political songs that reflected the growing unrest with racism, war, social injustice and bigotry. His first serious protest song which condemns racial violence and segregation was written for a benefit concert in aid of the Congress for Racial Equality (CORE) on 23 February 1962. It was entirely congruent with the work of CORE, but not strictly speaking a 'topical' song in that its subject was a racial murder that had been committed in 1955. 'The Death of Emmet Till' relates the story of a white gang murder of a young black man, and the subsequent acquittal of two brothers by a jury that included some of their accomplices. The song says that there was a reason for the killing, but it doesn't say what it was. In fact, Emmet Till had whistled at a white woman. The song lacks the subtlety that Dylan was gradually to develop, and was indistinguishable from the type of expression common among fellow finger-pointers, who spelt out the problem in great detail and gave the prescriptions for solving it. More explicitly than most of his protest songs he is forceful in his injunction to resist and to condemn the Ku Klux Klan and all racial hatred. He followed this song with a powerful attack upon the extreme right-wing John Birch Society, ridiculing their paranoia about communists by using humour. He was nevertheless uncomfortable about being called a writer of protest songs. Most of the songs have not appeared on his officially released albums and exist only in bootleg versions or in radio archives. In 1991 Sony released a set of three bootleg albums, the first of which includes such songs as 'Let Me Die in My Footsteps', 'Talkin' John Birch Paranoid Blues', 'Walls of Redwing' and 'Who Killed Davey Moore?'.

The early protest songs are clearly injunctive in their intent. They are preconceived both in purpose and practical effect. Most even draw the moral for the listener. These songs are meant to charge the audience emotionally, channelling this emotion into active support for political causes. Some are direct exhortations to act, in other words calling upon the audience to do something about a particular situation or injustice. 'Let Me Die in My Footsteps' is a representative example:

> If I had rubies and riches and crowns
> I'd buy the whole world and change things around
> I'd throw all the guns and the tanks in the sea
> For they are mistakes of past history.
> Let me die in my footsteps
> Before I go down under the ground.

In an interview in 1963 Dylan is explicit about his intent: 'What comes out in my music is a call to action' (cited in Heylin 1998: 77). In other songs, he seeks the same effect more subtly through graphic images, like the powerful

'Only a Pawn in Their Game' — about the murder of Medgar Evers the leader of the Mississippi wing of the National Association for the Advancement of Colored People, in June 1963 — and 'The Lonesome Death of Hattie Carroll', or sometimes in a poignant tale of hardship, like 'North Country Blues' which are meant to evoke the appropriate emotion, dread, disgust, despair, anger, sympathy, but rarely resignation. Their purpose is to generate a collective revulsion, a growing tide of outrage against the 'system'. 'North Country Blues', for example, is sung in the first-person singular and laments the decline and death of the iron ore industry in the region where Dylan grew up. The message is effectively the same as that of his later song, 'Union Sundown'. It blames the decline of rural American industries on imports produced by cheaper labour:

> They complained in the East,
> They are paying too high.
> They say that your ore ain't worth digging.
> That it's much cheaper down
> In the South American towns
> Where the miners work almost for nothing.

The song goes on to predict the demise of the community resulting from the enforced exodus of the youth in search of work. It is a maudlin, melancholy lament, resigned to the cruelty of market forces, but nevertheless regretful of the real and uncompromising impact. The song doesn't spell it out, but it is implied that trade tariffs should be imposed in order to protect endangered communities from unfair competition.

A number of songs sum up his whole attitude to the conventional and accepted inheritance from the previous generation. Dylan's topical songs of this period are both typical, yet distinctive in the civil rights movement. They are songs which engender collective identity, not through the originality of their lyrics or innovative musical style, but because they lent themselves to be communally sung. The folk revival was very much based on a collective identity and common form of expression, and the success of performers such as Tom Paxton, Phil Ochs, Pete Seeger, Joan Baez, Judy

Collins and Buffy Saint Marie was the participatory nature of their songs, and the emotive content of their lyrics. The singers demanded participation and often led by example in gathering an ensemble of performers on stage. These songs include 'Playboys and Playgirls', 'Blowin' in the Wind' and 'The Times They are A Changin''. In 'Playboys and Playgirls' he defiantly announces that he won't be beaten into submission by fashionable society, war profiteers, racist lynch mobs and Jim Crow (segregationist) laws. He will not, he says, allow any of these to dictate his own way of behaving, 'not now or no other time'. When he says in the first verse that they 'Ain't gonna run my world', it is a rallying cry to the collective, not a personal statement, but the expression of the stance of a generation of people determined to bring about political change, emotionally charged and willing to give their practical support to political causes, anti-war, anti-racist, etc.:

> The laughing in the lynch mob
> Ain't a-gonna do no more
> Ain't a-gonna do no more,
> Ain't a-gonna do no more.
> The laughter in the lynch mob
> Ain't a-gonna do no more,
> Not now or no other time
> (© 1964, 1966 Warner Bros. Inc.).

In fact, the recording that we have Dylan sang with Pete Seeger at the 1963 Newport Folk Festival (*Newport Broadside*, Vanguard records), and in which the audience is encouraged to sing along, emphasising the collective rather than the individual defiance of the song. Another song sung at this festival and to the same purpose and effect was 'Blowin' in the Wind', which Dylan sang with Peter, Paul and Mary, Joan Baez, The Freedom Singers, Pete Seeger and Theo Bikel (*Evening Concerts at Newport vol. 1*, Vanguard). This is one of the classic protest songs of the 1960s and appeared first on *The Freewheelin' Bob Dylan*.

The album *The Times They are A-Changin'* has been criticised by Clinton Heylin for its almost unrelenting pessimism, its monotone, even monotonous, intensity and high moralism, adding up to a 'gruelling listening experience' (Heylin 1998: 78 and 79). This seems to me to be an unduly harsh criticism of a collection of material which is far from homogeneous, and continues the transformation of the finger-pointing songs into a different form which he had begun in *The Freewheelin' Bob Dylan*. Both 'The Times They are A-Changin'' and 'When the Ship Comes In' are far from pessimistic. It is true that they are songs about destruction, but they exude a confidence in renewal—a renewal that transcends the injustices and corruption of the present. They are both redemptive songs and have similar messages. They are defiantly optimistic in the face of adversity because of the belief in the inevitability of the tide of change. The metaphor of water is used to drive home the same message in both songs: accept the inevitability of change or drown, like Pharoah's tribe, in the growing tide of resistance and demand for social justice.

'The Times They are A Changin'' became the rallying call or anthem of a generation. Such anthems are songs that unite people in fostering a sense of belonging to a like-minded community, nation or the same cause. 'The Times They Are A-Changin'' exudes confidence, hailing a new dawn and clearly articulates for the first time a social change that began to occur in the 1950s, and which later became known as the generation gap. It is conciliatory in that it offers the opportunity for the older generation, particularly politicians, not merely to accept, but also to go with the flow. It is uncompromising in that the older generation is told to participate on the terms of the younger, or step out of the way.

> Come mothers and fathers throughout the land
> And don't criticize what you can't understand
> Your sons and your daughters are beyond your command
> The old road is rapidly aging
> Please get out of the new one if you can't lend your hand
> The times they are a changin'.

As Dylan himself explains in the notes to his retrospective album *Bio-graph*, it is definitely a song with a preconceived purpose and a clear sense of who his audience is. In this respect it is an example of what Collingwood called craft with a clear means-end relation between the author and the lyrics, premeditated with the intention of achieving a desired effect.

Dylan continued to mine the rich seam of topical 'song material', particularly the division between black and white. 'The Ballad of Donald White', 'The Death of Emmett Till' and the 'Lonesome Death of Hattie Carroll' are songs which deal with the injustices and prejudices of the American legal justice system from the point of view of the 'victim'. In the first, the victim is the convicted murderer himself who sought help but whose voice was not heard. He was a man who had no parents, no friends and who could not adjust to society. He realised that society needed protecting from him and asked to be returned to an institution. He was sentenced to death for his crime, and the song ends with White wondering how many had taken heed of his words and how many unfortunate boys deprived of opportunities in life would walk the same road as him, and asks are they really the enemies or victims of society. The second is preserved as a broadcast on a show called 'Broadside' in May 1962. It tells of the murder of a black man from Chicago by a group of white men out for some fun in a Mississippi town, and who were acquitted by a jury, some members of which, according to Dylan, were accomplices in the crime. After stirring the emotions of the listener, the song ends with an exhortation to all like-minded people, who want to make the great land of America a greater place in which to live, to act in order to bring justice about and make human rights a reality. It is very much in the populist rousing style of Woody Guthrie, patriotic with a sharp, cutting-edge, anti-establishment, pro-people and patriotic.

Finally, to illustrate Dylan's use of art to arouse emotion and motivate a politically conscious public to act, is his anti-war songs, and among them we find reflected the growing fear among the population in general of nuclear war. On *The Freewheelin' Bob Dylan* there are two explicitly anti-nuclear war songs, 'Masters of War' and 'Talking World War III Blues'. There was to have been a third, 'Let

Me Die in my Footsteps' (to which I referred earlier). 'Masters of War' is a venomous attack on those in authority who use war as an extension of policy, orchestrating destruction and hiding behind their desks while young men are sent to their deaths. It is an expression of utter contempt for the evil inflicted on the world by these men. He likens them to the filth that runs down drains, and spits out his desire that they should all die, leaving the world a much better place. Their sins are so horrendous that 'even Jesus would never forgive' what they do. He has dropped this last statement from the song since he became a Christian fundamentalist, because, of course, to paraphrase Samuel Butler, it is his trade to save and forgive. This is a song that Dylan continuously includes in his repertoire and demonstrates the extent to which his audience has never ceased to associate him with his political stance, or finger-pointing songs. On Veteran's Day 2002, for example, at Madison Square Garden in the evening after the Parade had marched down Fifth Avenue in the morning, and which the President had dedicated to those fighting the war against terrorism, Dylan pointedly sang 'Masters of War' and 'It's Alright Ma'. The audience roared in recognition and approval when he sang the lines, 'And I hope that you die, and your death'll come soon' and 'But even the president of the United States sometimes has to stand naked'. He elicited the same reaction to 'It's Alright Ma', but now in the context of the aftermath of the Iraq war, for example, at Wembley Arena, 15 November, 2003.

Dylan, of course, was one in a long line of protest singers and balladeers who chronicled the injustices of their societies. What made his protest songs so special? Michael Gray criticises Dylan's protest songs for having hardly anything in them but clichéd messages. He argues that it is not so much the clichés, but the fact that Dylan thinks clichés necessary for emphasis that mar the songs (Gray 2000: 22). Here, I think that Gray has missed the subtlety of the songs, and fails to appreciate their uniqueness in relation to the tradition to which he belongs. This is because he is too concerned to identify similarities between Dylan and his so-called influences, rather than detect the very real differences. Dylan elevates the protest song into an altogether more sophisticated medium.

Like Woody Guthrie, Dylan had a talent for using humour and irony, even sarcasm, in conveying a political message. But in addition, his songs were on the whole subtle, rather than sloganeering, powerful without being crass, emotional without being sentimental. Joan Baez thought the beauty of Dylan's protest songs in comparison with others was their understatement, 'he wrote songs that hadn't been written yet' (cited in Scaduto 1973: 111).

The music and delivery of the words is congruent with the subtlety of the message. There are songs, such as the 'Ballad of Donald White' and 'The Death of Emmet Till' in which Dylan plays the traditional role of the folk-singer, reporting and highlighting the social condition of his times, but he is never merely doing this. There is a strong sense of social conditioning in his songs, the perpetrators of crime are just as much victims as the victims themselves. Personal responsibility is often absorbed into societal responsibility. In both 'Who Killed Davey Moore?' and 'Only a Pawn in Their Game' the guitar is biting and the voice of the interrogator rasping and accusatory. In the former the accused are assertively defensive. 'Who killed Davey Moore, why, an what's the reason for?' elicits denials from the referee, the angry crowd, his manager, the gambler, the boxing writer and finally the opponent. The song doesn't actually attribute blame to any of them individually, but to society collectively for encouraging and condoning boxing as a sport. Dylan uses the same technique in his account of the murder of Medgar Evers. Evers had been killed in the front garden of his home in June 1963 in what appears to have been an irrational retaliation for the enrolment of two black people at the University of Alabama. The incident shocked more liberal-minded Americans and impelled J. F. Kennedy to abandon his attempts at appeasement and take a more aggressive stance towards desegregation in the South. Both he and his brother Robert, the Attorney General, attended the funeral, and the Evers family were invited to the White House as a gesture of solidarity. The incident was one that immediately aroused the condemnation of protest singers. Phil Ochs, for example, laboured the moral of the story in dull and dreary narrative form, doing little to arouse passion or indignation that wasn't already there because of its sanctimonious tone.

In Dylan's 'Only a Pawn in Their Game' the killer of Medgar Evers is himself portrayed as the victim of institutionalised racism, taught to believe that the laws justifiably protect his white skin. He is filled with irrational hatred and used by the officers of law and order to perpetuate racially motivated criminal acts which promote and protect their vested interests. It is an indictment of the whole of society, portraying the murderer and murdered as victims.

Again, in the 'Lonesome Death of Hattie Carroll' Dylan does not employ a simple hectoring style, but builds to an intensity of feeling by taking the listener through different degrees of indignation and pity, postponing their expression at the end of each verse with the words 'now ain't the time for your tears'. The particular incident itself, a true story of the murder by a young socialite of a black waitress in Maryland who was slow to bring the drink he had ordered, is used to build the emotional intensity, but the expression of grief and sadness is reserved for institutional failure and hypocrisy. The colour of neither the accused nor the victim is mentioned, but the relationship in which they stand, the treatment of the accused and the culmination in the sentence, strongly intimate the injustice of the white/black subordinate/superor-dinate relationship. The charade of courtroom dignity, honour, justice and equality before the law is exposed by the murderer's six-month sentence. In other words, what Dylan is saying is that while we have a deep sympathy with the victim, what we really need to do is weep for a society that feigns justice and equality with a false dignity and grace in establishment institutions which exude an appearance of equality divorced from the reality of racism.

The whole intonation and force of these songs is not merely in the words, but the performance. These songs are particularistic in that they identify a specific incident or subject from which generalisations are drawn, or from which they can be inferred, by the listener. He was also capable of writing protest songs without a specific point of reference, but which were nevertheless capable of summing up the human predicament in a way that resonated with every sympathetic and disaffected individual. 'Blowin' in the Wind', for example, is a song that celebrates the dynamic progressive feature of human kind, inquisitive-ness. It does not pretend to give answers, but instead emphasises the importance of the questioning activ-ity — there never will be any answers if the questions are not first asked. It has a surface appearance of fatality and resig-nation, with an undercurrent of self-assertion. It raises the question, how many — how many deaths, how many times — and implies that collectively we will determine when all such injustices cease. The inspiration for the song came from the idea that everyone who didn't speak out was betraying himself or herself by his or her silence (Gill 1998: 23). To be silent was to be complicit in the crime, to speak out, to ask questions, was at the very least to begin the pro-cess of collective self-reflection, a demand of the authorities to justify and defend what they take for granted.

Unlike many other protest singers of the 1960s he had an ability to conjure up the image, without having to spell out the message in literal terms. That is, an ability to stimulate the imagination of the listener, rather than foreclose it with too literal a representation of his message.

There are all sorts of things that we do with words with-out having to use the words themselves. A joke relies upon the audience picking up on the fact that in saying what you are saying you intend to be humorous. This is what John Austin called the illocutionary force of a sentence and what Quentin Skinner elaborated into the idea of what someone intends to mean *in* saying something as opposed to *by* say-ing it. *By* singing 'The Chimes of Freedom' on a specific occasion Dylan intended to fulfil his commitment to Gre-nada Television and pick up his pay cheque. *In* singing 'The Chimes of Freedom' he may have intended to convey a glimmer of hope to all those oppressed by psychological, sociological or physiological afflictions, without explicitly articulating the idea that fate or destiny is on their side in the tolling of the bells of liberty. In Phil Ochs' 'There but for Fortune' and Ralph McTell's 'Streets of London', whose melodies and intonations are incongruous with the lyrics, we are introduced to the victims of society and told not to be judgemental on them, but on the system. There but for the grace of God we could all be the drunk, the down-and-out, the prisoner.

Using his art as magic, the arousal of emotions for their practical effects, is only one side of Bob Dylan in the early albums, and of course, he revisits this form of expression throughout his career in such songs of criminal injustice as 'George Jackson' and 'Hurricane', or in the prophetic evangelical 'Gotta Serve Somebody', 'When You Gonna Wake Up?' and 'When He Returns'. Whereas the earlier songs exude an optimism in the self-creating powers of humanity, the ability to change the world by imagining new possibilities, the finger-pointing songs of his born-again Christian phase asks us to put our faith in God. As Dylan confidently assures us in 'When He Returns': 'For Like a thief in the night, He'll replace wrong with right/When He returns'. It is interesting that when he returned to touring in 1974 he no longer wished to disown the old finger-pointing songs, nor other acoustic standards for which he was famous. At the start of his 1974 tour on 3 January 1974 in Chicago, Dylan sang solo immediately after the interval 'The Times They Are A Changin'', 'Song to Woody', 'Lonesome Death of Hattie Carroll' and 'It's Alright Ma (I'm Only Bleedin')'. Reviews of the concert are exuberant about the fact that Dylan could still do it, sing the message songs with conviction and that the message was timeless in the post-vice president Agnew era (Fong-Terres 1975a: 13). Throughout the 1990s Dylan included one of his first anti-military-industrial complex protest song in his live performances. The song was 'John Brown', which he never included on his early albums, and which in its message is rather direct and crude, but nevertheless powerful because of the graphic depiction of the effects of war upon one soldier who returns to his mother who was once so proud to see him go into combat. It is a song in the mode of 'Mrs McGrath', which tells of a soldier in the Napoleonic Wars returning from battle to his mother waiting on the sea shore:

> Then up jumped Ted without any legs.
> And in their place were two wooden pegs.
> She kissed him a hundred times or two
> Saying holy Moses it isn't you

Dylan uses the same tactic describing the battled-scarred John Brown whose face is mutilated and his hand blown off. When asked in an interview for *Rolling Stone* in 1974 why he had returned to the message songs, Dylan answered: 'For me, its just reinforcing those images in my head that were there, that don't die, that will be there tomorrow, and in doing so for myself, hopefully also for those people' (Fong-Terres 1975b: 104). Even during the early part of Dylan's career when the protest songs were at their most obviously politically pointed, there are intimations of the second of the categories I identified, art as the expression of emotion, that is, where there is no obvious preconceived intentional effect constructed on a means ends calculus, but instead where the emotion is expressed in writing the song. One of Dylan's most intense songs is 'Hard Rain's A-Gonna Fall'. In it Dylan expresses his emotions not in any literal, narrative or descriptive way, but abstractly, often through disconnected images, not through a story or a portrayal of a situation, and it is doubtful that he had any intention to arouse any particular emotions in his audience to any practical effect. The singer responds to a series of questions posed by an interested, non-judgemental, caring parent-figure. The questions are simple: Where have you been? What have you seen? What have you heard? Who have you met? What will you do now? The answers are a series of evocative images, mostly disconnected, but in the first three verses the number 10,000 is repeated. He has been '10,000 miles in the mouth of a graveyard': Saw '10,000 talkers whose tongues were all broken': Heard '10,000 whispering and nobody listening'. The notes to *Freewheelin'* suggest that this song was written during the Cuban missile crisis (although there is some doubt about this) and represents an expression of what feelings the crisis generated in Dylan (Marqusee 2003: 60). Scaduto is sensitive to what Dylan is doing when he writes: '*Hard Rain* is filled with spare, sparkling images that evoke the terrors of national injustice and of international-insanity-diplomacy. Never mentioning nuclear war or fallout, the evils of segregation or man's inhumanity to his own kind, but forcing the listener to conjure with such terror out of his own emotions' (Scaduto 1973: 127). It is not a polemical protest song, but as Nat Hentoff says in the notes, it is a transmutation of Dylan's 'fierce convictions into what can only be called art'. Tom Paxton, one of the first to hear it, said that it very quickly became acclaimed by Dylan's fans as his greatest work to date, and Dave van Ronk maintained that everyone became intensely aware that it heralded an artistic revolution (Gill 1998). Paul Williams talks about this song in terms similar to those that inform Collingwood's characterisation of art proper. He suggests that Dylan wrote this song with no preconceived idea of what it should mean, nor with a calculated intent in what it should evoke in his audience, but nevertheless with a sensitivity to the effect upon the listener.[11]

By the end of 1964 Dylan had already distanced himself considerably from those who hailed him as a great topical songwriter, as Dylan's disturbed comment to Joan Baez about not wanting to be responsible for the political aspirations of his audience, and Silber's complaint about Dylan's entourage serving to distance him from reality testifies. By the middle of 1965 he was consciously rejecting the significance that those songs had for the civil rights movement. Asked about those songs in an interview in September of that year Dylan reacted by saying: 'I'm not a preacher. Songs can't save the world, I know that. Whatever you have

---

[11]   He says that the poet, in whose company he includes Dylan at this point, 'does not premeditate, and in a real sense is inspired, and yet at the same time must work very hard and have a talent that is uniquely his own, in order to seize the moment and be the voice of his times, his generation' (Williams 1994: 60).

to give, you give. That's the way it is'. (Beverly Hills press conference, 1965). The fact that Dylan moves away from what he called finger-pointing songs, does not mean that his songs become apolitical.

We also get intimations of a sense of art as the expression of emotion in the earlier works. 'Don't Think Twice its All Right' (*Freewheelin'*) and 'Spanish Boots of Spanish Leather' (*Times They are A-Changin'*) are love songs about the personal relationship he had with Suze Rotolo. These songs present art as representation. The subject matter is unambiguous, although its point of reference may not be explicit. They are emotionally expressive songs depicting a state or condition in which the singer finds himself. These are essentially a foretaste of the personal exploration of relationships that we find on *Another Side of Bob Dylan*, the album which generated a great deal of criticism from his Greenwich Village friends. In relation to these songs you could ask questions about outside referents. Take, for example, 'My Back Pages'. It is a lyric poem that on the surface could be taken to be a series of images: 'Crimson flames tied through my ears /Rolling high and mighty traps'. But if taken merely as images, the import of the song is lost. Knowing its referents makes a difference to our appreciation, despite the fact that it does not take a narrative form. It is a song of self-criticism, criticism of talking in certainties and absolutes and of being too arrogant and sanctimonious to realise it. It is a thinly veiled criticism of those whom he felt had used and tried to control him, and of himself for being so easily fooled:

> A self-ordained professor's tongue
> Too serious to fool
> Spouted out that liberty
> Is just equality in school
> 'Equality', I spoke the word
> As if a wedding vow.
> Ah, but I was so much older then,
> I'm younger than that now.

In 'It's Alright Ma' we similarly have an expression of emotion that is generalised against a system, as opposed to be directed against the movement to which he once belonged.

The words exude the emotion of anger with no specific or particularistic referent:

> Old lady judges watch people in pairs
> Limited in sex they dare
> To push fake morals, insult and stare
> While money doesn't talk it swears
> Obscenity, who really cares
> Propaganda, all is phoney.

Here, then, the question of who the lady judges might be is irrelevant to the appreciation of the emotion being expressed. He is expressing anger at the false standards perpetrated by a society that is hypocritically moralistic, and in which the power of money and not sexual explicitness is obscene. It is what Lorca called poetry of the imagination, the exploration of the interconnectedness of reality, the unravelling of its contradictions in order to make sense of them. As Dylan himself commented, he wanted to write songs that worked on many different levels. The same words with an interchanging subject may be both sincere and ironic when approached from different perspectives. Because appreciation is a matter of fusion between horizons, a work of art may mean nothing to a person whose horizon is not open to the experience.

The third category, what Lorca called inspirational, Bob Dylan calls 'hallucination … atery' songs. What, then, did he mean by 'hallucination … atery song'? Essentially he is talking about an abstract song, not necessarily induced by hallucinogenics, whose lyrics conjure up images with scattered referents, with no particular story, but which may have a point or many points, without needing to be stated. Dylan maintains at this time that 'I've stopped composing and singing anything that has either a reason to be written or a motive to be sung.... The word 'message' strikes me as having a hernia-like sound' (cited in Williams 1996: 16–17). These songs are most strongly influenced by the French Symbolist Rimbaud. Rimbaud was a rebel who wanted to reach a wider popular audience with his poetry in which he questioned all types of establishment authority, including Church and State. Like Woody Guthrie he almost lived the life of a vagrant, and drank very heavily. In addition, Rimbaud indulged heavily in marijuana and opium. Rimbaud claimed that in order to transform the poet into a seer or visionary, the senses must become disordered or disturbed by a prolonged process of disorientation. Dylan's own well-documented drunkenness and excessive abuse of drugs coincides with the development of his abstract, almost surreal poetic phase. Here art is no longer representation, but fragmentation, abstract images, emotionally demanding, but having no direct intent. It is the world around him that provides the inspiration, often a specific incident or event, which stimulates his creative talent resulting in a series of images, mostly abstract, evocative of a mood or feeling, but you could not say that the songs were about the particular situations that proved inspirational. It would be difficult on hearing 'Hard Rain's A-Gonna Fall' to identify the Cuban missile crisis as the subject matter, and even though the Vietnam War weighed heavily on Dylan's mind when he wrote 'Tombstone Blues' (*Highway 61 Revisited*), and the poetic images are inspired by it, the song is not a narrative but instead a series of metaphors whose inspiration happens to be the Vietnam war:

> The king of the Philistines his soldiers to save
> Put jawbones on their tombstones and flatters their graves
> Puts the pied piper in prison and fattens the slaves
> Then sends them out to the jungle.

President Lyndon Johnson is the Philistine leader who throws the draft-dodgers in prison, has a programme of inner-city rejuvenation meant to improve the condition of the blacks, who are disproportionately represented in the battalions in Vietnam. These may or may not be the referents to the images, but the images are meant to stand alone. In other words a song can evoke the mood of an era, without having specific referents within it. Jon Landau realises this in his review of *John Wesley Harding*. He contends that Dylan exhibits a profound awareness of the war and the effect that it is having upon everyone, just as the country is about to split apart over the assassinations of Martin Luther King and Robert Kennedy, over race, political and police riots, the presidential election and the carnage in Vietnam. Landau does not claim that any of the songs are about Vietnam, or a protest against it: 'All I mean to say is that Dylan has felt the war, and there is an awareness of it contained within the mood of the album as a whole' (cited in Marcus 1998: 55).

The songs that most epitomise this phase of Dylan's career are, for example, 'Desolation Row', 'Stuck Inside of Mobile with the Memphis Blues Again', 'Sad Eyed Lady of the Lowlands' and 'Visions of Johanna'. In these songs many names are mentioned, some quite familiar, such as 'John the Baptist', 'Casanova', 'Galileo', 'Einstein', 'T. S. Eliot', 'Cecil B. DeMille', 'Shakespeare', 'Mona Lisa', 'The Madonna' and 'Ezra Pound'. Other names have no apparent obvious referent, such as 'Brother Bill', 'Dr Filth', 'Louise' and 'Ruthie'. What all the names have in common is that they are contemplative images, not persons:

> Einstein disguised as Robin Hood
> With his memories in a trunk
> Passed this way and hour ago
> With his friend a jealous monk
> He looked so immaculately frightful
> As he bummed a cigarette
> Then went off sniffing drainpipes
> And reciting the alphabet
> Now you would not think to look at him
> That he was famous long ago
> For playing the electric violin on Desolation Row

This is an example of what Lorca called *duende*. It is, as Christopher Ricks points out, 'the extraordinary vision of hell on earth where civilisation doesn't know what to value or when it does know—it doesn't know how to value it (Ricks 2008: 2). By this time Dylan had come to see his songs as experiences, and comprehending the meaning of the words was not necessary to under-standing the experience; indeed, too much intellectualising could destroy the experience. Even though 'John Wesley Harding' signalled another musical transformation, it did not herald a transformation in his poetry, but instead a steadier control of the imagery. The songs are still characterised by the presentation of images unfolding as narratives in dramatic form, but at the same time the songs elude those who seek to discern a meaning by appearing to have a direction and point, but suddenly veer off in a different direction, or unexpected turn. One reviewer, commenting on 'The Ballad of Frankie Lee and Judas Priest', asserts that: 'There is a frightening delight in meaninglessness: drawled words ... irrelevant details and non-sequiturs' (Strause 1998: 87).

I have argued that the protest song phase in Dylan's early career may best be understood as pseudo-art, or what Collingwood called art as magic. The songs are faithful in many respects to the form of the genre, but also unique in the subtlety of the message, portraying the murderers and murdered as victims of a sick society. He is not offering a structural analysis of society in which the forces at work are impersonal. Instead, he attributes agency to the officers of the institutions who have vested interests in perpetuating racism, the arms race or the running-down of traditional industries. These songs, I have suggested, are quite different from those that are expressive of personal rather than collective emotion and whose referents are still anchored in the logic of everyday reality, what Lorca called imaginative poetry. Finally, both forms of lyric are to be distinguished from the abstract expressionism of the 'inspirational' phase. Here we are presented with a parallel universe made up of the accentuated absurdities of our own, a series of images, but not propositions, about which it makes no sense to ask whether they are right or wrong, and whose images, to use Oakeshott's words, are to be delighted in.

## References

Benson, Carl (1998) *The Bob Dylan Companion: Four Decades of Commentary*. New York: Schirmer Books.

Betti, Emilio (1980) 'Hermeneutics as the Methodology of the *Geisteswis-senschaften*', in Joseph Bleicher (ed.), *Contemporary Hermeneutics: Hermeneuticsas Method, Philosophy and Critique*. London: Routledge and Kegan Paul.

Benson, Carl (ed.) (1998) *The Bob Dylan Companion*. New York: Schimmer. Beverly Hills press conference, 4 September 1965. Reproduced in *The Bob Dylan Companion*, ed. Benson (1998). New York: Schimmer.

Booklet accompanying *Biograph*. 1985.

Boucher, David (2004) *Dylan and Cohen: Poets of Rock and Roll*. New York: Continuum.

Butler, Christopher (2002) 'Dylan and the Academics', in Neil Corcoran (ed.) *'Do You Mr Jones' Bob Dylan with the Poets and Professors*. London: Chatto and Windus.

Collingwood, R. G. (1924) *Speculum Mentis, or the Map of Knowledge*. Oxford: Clarendon Press.

Collingwood, R. G. (1937) *The Principles of Art*. Oxford: Oxford University Press.

Collingwood, R. G. (1939) *An Autobiography*. Oxford: Oxford University Press.

Corcoran, Neil (ed.) (2002) *'Do You Mr. Jones?': Bob Dylan with the Poets and Professors*, London: Chatto and Windus.

Denisoff, R. Serge (1972) *Sing a Song of Significance*. Bowling Green, Ohio: Bowling Green University Press.

Devlin, Jim (ed.) (1958) *In His Own Words, Leonard Cohen*. London: Omnibus.

Fong-Torres, Ben (1975a) 'Dylan Opens to a Hero's Welcome', in *Knocking on Heaven's Door*. London: Dempsey in association with Cassell.

Fong-Torres, Ben (1975b) 'Transcript of an interview with Bob Dylan', 12 January, Chateau Champlain hotel in Montreal, in *Knocking on Dylan's Door*, by the authors of *Rolling Stone Magazine*.

Fowlie, Wallace (1994) *Rimbaud and Jim Morrison*, Durham, NC and London: Duke University Press.

Gadamer, Hans-Georg (1985) *Truth and Method*. London: Sheed and Ward.

Gibbens, John (2001) *A Nightingale's Code: A Poetic Study of Bob Dylan*. London: Touched Press.

Gill, Andy. (1998). *My Back Pages: Classic Bob Dylan 1962-69*. London: Carlton.

Ginsberg, Allen (1992) 'Bob Dylan and Renaldo and Clara', in *Wanted Man,* in John Bauldie (ed.) *Wanted Man: In Search of Bob Dylan*. London: Penguin.

Glaister, Dan (1997) 'Fade Far Away, Dissolve … to Dylan', *The Guardian*, 27 March.

Gray, Michael (2000) *Song and Dance Man III*. London and New York: Cassell.

Harris, Derek, cited in Christopher Maurer (1990) Introduction to Federico Garcia Lorca, *Poet in New York*.London: Penguin.

Harris, John (2000) 'In Praise of Bob Dylan', Q *Dylan*.

Hajdu, David (2001) *Positively 4thStreet*. London: Bloomsbury.

Heylin, Clinton (1992) *Dylan: Behind the Shades*. Harmondsworth: Penguin.

Hirsch, Jr, E. D. (1976) *The Aims of Interpretation*. Chicago: University of Chicago Press.

Jones, Henry (1892) *Browning as a Philosophical and Religious Teacher*. Glasgow: Maclehose, 2nd edition.

Kermode Frank and Spender, Stephen (2001) The Metaphor at the End of the Tunnel', in Elizabeth Thomson and David Gutman (eds) *The Dylan Companion*. New York: Da Capo. Originally published in *Esquire*, May 1972.

Lee, J. L. (2002) *Like the Night*, London: Helter Skelter.

Lorca, Federico Garcia (1997) 'Imagination, inspiration, evasion', in *Obras com-pletas III*: prosaed, Miguel Garcia-Posada. Barcelona: Galaxia Gutenberg.

Lorca, Federico Garcia (2004) 'Theory and Practice of the *Duende'* translated by A. S. Klein, http://www.tonykline.co.uk/PITBR/Spanish/LorcaDuende.htm

Lumsden, Roddy (1999) 'While the King was Looking Down', in Roddy Lumsden and Stephen Trousse (eds) *The Message: Crossing the Tracks Between Poetry and Pop*, London: The Poetry Society.

McClure, Michael. 'The Poet's Poet', in *Knocking on Dylan's Door*.

Malanga, Gerard (1978) 'Dylan: Poet' in the 1978 European Tour Programme.

Marcus, Greil (1998) *Invisible Republic: Bob Dylan's Basement Tapes*, London: Picador.

Marqusee, Mike (2003) *Chimes of Freedom: The Politics of Bob Dylan's Art*. New York: The New Press.

Maurer, Christopher (1990) Introduction to Federico Garcia Lorca, *Poet in New York*. London: Penguin.

Motion, Andrew (1999) 'On Bob Dylan', in Roddy Lumsden with Stephen Trousse (eds) *The Message: Crossing the Tracks between Poetry and Pop*, London: PoetrySociety.

*The New Oxford Book of English Prose* (1998) Oxford: Oxford University Press.

Mulhall, Stephen (1992) 'Expression', in David Cooper (ed.) *A Companion to Aesthetics*, Oxford: Blackwell.

Oakeshott, Michael (1991) The Voice of Poetry in the Conversation of Mankind', in Oakeshott, *Rationalism in Politics*, new and expanded edn. Indianapolis: Liberty Press.

Rasky, Harry (2001) *The Songs of Leonard Cohen*, Oakville, Ontario: Mosaic Press.

Rawlings, Adrian (1966) 'What's Happening, Mr. Jones?', *Farrago*, 29 April. Reprinted in *The Bob Dylan Companion*, ed. Benson, 1973.

Ricks, Christopher (2003) *Dylan's Visions of Sin*. London: Penguin/Viking.

Ricks, Christopher (2008)'A lesson in Dylan Appreciation', an interview with Ieva Lesinska, *Rigas Laiks, Eurozine*. http://www.eurozine.org/articles/2008-04-11-ricks-en.htmlaccessed 15 October, 2008.

Scaduto, Anthony (1973) *Bob Dylan*, London: Helter Skelter, revised edn.

Shelton, Robert (n.d.) 'The Man behind the Songs', in *Bob Dylan Songbook*.London: Warner Bros., 14.

Shelton, Robert (1999) 'Singers and Song Writers Racing Down Dylan's Road', in Craig McGregor (ed.) *Bob Dylan: The Early Years*. New York: Da Capo. First published in *New York Times*, 27 August 1965.

Stein, George (1983) *Edie: An American Biography*, ed. George Plimpton. New York: Dell.

Strouse, Jean (1968) 'Bob Dylan's Gentle Anarchy', *Commonweal* Reprinted in *The Bob Dylan Companion*, ed. Benson, 1987.

Trousse, Stephen (1999) 'Stupid and Contagious: The Pleasures of the Text' in Roddy Lumsden and Stephen Trousse (eds) *The Message: Crossing the Tracks Between Poetry and Pop*. London: The Poetry Society. Abbott McNeill.

Whistler, James (1998). *The Ten o'clock Lecture*, in *The New Oxford Book of English Prose*. Oxford: Oxford University Press.

Williams, Paul (1994) *Bob Dylan: Performing Artist 1960-1973 The Early Years.* London: Omnibus.

Williams, Paul (1996) *Bob Dylan: Watching the River Flow: Observations in Progress 1966-1995*, London: Omnibus. www.geocites.com/Athens/Forum/2667.

Yurchenco, Henrietta (1966) 'Folk-Rot: In Defence', *Sound and Fury*, April. Reprinted in Carl Benson (ed.) *The Bob Dylan Companion*. New York: Schimer, 1987.

# Bob Dylan Time Line

### 1941

*May, 24.* Born Robert Allen Zimmerman (also given the Hebrew name of Shabtai Zisel ben Avraham). Duluth, Minnesota. America still not at war with Germany.

*December, 7.* Attack on Pearl Harbour by the Japanese.

### 1943

*March.* Woody Guthrie's *Bound for Glory* Published.

### 1946

Zimmerman family fortunes declined and Dylan's father Abe lost his job.

### 1947

Moved to Hibbing, Minnesota. Attended Nettleton Elementary School and later Hibbing High School (known as Zimbo in High School).

Hibbing had built its prosperity on iron ore, and had gone through a boom supply the ore during World War II. These deposits of ore were declining when Dylan grew up and unemployment and poverty rose. Subject of Dylan's 'North Country Blues' in 1964.

Fathers' circumstances improved after setting up a business selling electrical goods and furniture.

### 1950

Outbreak of the Korean War and manifestation of containment and anti-communism policy of USA.

Folk music firmly established in Greenwich Village when Allan Block opened his sandal shop on West 4th Avenue, and became a meeting place for those interested in folk culture. Included Cisco Houston, Leadbelly, Josh White, Will Geer and Woody Guthrie.

## 1951

*Sing Out* first appeared. Edited from 1951 to 1967 by Irwin Silber who was one of the leading lights behind the Newport Folk Festival.

Topical songs became a popular form of expression in Greenwich Village, and *Sing Out* was not able to keep up with the demand for space and came to focus upon the songs of movements rather than individual songwriters. *Broadside* came to fill the gap as a topical song magazine featuring the work of the new generation of finger-pointers.

## 1952

Dwight David Eisenhower elected president. Re-elected in 1956. Negotiated a Truce in the Korean War in 1953.

*September.* Woody Guthrie diagnosed with Huntington's Chorea.

## 1953

*January, 1.* Hank Williams Dies at the age of 29. He was to be a musical inspiration to Dylan thereafter.

## 1954

*May, 17.* Brown v. Board of Education, 347 U.S. 483 (1954) (USSC+). Landmark Supreme Court decision. Declared that the discriminatory racial segregation 'violates the 14th amendment to the U.S. Constitution, which guarantees all citizens equal protection of the laws'.

*April.* Pete Seeger toured campuses popularizing Woody Guthrie's songs to new audiences.

*May.* Bar Mitzvah.

*July.* After two visits that proved to be unsuccessful Elvis Presley was back in Sam Phillip's studio singing 'That's Alright Mama'. Phillips suggested that Scotty Moore play guitar and Bill Black bass. Phillips at last had found a white man who sounded and felt like a black R&B artist. Elvis joined Sun Records' 'Million Dollar Quartet' — Jerry Lee Lewis, Carl Perkins, Johnny Cash (with whom Dylan later collaborated) and Elvis Presley himself. Bill Black, Elvis Presley, Scotty Moore first played the Hillbilly Cat and the Blue Moon Boys.

*September*. Woody Gurhtrie checked into Brooklyn State Hospital.

## 1955

Emmet Till shot and thrown into the Tallahassee River. Subject matter of Bob Dylan's first finger-pointing song in early 1962.

James Dean appears in *Rebel Without A Cause*. Great influence on Dylan.

*May*, James Dean dies in a motor car accident.

## 1956

Dylan becomes a member of The Jokers, a band formed in a Jewish Summer Camp.

*May*. Guthrie checked out of Brooklyn State Hispital.

*May*. Guthrie involuntarily checked into Greystone Park in Morris Plains New Jersey.

## 1957

Dylan forms a band called The Shadow Blasters with a group of school friends.

## 1958

Dylan playing in a band called The Golden Chords.

High School graduation Dylan's uncle gave him a stack of 78rpm records of Ledbelly.

Took off to Fargo North Dakota and got a job as a busboy at the Red Apple Café. Although limited in his talents as a pianist he managed to persuade Bobby Vee's brother Bill to let him play with the band. Restricted to the range of C he played a few gigs and was let go.

## 1959

Bob and Sidsel Gleason started to bring Guthrie to their home every Sunday in East Orange, New Jersey. Regular gathering of folk singers of which Dylan later became one.

*January.* Dylan and his friends appeared as Elston Gunn and His Rock Boppers at Hibbing High School dance.

*January, 31.* Dylan sees Buddy Holly, Richie Valens and The Big Bopper in Duleth at the National Guard Armoury.

*February, 3.* Holly, Valens and The Big Bopper die in an air crash. Subject of Don Mclean's 'American Pie' — the day the music died.

The Newport Folk Festival started by George Wein, impresario and Dylan's future manager Albert Grossman capitalising on the success of Wein's Newport Jazz Festival. The project of the Newport Folk Festival was from the beginning both cultural and political. The likes of Theodore Bikel, Pete Seeger and Alan Lomax were driving forces.

*Autumn.* Dylan enrols in the University of Minnesota and lived in the Jewish fraternity house, Sigma Alpha Mu. He dropped out after one semester. He played acoustic guitar around various venues in the Twin Cities of Minneapolis and St. Paul, including the Ten O'Clock Scholar.

## 1961

*January, 21.* Dylan arrives in New York and visits Woody Guthrie in Greystone Park Hospital, New Jersey, a few days later. During the Spring Guthrie was transferred to Brooklyn State Hospital. Guthrie was already incapacitated by Huntington's Chorea.

*April.* Bay of Pigs. Failed invasion of Cuba by USA forces.

Dylan played his first shows in New York at Café Wha, MacDougal Street, Greenwich Village.

*September, 29.* Robert Shelton publishes review of Dylan in *New York Times*. Raves about Dylan concert in Gerdes Folk City, Greenwich Village. Shelton was later to write *No Direction Home: The Life and Music of Bob Dylan*.

*November.* Signed to Columbia by John Hammond. Recorded *Bob Dylan*.

## 1962

*March.* US release of *Bob Dylan*. UK release July. Shows he is deeply immersed in the tradition reflected in Harry Smith's *Anthology of American Folk Music*.

*April.* Dylan writes 'Blowin' in the Wind' to the melody of 'No More Auction Block'.

Late Spring, early summer, Albert Grossman becomes Dylan's manager.

*Summer.* Met Suze Rotolo the inspiration for many songs including 'Boots of Spanish Leather'. Memoir published in 2008, *A Freewheelin' Time*. She is pictured on the cover of Bob Dylan's *'Freewheelin'* album.

*October.* Cuban Missile Crisis. Said to have inspired 'A Hard rain's A-Gonna Fall', but he had in fact played it three weeks earlier at the Carnegie Hall.

Dylan played few dates around the clubs of Greenwich Village in 1962, but preferred concert halls. The transition between his first album and *The Freewheelin' Bob Dylan* can be discerned from recordings of his live appearances. He played at the Gaslight in October, 1962 and the recording released in 2005 and sold through Starbucks coffee shops, entitled *Bob Dylan Live at the Gaslight* is probably an authentic recording of that set.

*December, 17.* Dylan arrives in London to appear in the TV play 'Madhouse on Castle Street'. He sang 'Ballad of a Gliding Swan' which has recently resurfaced in a very poor recording. Met Martin Carthy, Bob Davenport and Dominic Behan from whom he picked up melodies he was to use on 'Girl From the North Country', 'Masters of War', 'Bob Dylan's Dream', 'A Hard Rain's A-Gonna Fall', 'With God on Our Side'.

## 1963

*March, 21.* Davey Moore, featherweight champion, knocked out by the undefeated featherweight No 1 contender Cuban Ultiminio 'Sugar' Ramos at 1-year-old Dodger Stadium. Moore failed to regain consciousness and died March 25. The the fatal injury was caused by Moore's head striking the bottom rope while falling to the canvas. The subject matter of Dylan's 'Who Killed Davey Moore' in which he absolves no one of blame.

*May.* US release of *The Freewheelin' Bob Dylan*. UK release November.

*May, 12.* Bob Dylan walks out on the Ed. Sullivan Show for denying him the right to sing the anti right-wing song 'Talkin' John Birch Society Paranoid Blues'.

*May.* Dylan and Joan Baez play the Monteray Folk Festival. He goes to Carmel where she lived and stays. Meets Mimi Baez and Richard Farina. Dylan and Baez became the King and Queen of Folk Music until it all fell apart. *Don't Look Back,* Pennebaker's film, clearly captured the strain. Baez had remained overtly political and acquired the nickname of 'St. Joan'.

*June, 12.* Medgar Evers murdered in Jackson by Ku Klux Klan members. Subject-matter of 'Only a Pawn in Their Game'.

*July.* Black Voter Registration Rally, Greenwood, Mississippi, premiered 'Only a Pawn in Their Game'.

*July, 26–28.* Newport Folk Festival. Friday evening Dylan billed with the likes of The Freedom Singers, Brownie McGhee and Sonny Terry, Peter Paul and Mary and the legendary Doc Watson. Sang 'With God on our Side' with Joan Baez, and 'Blowin' in the Wind' with Baez, Seeger, Peter Paul and Mary, and The Freedom Singers. Testament to Dylan's growing importance and spokesperson for the 'Movement'.

*August, 28.* Civil rights march on Washington, 200,000 protesters. Dylan and Baez just a few feet away from Martin Luther King as he proclaimed 'I have a dream'.

*October, 26.* Dylan plays Carnegie Hall. The songs he played further traces his evolution between *Freewheelin'* and *The Times They are A-Changing.* Six of the songs appear on a promotional cd *Bob Dylan Live at Carnegie Hall 1963.*

*November.* Beatles' first visit to the States.

*November, 22.* Assassination of John F. Kennedy. Malcolm X of the Nation of Islam comments that it was a case of 'chickens coming home to roost'. He was suspended for this and other comments.

*December.* Dylan receives the Tom Paine Award at the annual Bill of Rights Dinner. Is drunk and offensive to audience.

## 1964

*January.* US release of *The Times They Are A-Changin'*. UK release, May.

*March.* Malcolm X leaves the Nation of Islam and establishes the Organisation of Afro-American Unity.

Extended play from 1963 Newport Folk Festival, featuring Bob Dylan and assembled friends singing 'Blowing in the Wind' (Fontana TFE 18010), cover states: 'A number of people from every background have joined hands with the Negroes in the movement against segregation and for equal rights. Those in the folk song movement are proud that so many of its leading figures have become identified, personally and musically, with this major social current of our time'.

*May, 17.* Dylan played his first public London concert at the Royal Festival Hall, at 3:00 pm. Dylan's first UK tour was followed in May by a holiday in Greece where he wrote most of the songs for the album *Another Side of Bob Dylan*.

Newport Folk Festival. Dylan's transformation from the previous year was immediately obvious. His hair was now longer, and he wore dark glasses, but his songs were more intensely personal. Here he showcased 'Mr Tamberine Man'. 'Gates of Eden' enthralled and enthused the audience to the point where they were rebelling against the ordained order of appearance. This was the first glimpse that many had of Dylan striking out for independence. He closed his set with Joan Baez singing with 'God on Our Side' but the whole atmosphere had changed.

*August.* US release of *Another Side of Bob Dylan*. UK release November.

Vietnam War. USA militarily supported South Vietnam in attempt to stem the spread of communism. North Vietnam attacked US ships in 1964 and President Lyndon Johnson ordered retaliatory bombing of North Vietnam. War was never officially declared, but Congress passed the Gulf of Tonkin resolution which authorised US forces to repel North Vietnamese attacks. Inspiration for lines in 'Tombstone Blues'.

## 1965

*January.* Dylan records electric accompanied songs including 'Subterranean Homesick Blues'.

*February, 21.* Malcolm X shot dead in Harlem. Three Black Muslims were later found guilty of murder.

*March.* US release of *Bringing It All Back Home.* Dylan's appearance on the cover indicates a complete change of style. He is holding a blue Persian cat named 'Rolling Stone'.

*April, 30–May 10.* Dylan tours England. D. A. Pennebaker shoots cinéma vérité for *Don't Look Back.*

*May.* Dylan tried to record with John Mayall and the Blues-breakers, including Eric Clapton. Disappointed and aborted outcome.

Dylan's relationship with Sara Lowndes flourishing. Takes room in the Chelsea hotel to be near her.

America's involvement in the Vietnam War becomes increasingly more committed, and protests become more radical and violent. Dylan's reaction is to withdraw into himself with increasingly more self-reflective songs, which betray a dark deep disturbing character—what the poet Lorco calls 'Duende'.

*June.* Mike Bloomfield and Al Kooper (organ) play on 'Like a Rolling Stone'.

Under the influence of Lowndes and Alan Ginsberg Dylan became a devotee of *I Ching.*

*July, 22–25.* Dylan played electric set, including 'Like a Rolling Stone' that had just been released as a single and was climbing the charts, at the Newport Folk Festival with the Paul Butterfield Band, minus Paul Butterfield. Pete Seeger said to have tried to cut the electricity cable. Murray Lerner's Film, *The Other Side of The Mirror* (2007), captures the transitions from 1963 to 1965 in Dylan's Newport performances.

*July–August.* completing recordings for Highway 61 Revisited released in the US in August and the UK September.

*August, 28.* concert at Forest Hills adding to the line-up of Al Kooper and Garth Brooks, were Robbie Robertson and Levon Helm (to be replaced by Sandy Konikoff, and later by Mickey Jones on drums) of the Canadian band The Hawks.

*September, 24.* Dylan starts tour with the Hawks and enters the recording studio October, 1965, adding Bobby Gregg and Al Kooper to the line-up for some songs.

## 1966

*March.* completed the sessions for *Blonde on Blonde* and released US May 1966, and UK August.

*April.* World leg of the tour begins.

*May, 17.* The infamous 'Royal Albert Hall' concert, actually recorded at Manchester. It was here that a heckler called him 'Judas'. The recording was released as vol 4 in the bootleg series, *Bob Dylan Live*, 1966.

*May, 27.* Last concert with the Hawks at London's Royal Albert Hall before retreat to Spain for a holiday.

*June/July.* Woodstock, re-editing Pennebaker's film of the 1966 tour. It became the infamous and rarely seen *Eat the Document* which CBS turned down.

*July.* Motorcycle accident, fracturing Dylan's neck. Goes into complete seclusion.

Records demos with the newly named Band in the Big Pink.

## 1967

*March.* Astoria in London, Jimi Hendrix set fire to his guitar and suffered burnt hands.

*March.* Release of UK version of Dylan's *Greatest Hits*. US version released March.

*May, 17.* Premiere of *Don't Look Back* at the Presidio Theatre in San Francisco, and opened in New York September 6 at the 34th Street East Theatre. In 2006 a special edition of the film was released, 'The 1965 Tour Deluxe Edition' with additional footage comprising a second DVD '1965 Revisited'.

*June. Sgt. Pepper*, the Beatles' psychedelic album released. Pink Floyd's first album *Piper at the Gates of Dawn*.

Summer of Love. The music that changed everything came from California. It was a 28-year-old Floridian called Scott McKenzie singing: 'If you're going to San Francisco/Be sure to wear some flowers in your hair ... '. The song, 'San Francisco', written by John Phillips of the Mamas & the Papas, was a hit all over the world.

*October, 3.* Death of Woody Guthrie at Brooklyn State Hospital. Posthumously inducted into Songwriters' Hall of Fame; Posthumously inducted into Nashville Songwriters Foundation, Inc.; Posthumously inducted into Rock and

Roll Hall of Fame; Posthumously awarded Lifetime Achievement Award by North American Folk Music and Dance Alliance.

*October, 26.* Levitation of the Prentagon. Planned by the National Mobilization Committee to End the War in Vietnam—loose coalition of groups ranging from religious organizations to the leftist Students for a Democratic Society. David Dellinger took leading roll—edited a radical journal called *Liberation*. Why the Pentagon—the centre of the military industrial complex and the real source of power.

*October–November.* Dylan records songs for new Album at Columbia Music Row Studios in Nashville.

## 1968

*January.* Dylan's first public appearance after the motorcycle crash. Woody Guthrie Memorial Concert at Carnegie Hall where Dylan and the Band played 'I Ain't Got no Home', 'Dear Mrs Roosevelt', and 'Grand Coulee Dam'. They joined others in collectively singing 'This Land is Your Land' and 'This Train is Bound for Glory'. The songs appear on *A Tribute to Woody Guthrie* vols 1 and 2. 1972.

*January.* US release of *John Wesley Harding*. Released in UK February. Strips back the sound to bass, drums, rhythm and lead, with harmonica. Song structure change and the songs are more narrative based and firmly rooted in the American fold tradition.

*March, 18.* 17 year old Bobby Hutton killed in a police ambush of Eldridge Clever, the minister for information of the Black Panther Party for Self Defence. By now the folk Movement had become an irrelevance.

*April, 4.* Assassination of Martin Luther King in Memphis Tennessee.

*June, 6.* Assassination of Robert Kennedy in Los Angeles while campaigning for the Democratic Party nomination.

*June.* Death of Dylan's father occasioned a move towards Judaism. Learned Hebrew and visited Israel.

## 1969

*April.* Release of *Nashville Skyline*. Completely different in sound and tone from *John Wesley Harding*. Dylan thought the songs more indicative of his inner self than previous albums, there were less words and they were easier to remember. It is overtly country and western.

*August, 31.* Dylan and the Band played a set at the Isle of Wight Festival. He played for only one hour. His performance and the sound were so lack-lustre that he abandoned his plans to tour.

## 1970

Dylan becomes associated with Rabbi Meir Kahane's Jewish Defence League. Resented the fact that he was being claimed by Zionists and distanced himself.

*June.* Release of *Self Portrait*. Unusually large number of tracks not penned by Dylan. Includes four tracks from Dylan's Isle of Wight performance. Hugely disappointed fans. Greil Marcus exclaimed in his review in *Rolling Stone* 'what is this shit'.

*October.* Release of *New Morning*. The core of the album centres on three songs that Dylan wrote for Archibald MacLeish's *Scratch*, which were not used for that project.

Publication of *Culture and Commitment a Study of the Generation Gap* by Margaret Mead. The generation gap: was the subject of a great deal of discussion, and what made it a unique phenomenon was that it was world-wide. Margaret Mead saw this as evidence that the young had truly become part of a world community, a cosmopolitan culture. Mead argued that global communications and instantaneous transmission of pictures make the same images available to all of us.

## 1971

*August, 21.* Black Panther George Jackson, author of *Soledad Brother*, was murdered in San Quentin prison while awaiting trial for the alleged murder of a white prison guard.

*September.* Live performance at the Concert for Bangla Desh.

*November, 17.* US release of *More of Bob Dylan's Greatest Hits*. Released in UK, December.

*November.* Dylan records 'George Jackson'. A return to the protest genre.

## 1972

Dylan accepts the small part of Alias in Sam Peckinpah's *Pat Garrett and Billy the Kid*. Alias is a printer's apprentice who joins up with Billy the Kid.

Dylan writes his first sountrack for the film.

Filming begins in Durango, Mexico.

## 1973

Yom Kippur War. Broke out towards the end of Golda Meir's last term as Isreal's Premier. Egypt attacked the state of Israel on Yom Kippur, the holiest day in the Jewish Calendar.

*July, 13*. US release of *Pat Garrett and Billy the Kid*: *Original Soundtrack Recordings*. Dylan's first film soundtrack. Dylan plays the part of Alias in the film.

*November*. Release of an album of 'warm-up' songs that Dylan did not intend for release. Columbia released *Dylan* after he left the label. On returning Dylan insisted that it be deleted.

## 1974

*January*. Release of *Planet Waves*. Disappointing sales of only half a million.

*June*. Release of the live double album *Before the Flood* with songs taken from Bob Dylan and the Band's first tour since 1966.

## 1975

*January*. Release of *Blood on the Tracks*. Despite getting mixed reviews, the album has rightly become one of the most revered in Dylan's catalogue. It went to number one on the American album charts. Its songs have been interpreted as charting the struggles within Dylan's marriage, though Dylan himself rejects the crassness of projecting his personal life directly onto his records. The sadness and inwardness of the album echoes a more general disenchantment in the context of Watergate, the proceedings to impeach the President and Nixon's resignation in August 1974.

*July*. Release of *The Basement Tapes*, an album put together by Robbie Robertson and drawing on songs Dylan recorded with the Band in Woodstock during 1967, while he was recuperating from his motorcycle accident, a number of which, such as 'Tears of Rage' and 'This Wheel's On Fire' were well-known via cover versions.

*September*. Fall of Saigon.

*October*. Rolling Thunder Revue — a touring troupe of rock musicians flanked by Sam Shepard, Allen Ginsberg and orchestrated by Jacques Levy — opens in Plymouth, Massachusetts. It continues over the next two years.

*December, 8*. First leg of the Rolling Thunder tour culminates in a benefit concert in Madison Square Garden — The Night of the Hurricane — to raise money for the boxer Rubin 'Hurricane' Carter, whose imprisonment inspires the song, 'Hurricane' on Desire.

## 1976

*January*. Release of *Desire*. Like *Blood on the Tracks*, this reaches number one in the album charts and goes platinum. The album is largely co-written with Jacques Levy and contains a variety of narratives, including the denunciation of Rubin 'Hurricane' Carter's imprisonment. The song, 'Joey', narrating the story of the murder of the gangster Joey Gallo evokes controversy, due to its sympathetic treatment of Gallo.

*September*. Release of *Hard Rain*, a raucous, raw concert recording of the Rolling Thunder Revue, which features an explosive and raging version of 'Idiot Wind'.

*October*. Suicide of Phil Ochs, political activist and folksinging associate of Dylan in the 1960s.

## 1977

*January*. Ronald Reagan becomes President of the USA.

*August*. Death of Elvis Presley. 'Went to See the Gypsy' on *New Morning* has been seen as a song about Elvis Presley and his influence.

## 1978

*January*. Opening of Dylan's film of the Rolling Thunder Revue — *Renaldo and Clara*. A long, rambling film, with moments of interest and terrific concert footage. It is panned critically and fails at the box office.

*March.* Release of *Bob Dylan, Masterpieces* (released in Japan, Australia and New Zealand).

*March.* Sara Dylan files for divorce and it is granted quickly, though dispute over custody of the children dragged.

*April.* Release of *The Last Waltz* — a Martin Scorsese film and soundtrack of the Band's farewell concert of 1976, to which artists, such as Dylan, who had figured in the story of the Band were invited.

*June.* Release of *Street Legal*, an album of dense, lyrically intriguing songs with Dylan singing against a muddy big band sound and backing singers. Intimations of change and personal crisis can be detected in songs such as 'Changing of the Guards' 'No Time to Think' and 'Senor (Tales of Yankee Power)'.

## 1979

*January.* Dylan begins Bible classes, which he attends for three months, at the Vineyard fellowship as he converts to Christianity and releases Christian albums in the succeeding three years.

*May.* Release of *Bob Dylan at Budokan*. A reworking of many famous songs with radically new arrangements and a rich backing.

*August.* Release of *Slow Train Coming*. Dylan's first Christian album, which earns him a Grammy for best solo rock vocal, for his performance on 'Gotta Serve Somebody'.

*September.* Tours and for the next six months he plays his new Christian songs rather than dipping into his secular back catalogue.

*November.* U.S. Embassy in Iran is seized and hostages taken.

## 1980

*June.* Release of *Saved*. Less successful commercially than its predecessor, *Slow Train Coming*, but subsequent cover versions of its tracks testify to the strength of the songs.

*December.* Murder of John Lennon.

## 1981

*January.* Ronald Reagan begins second term as President.

*March.* Retirement of long-term CBS news anchorman, Walter Cronkite, namechecked in the song, 'Black Diamond Bay' on *Desire*.

*June.* Israeli planes bomb a nuclear plant in Iraq, which is referred to in the song 'Neighbourhood Bully' on *Infidels*.

*August.* Release of *Shot of Love*. A more varied collection of songs than on the previous religious albums and containing the spiritually evocative, 'Every Grain of Sand'.

## 1982

*June.* Falklands War.

## 1983

*November.* release of *Infidels*. A well-received album of strong songs, incorporating 'Union Sundown', which critiques modernity and globalization, but not including some of the subsequently most acclaimed songs of the recording sessions, notably 'Blind Willie McTell', eventually released on *Bob Dylan – the Bootleg Series Volumes 1–3 (Rare and Unreleased), 1961–1991*.

## 1984

*December.* Release of *Real Live*. A rocking reworking of famous songs, including a rewritten, 'Tangled Up in Blue'.

## 1985

*January.* George Bush is inaugurated as President.

*January.* *We Are the World* – a charity record organized by Bob Geldof in which Dylan participates.

*March.* Gorbachev becomes President of the USSR.

*June.* Release of *Empire Burlesque*. A mix of songs, personal, religious and political with elaborate backing save for the stark, 'Dark Eyes' and including 'Clean-Cut Kid', a narrative of the demise of a Vietnam veteran.

*July.* Dylan participates in the charity concerts, *Live Aid*. His performance at the climax of the American event in Philadelphia, flanked by Keith Richards and Ron Wood, is ragged and sparks controversy due to the comments he makes at the outset over the possibility of offering some of the money to debt-ridden American farmers.

*September. Farm Aid,* a concert for the benefit of struggling American farmers is staged in Champaign Illinois, at which Dylan performs with Tom Petty and the Heartbreakers (For analysis of Dylan at Live Aid and his inspiration of Farm Aid, see the chapter by Chris Brown).

*November.* Release of *Biograph.* A career review of Dylan, including some of his most celebrated songs and unreleased gems such as 'Percy's Song', 'Up to Me' and 'Abandoned Love'.

## 1986

*January.* Performs 'I Shall Be Released' at a tribute concert in memory of Martin Luther King.

*March.* Suicide of Richard Manuel, member of the Band.

*March.* Release of *A Vision Shared – A Tribute to Woody Guthrie and Leadbelly,* on which Dylan sings 'Pretty Boy Floyd'.

*June.* Marries his backing singer, Carolyn Dennis. The marriage was publicized by Howard Sounes in his biography, *Down the Highway.*

*August.* Release of *Knocked Out Loaded.* Widely criticized on its release but containing the long, intriguing narrative song, 'Brownsville Girl'.

*October.* Release of *Hearts of Fire* : a film and soundtrack. The film was panned critically and its director Richard Marquand dies shortly after its release.

## 1988

*January.* Birth of Dylan's daughter, Desiree Gabrielle Dennis-Dylan.

*January.* Inducted into the Rock and Roll Hall of Fame.

*February.* 'Hurricane' Carter is finally released from prison. *Hurricane,* a film of Carter's imprisonment and the struggle for his freedom, directed by Norman Jewison and starring Denzil Washington, with a glimpse of Dylan, is released in 1999.

*June*. Release of *Down in the Groove*. Widely criticized on its release. It incorporates a range of interesting cover songs, a few of Dylan's own, including the eerie 'Death is Not The End' and collaboratively written songs with Robert Hunter, the Grateful Dead lyricist.

*June*. Dylan performs in what has become known as The Never Ending Tour, as he has continued to tour extensively with an evolving group of backing musicians.

*December*. Death of Roy Orbison, whose voice is recalled vividly in *Chronicles: Volume 1* as being the kind that made you want to drive your car over a cliff. Orbison's voice contributes greatly to the charm of the first Travelling Wilburys album.

## 1989

*January*. George Bush begins second term as President.

*June*. Massacre of protestors in Tiananmen Square, China.

*June*. Release of *Dylan and the Dead*. A record of Dylan's collaboration with the Grateful Dead at various concerts over the preceding years. Dylan recognizes the collaboration to be instrumental to his recovery of self-belief in making music, but the chemistry between the Dead and Dylan on this album has generally been judged to be unconvincing.

*September*. Release of *Oh Mercy*. Produced by Daniel Lanois and discussed in Dylan's *Chronicles Volume One*, it contains fine songs covering a variety of spiritual and ethical concerns. 'Ring Them Bells' and 'What Good Am I?' raise questions of personal and spiritual responsibility while 'Everything is Broken' is an unblinking dismissal of the state of the world.

*October*. Release of *Travelling Wilburys Volume 1*. The super group of Dylan (Lucky Wilbury), George Harrison, Roy Orbison, Tom Petty and Jeff Lynne wins a Grammy award for the Best Rock Performance by a duo or group. Easy, uncomplicated rock, which yields a beguiling pastiche on Springsteen, 'Tweeter and the Monkey Man'.

## 1990

*January*. Death of Beatty Rutman, Dylan's mother.

*September*. Release of follow-up to vol. 1 of *Travelling Wiburys Volume 3*. Dylan is Boo Wilbury.

*October.* Unification of East and West Germany.

*November.* Release of *Under the Red Sky*. All star backing for a mixed bag of songs, some of which echo nursery rhymes. Dylan has hinted it suffered from his simultaneous work on the second Travelling Wilburys album.

### 1991

*February.* 1st Gulf War.

*February.* Grammy Lifetime Achievement Award. At the Ceremony Dylan gives an enigmatic acceptance speech and plays a blistering version of 'Masters of War'.

*March.* Release of *Bob Dylan – the Bootleg Series Volumes 1-3(Rare and Unreleased), 1961-1991*. Much admired collection of previously unreleased material spanning Dylan's career, and featuring some early songs, such as 'Who Killed Davey Moore?' and 'Talkin' John Brich Paranoid Blues?' that criticize aspects of 1960s American society.

### 1992

*October.* Divorces from Carolyn Dennis.

*October.* The 30th Anniversary Concert Celebration, held at Madison Square Garden, at which Dylan appeared along with a host of rock and folk artists, such as Neil Young, Eric Clapton and George Harrison, who had collaborated with and, or, admired Dylan.

*November.* Release of *Good As I Been to You*. A return to acoustic music and traditional songs, which Greil Marcus has identified as the precursor to Dylan's return to form in the 1990s.

### 1993

*January.* Bill Clinton becomes President of the USA.

*August.* Release of *Bob Dylan The 30th Anniversary Celebration*.

*October.* Release of *World Gone Wrong*, which wins a Grammy award for the Best Traditional Folk Album. A tough, uncompromising set of acoustic performances of songs to which Dylan testifies his commitment in sleeve notes, manifestly at odds with the contemporary world and yet prefiguring the subsequent vogue for roots music.

## 1994

*November.* Release of *Bob Dylan's Greatest Hits, Volume 3,* featuring a Grammy nominated unreleased track from the *Oh Mercy* sessions, 'Dignity'.

## 1995

*November.* Release of *MTV Unplugged,* interesting collection of acoustically performed Songs.

## 1997

*January.* Bill Clinton begins his second term as President.

*April.* Death of Allen Ginsberg, beat poet and associate of Dylan over the years, appearing in the cue card video in *Don't Look Back,* touring with Dylan on *The Rolling Thunder Revue* and making as yet unreleased recordings Dylan was hospitalized with a life-threatening heart infection.

*September.* Release of *Time Out of Mind,* which gains three Grammy Awards including Best Album and Best Rock Solo Vocal Performance. The Wallflowers, the group headed by Dylan's son, Jakob, also pick up 2 Grammy awards in 1998.

*September.* Performs before Pope John Paul II in Bologna, Italy.

*December.* Awarded Kennedy Center Honour by US President Bill Clinton.

## 1998

*October.* Release of *Bootleg Series Volume 4: The 'Royal Albert Hall' Concert.* (For analysis of this concert of 1966, see the chapter by Michael Jones).

## 2000

Release of *Things Have Changed* — it forms part of the soundtrack to the critically acclaimed *Wonder Boys.* The song wins a Gloden Globe and an Academy Award.

*November.* Release of *The Essential Bob Dylan,* a platinum album incorporating tracks from throughout Dylan's career.

## 2001

*January.* George. W. Bush Jnr. becomes President of the USA.

*July.* Release of *Live 1961–2000.* A limited edition record featuring live recordings spanning thirty nine years of concerts.

*September.* Terrorist attacks in the USA.

*September.* Release of *'Love and Theft'*, which wins A Grammy Award for The Best Contemporary Folk Album. A tough and well-received album that includes a variety of old-time music, jazz, crooning, swing, blues and folk.

*November.* Death of George Harrison, long-term associate of Dylan and fellow Traveling Wilbury.

## 2002

*November.* Release of *Bootleg Series Volume 5: Bob Dylan Live 1975 – The Rolling Thunder Revue.* A fine representative record of Rolling Thunder Revue, featuring Dylan solo and with Joan Baez.

## 2003

*March.* Invasion of Iraq by USA and allies.

*April.* Release of the film *Masked and Anonymous*, which is co-written and co-directed by Dylan and Larry Charles. It stars Dylan as Jack Fate and deals with the music business, politics and fame; its soundtrack consists of interesting and maverick cover versions of Dylan songs and fine live performances by Dylan. (For analysis of this film, see the chapter in this book by Elizabeth Brake).

*September.* Death of Johnny Cash, who had championed Dylan's cause when he had gone electric, and had duetted with Dylan on *Nashville Skyline.*

## 2004

*March.* Release of *Bootleg Series Volume 6: Bob Dylan Live 1964.* Belated release of the Halloween Concert at Philharmonic Hall, where Dylan is lively and talkative between songs.

*October. Chronicles: Volume One* is published. It earns universal plaudits for its literary worth and becomes a best seller.

Performs in a TV advertisement for Victoria's Secret lingerie.

## 2005

*January.* George W. Bush begins his second term as President.

*June.* Release of *Live at the Gaslight 1962*, a recording of early concerts at the Gaslight café in Greenwich Village, New York. Powerful performances, somewhat controversially released initially via Starbucks.

*August.* Hurricane Katrina causes widespread devastation, particularly in New Orleans, Louisiana. The US government is criticised for its uncertain response to the emergency. Dylan's 'The Levee's Gonna Break' on *Modern Times* is a reworking of an old blues song that echoes the disaster.

*September.* Martin Scorsese's critically acclaimed biographical film, *No Direction Home* is released. The soundtrack featuring unreleased material from the 1960s, including the haunting *Dink's Song* and alternative recordings and live versions of songs, where he is backed by his early electric sidemen, Mike Bloomfiled and Al Kooper.

## 2006

*May.* Dylan begins highly successful DJ career, hosting a weekly *Theme Time Radio Hour* for XM Satellite Radio.

*August.* Release of *Modern Times*. It entered the US charts at number one and won a Grammy for Best Contemporary Folk/Americana album and best solo rock vocal performance for 'Someday Baby'.

*August.* Release of *Bob Dylan: The Collection* by iTunes Music Store (773tracks).

## 2007

*August.* Release of Todd Haynes' award-winning film *I'm Not There*, a highly individual and experimental biographical study of the multiple persona of Dylan.

*August.* Release of the soundtrack for *I'm Not There*, including songs covered by a variety of contemporary and established artists including Ramblin' Jack Elliott, Richie Havens and Sonic Youth. Dylan and the Band's version of 'I'm Not There' is also featured on the album.

*October.* First showing of the film, *The Other Side of the Mirror: Bob Dylan at the Newport Folk Festival,* directed by Murray Lerner. It is a fascinating portrait of Dylan's development as an artist over the years 1963, 1964 and 1965.

*October.* Release of *Dylan*—a triple CD retrospective surveying Dylan's career.

*October.* Dylan stars in a multi-media campaign for the 2008 Cadillac Escalade.

*October.* Exhibition of Dylan's art— *The Drawn Blank Series,* opened in October 2007 in, Germany.

## 2008

*July.* In an interview with *The Times,* Dylan comments on how Barack Obama is redefining politics. In February 2008, Dylan's son Jesse had directed a video, *Yes, We Can* in support of Obama.

*August.* Dylan receives a Pulitzer Prize Special Citation.

*October.* Release of, *Tell Tale Signs: Rare And Unreleased 1989–2006.* Evidence of Dylan's artistry in performing radically differing out-takes of songs such as 'Most of the Time' and 'Dignity'.

# *Index*

# Healing, Hype or Harm? Scientists Investigate Complementary or Alternative Medicine

*Edzard Ernst (ed.)*

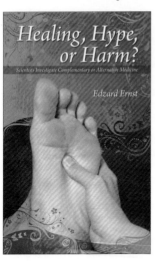

The scientists writing this book are not 'against' complementary or alternative medicine (CAM), but they are very much 'for' evidence-based medicine and single standards. They aim to counter-balance the many uncritical books on CAM and to stimulate intelligent, well-informed public debate.

TOPICS INCLUDE: What is CAM? Why is it so popular? Patient choice; Reclaiming compassion; Teaching CAM at university; Research on CAM; CAM in court; Ethics and CAM; Politics and CAM; Homeopathy in context; Concepts of holism in medicine;  Placebo, deceit and CAM; Healing but not curing; CAM and the media.

Edzard Ernst is Professor of Complementary Medicine, Universities of Exeter and Plymouth.

190 pp., £8.95/$17.90, 9781845401184 (pbk.), Sept. 2008, *Societas,* Vol.36

# The Balancing Act: National Identity and Sovereignty for Britain in Europe

*Atsuko Ichijo*

This is a careful examination of the historical formation of Britain and of key moments in its relations with the European powers. The author looks at the governing discourses of politicians, the mass media, and the British people.

The rhetoric of sovereignty among political elites and the population at large is found to conceive of Britain's engagement with Europe as a zero-sum game. A second theme is the power of geographical images – island Britain – in feeding the idea of the British nation as by nature separate and autonomous. It follows that the EU is seen as 'other' and involvement in European decision-making tends to be viewed in terms of threat. This is naive, as nation-states are not autonomous, economically, militarily or politically. Only pooling sovereignty can maximize their national interests.

Atsuko Ichijo is Senior Researcher in European Studies at Kingston University.

150 pp., £8.95/$17.90, 9781845401153 (pbk.), Nov. 2008, *Societas,* Vol.37

# The Enemies of Progress

*Austin Williams*

This polemical book examines the concept of sustainability and presents a critical exploration of its all-pervasive influence on society, arguing that sustainability, manifested in several guises, represents a pernicious and corrosive doctrine that has survived primarily because there seems to be no alternative to its canon: in effect, its bi-partisan appeal has depressed critical engagement and neutered politics.

It is a malign philosophy of misanthropy, low aspirations and restraint. This book argues for a destruction of the mantra of sustainability, removing its unthinking status as orthodoxy, and for the reinstatement of the notions of development, progress, experimentation and ambition in its place.

Al Gore insists that the 'debate is over'. Here the auhtor retorts that it is imperative to argue against the moralizing of politics.

Austin Williams tutors at the Royal College of Art and Bartlett School of Architecture.

96 pp., £8.95/$17.90, 9781845400989 (pbk.), May 2008, *Societas,* Vol.34

# Forgiveness: How Religion Endangers Morality

*R.A. Sharpe*

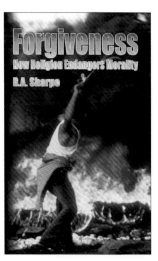

In his book *The Moral Case against Religious Belief* (1997), the author argued that some important virtues cease to be virtues at all when set in a religious context, and that, consequently, a religious life is, in many respects, not a good life to lead. In this sequel, his tone is less generous to believers than hitherto, because 'the intervening decade has brought home to us the terrible results of religious conviction'.

R.A. Sharpe was Professor Emeritus at St David's College, Lampeter. The manuscript of *Forgiveness* was prepared for publication by his widow, the philosopher Lynne Sharpe.

128 pp., £8.95 / $17.90, 9781845400835 (pbk.), July 2008, (*Societas* edition), Vol.35

# Who Holds the Moral High Ground?

### Colin J Beckley and Elspeth Waters

Meta-ethical attempts to define concepts such as 'goodness', 'right and wrong', 'ought' and 'ought not', have proved largely futile, even over-ambitious. Morality, it is argued, should therefore be directed primarily at the reduction of suffering, principally because the latter is more easily recognisable and accords with an objective view and requirements of the human condition. All traditional and contemporary perspectives are without suitable criteria for evaluating moral dilemmas and without such guidance we face the potent threat of sliding to a destructive moral nihilism. This book presents a possible set of defining characteristics for the foundation of moral evaluations, taking into consideration that the female gender may be better disposed to ethical leadership.

128 pp., £8.95/$17.90, 9781845401030 (pbk.), January 2008, *Societas,* Vol.32

# Froude Today

### John Coleman

A.L. Rowse called fellow-historian James Anthony Froude the 'last great Victorian àwaiting revival'. The question of power is the problem that perplexes every age: in his historical works Froude examined how it applied to the Tudor period, and defended Carlyle against the charge that he held the doctrine that 'Might is Right'.

Froude applied his analysis of power to the political classes of his own time and that is why his writings are just as relevant today. The historian and the prophet look into the inner meaning of events – and that is precisely what Froude did – and so are able to make judgments which apply to ages far beyond their own. The last chapters imagine what Froude would have said had he been here today.

96 pp., £8.95/$17.90, 9781845401047 (pbk.), March 2008, *Societas,* Vol.33

**Imprint Academic, PO Box 200, Exeter EX5 5HY, UK**
Tel: +44(0)1392 851550.    Email: sandra@imprint.co.uk

2008–2009

# SOCIETAS

essays in political and cultural criticism
imprint-academic.com/societas

# Progressive Secular Society and other essays relevant to secularism

*Tom Rubens*

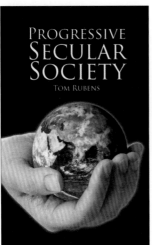

A progressive secular society is one committed to the widening of scientific knowledge and humane feeling. It regards humanity as part of physical nature and opposes any appeal to supernatural agencies or explanations. In particular, human moral perspectives are human creations and the only basis for ethics.

Secular values need re-affirming in the face of the resurgence of aggressive supernatural religious doctrines and practices. This book gives a set of 'secular thoughts for the day' – many only a page or two long – on topics as varied as Shakespeare and Comte, economics, science and social action.

Tom Rubens teaches in the humanities at secondary and tertiary levels.

128 pp., £8.95/$17.90, 9781845401320 (pbk.), May 2009, *Societas,* Vol.40

# Self and Society (enlarged second edition)

*William Irwin Thompson*

The book contains a series of essays on the evolution of culture, dealing with topics including the city and consciousness, evolution of the afterlife, literary and mathematical archetypes, machine consciousness and the implications of 9/11 and the invasion of Iraq for the development of planetary culture.

This enlarged edition contains an additional new second part, added to include chapters on 'Natural Drift and the Evolution of Culture' and 'The Transition from Nation-State to Noetic Polity' as well as two shorter reflective pieces.

The author is a poet, cultural historian and founder of the Lindisfarne Association. His many books include *Coming into Being: Artifacts and Texts in the Evolution of Consciousness.*

150 pp., £8.95/$17.90, 9781845401337 (pbk.), July 2009, *Societas,* Vol.41

# Seeking Meaning and Making Sense

*John Haldane*

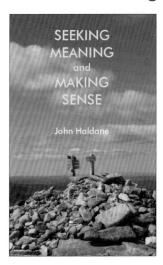

Here is an engaging collection of short essays that range across philosophy, politics, general culture, morality, science, religion and art.

The author contributes regularly to *The Scotsman* and a number of radio programmes. Many of these essays began life in this way, and retain their direct fresh style.

The focus is on questions of Meaning, Value and Understanding. Topics include: Making sense of religion, Making sense of society, Making sense of evil, Making sense of art and science, Making sense of nature.

John Haldane is Professor of Philosophy and Director of the Centre for Ethics, Philosophy and Public Affairs in the University of St Andrews.

128 pp., £8.95/$17.90, 9781845401221 (pbk.), Jan. 2009, *Societas,* Vol.38

# Independent: The Rise of the Non-aligned Politician

*Richard Berry*

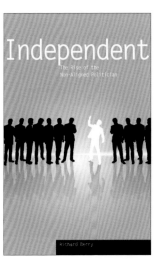

Martin Bell, Ken Livingstone and Richard Taylor (the doctor who became an MP to save his local hospital) are the best known of a growing band of British politicians making their mark outside the traditional party system.

Some (like Livingstone) have emerged from within the old political system that let them down, others (Bell, Taylor) have come into politics from outside in response to a crisis of some kind, often in defence of a perceived threat to their local town or district.

Richard Berry traces this development by case studies and interviews to test the theory that these are not isolated cases, but part of a permanent trend in British politics, a shift away from the party system in favour of independent non-aligned representatives of the people.

Richard Berry is a political and policy researcher and writer.

128 pp., £8.95/$17.90, 9781845401283 (pbk.), March 2009, *Societas,* Vol.39

# Universities: The Recovery of an Idea (revised second edition)
## *Gordon Graham*

RAE, teaching quality assessment, student course evaluation, modularization – these are all names of innovations in modern British universities. How far do they constitute a significant departure from traditional academic concerns? Using themes from J.H.Newman's *The Idea of a University* as a starting point, this book aims to address these questions.

'It is extraordinary how much Graham has managed to say (and so well) in a short book.' **Alasdair MacIntyre**

£8.95/$17.90, 9781845401276 (pbk), *Societas* V.1

# God in Us: A Case for Christian Humanism
## *Anthony Freeman*

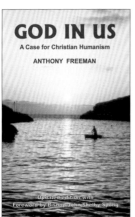

*God In Us* is a radical representation of the Christian faith for the 21st century. Following the example of the Old Testament prophets and the first-century Christians it overturns received ideas about God. God is not an invisible person 'out there' somewhere, but lives in the human heart and mind as 'the sum of all our values and ideals' guiding and inspiring our lives.

The Revd. Anthony Freeman was dismissed from his parish for publishing this book, but remains a priest in the Church of England.

'Brilliantly lucid.' *Philosophy Now*
'A brave and very well-written book' *The Freethinker*

£8.95/$17.90, 9780907845171 (pbk), *Societas* V.2

# The Case Against the Democratic State
## *Gordon Graham*

This essay contends that the gross imbalance of power in the modern state is in need of justification and that democracy simply masks this need with the illusion of popular sovereignty. The book points out the emptiness of slogans like 'power to the people', as individual votes do not affect the outcome of elections, but concludes that democracy can contribute to civic education.

'Challenges the reigning orthodoxy'. *Mises Review*

'Political philosophy in the best analytic tradition… scholarly, clear, and it does not require a professional philosopher to understand it' *Philosophy Now*

'An excellent candidate for inclusion on an undergraduate syllabus.' *Independent Review*

£8.95/$17.90, 9780907845386 (pbk), *Societas* V.3

# The Last Prime Minister
### *Graham Allen MP*

This book shows how Britain has acquired an executive presidency by stealth. It is the first ever attempt to codify the Prime Minister's powers, many hidden in the mysteries of the royal prerogative. This timely second edition takes in new issues, including Parliament's impotence over Iraq.

'Iconoclastic, stimulating and well-argued.' **Vernon Bogdanor**, *Times Higher Education Supplement*

'Well-informed and truly alarming.' **Peter Hennessy**

'Should be read by anybody interested in the constitution.' **Anthony King**

£8.95/$17.90, 9780907845416 (pbk), *Societas* V.4

# The Liberty Option
### *Tibor R. Machan*

*The Liberty Option* advances the idea that it is the society organised on classical liberal principles that serves justice best, leads to prosperity and encourages the greatest measure of individual virtue. The book contrasts this Lockean ideal with the various statist alternatives, defends it against its communitarian critics and lays out some of its more significant policy implications. The author teaches ethics at Chapman University. His books on classical liberal theory include *Classical Individualism* (Routledge, 1998).

£8.95/$17.90, 9780907845638 (pbk), *Societas* V.5

# Democracy, Fascism & the New World Order
### *Ivo Mosley*

Growing up as the grandson of Sir Oswald, the 1930s blackshirt leader, made Ivo Mosley consider fascism with a deep and acutely personal interest. Whereas conventional wisdom sets up democracy and fascism as opposites, to ancient political theorists democracy had an innate tendency to lead to extreme populist government, and provided unscrupulous demagogues with the ideal opportunity to seize power. In *Democracy, Fascism and the New World Order* Mosley argues that totalitarian regimes may well be the logical outcome of unfettered mass democracy.

'Brings a passionate reasoning to the analysis'. *Daily Mail*

'Read Mosley's, in many ways, excellent book. But read it critically.' **Edward Ingram**, *Philosophy Now*

£8.95/$17.90, 9780907845645 (pbk), *Societas* V.6

## Off With Their Wigs!
### Charles Banner and Alexander Deane

On June 12, 2003, a press release concerning a Cabinet reshuffle declared as a footnote that the ancient office of Lord Chancellor was to be abolished and that a new supreme court would replace the House of Lords as the highest appeal court. This book critically analyses the Government's proposals and looks at the various alternative models for appointing judges and for a new court of final appeal.

'A cogently argued critique.' *Commonwealth Lawyer*

£8.95/$17.90, 9780907845843 (pbk), *Societas* V.7

## The Modernisation Imperative
### Bruce Charlton & Peter Andras

Modernisation gets a bad press in the UK, and is blamed for increasing materialism, moral fragmentation, the dumbing-down of public life, declining educational standards, occupational insecurity and rampant managerialism. But modernisation is preferable to the likely alternative of lapsing back towards a 'medieval' world of static, hierarchical and coercive societies – the many and serious criticisms of modernisation should be seen as specific problems relating to a process that is broadly beneficial for most of the people, most of the time.

'A powerful and new analysis'. **Matt Ridley**

£8.95/$17.90, 9780907845522 (pbk), *Societas* V.8

## Self and Society, *William Irwin Thompson*

£8.95/$17.90, 9780907845829 (pbk), *Societas* V.9
now superceded by Vol.41 (see above, p.S6)

## The Party's Over
### Keith Sutherland

This book questions the role of the party in the post-ideological age and concludes that government ministers should be appointed by headhunters and held to account by a parliament selected by lot.

'Sutherland's model of citizen's juries ought to have much greater appeal to progressive Britain.' *Observer*

'An extremely valuable contribution.' *Tribune*

'A political essay in the best tradition – shrewd, erudite, polemical, partisan, mischievous and highly topical.' *Contemporary Political Theory*

£8.95/$17.90, 9780907845515 (pbk), *Societas* V.10

# Our Last Great Illusion
## Rob Weatherill

This book aims to refute, primarily through the prism of modern psychoanalysis and postmodern theory, the notion of a return to nature, to holism, or to a pre-Cartesian ideal of harmony and integration. Far from helping people, therapy culture's utopian solutions may be a cynical distraction, creating delusions of hope. Yet solutions proliferate in the free market; this is why therapy is our last great illusion. The author is a psychoanalytic psychotherapist and lecturer, Trinity College, Dublin.

'Challenging, but well worth the engagement.' *Network*

£8.95/$17.90, 9780907845959 (pbk), *Societas* V.11

# The Snake that Swallowed its Tail
## Mark Garnett

Liberal values are the hallmark of a civilised society, but depend on an optimistic view of the human condition, Stripped of this essential ingredient, liberalism has become a hollow abstraction. Tracing its effects through the media, politics and the public services, the book argues that hollowed-out liberalism has helped to produce our present discontent.

'This arresting account will be read with profit by anyone interested in the role of ideas in politics.'
**John Gray**, *New Statesman*

'A spirited polemic addressing the malaise of British politics.' **Michael Freeden**, *The European Legacy*

£8.95/$17.90, 9780907845881 (pbk), *Societas* V.12

# Why the Mind is Not a Computer
## Raymond Tallis

The equation 'Mind = Machine' is false. This pocket lexicon of 'neuromythology' shows why. Taking a series of keywords such as calculation, language, information and memory, Professor Tallis shows how their misuse has a misled a generation. First of all these words were used literally in the description of the human mind. Then computer scientists applied them metaphorically to the workings of machines. And finally the use of the terms was called as evidence of artificial intelligence in machines *and* the computational nature of thought.

'A splendid exception to the helpless specialisation of our age' **Mary Midgley**, *THES*

'A work of radical clarity.' *J. Consciousness Studies*

£8.95/$17.90, 9780907845942 (pbk), *Societas* V.13

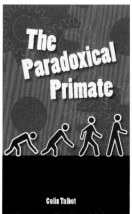

# The Paradoxical Primate
## Colin Talbot

This book seeks to explain how human beings can be so malleable, yet have an inherited set of instincts. When E.O. Wilson's *Consilience* made a plea for greater integration, it was assumed that the traffic would be from physical to human science. Talbot reverses this assumption and reviews some of the most innovative developments in evolutionary psychology, ethology and behavioural genetics.

> 'Talbot's ambition is admirable…a framework that can simultaneously encompass individualism and concern for collective wellbeing.' *Public* (The Guardian)

£8.95/$17.90, 9780907845850 (pbk), *Societas* V.14

# Tony Blair and the Ideal Type
## J.H. Grainger

The 'ideal type' is Max Weber's hypothetical leading democratic politician, whom the author finds realized in Tony Blair. He is a politician emerging from no obvious mould, treading no well-beaten path to high office, and having few affinities of tone, character or style with his predecessors. He is the Outsider or Intruder, not belonging to the 'given' of British politics and dedicated to its transformation. (The principles outlined are also applicable. across the parties, in the post-Blair period.) The author was reader in political science at the Australian National University and is the author of *Character and Style in English Politics* (CUP).

> 'A brilliant essay.' **Simon Jenkins**, *Sunday Times*
> 'A scintillating case of the higher rudeness.' *Guardian*

£8.95/$17.90, 9781845400248 (pbk), *Societas* V.15

# The Great Abdication
## Alex Deane

According to Deane, Britain's middle class has abstained from its responsibility to uphold societal values, resulting in the collapse of our society's norms and standards. The middle classes must reinstate themselves as arbiters of morality, be unafraid to judge their fellow men, and follow through with the condemnation that follows when individuals sin against common values.

> '[Deane] thinks there is still an element in the population which has traditional middle-class values. Well, maybe.' **George Wedd**, *Contemporary Review*

£8.95/$17.90, 9780907845973 (pbk), *Societas* V.16

Neil MacCormick

Who's Afraid of a
European
Constitution?

# Who's Afraid of a European Constitution?

*Neil MacCormick*

This book discusses how the EU Constitution was drafted, whether it promised any enhancement of democracy in the EU and whether it implied that the EU is becoming a superstate. The arguments are equally of interest regarding the EU Reform Treaty.

Sir Neil MacCormick is professor of public law at Edinburgh University. He was an MEP and a member of the Convention on the Future of Europe.

£8.95/$17.90, 9781845392 (pbk), *Societas* V.17

# Darwinian Conservatism

*Larry Arnhart*

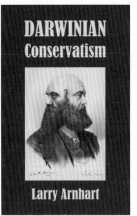

DARWINIAN
Conservatism

Larry Arnhart

The Left has traditionally assumed that human nature is so malleable, so perfectible, that it can be shaped in almost any direction. Conservatives object, arguing that social order arises not from rational planning but from the spontaneous order of instincts and habits. Darwinian biology sustains conservative social thought by showing how the human capacity for spontaneous order arises from social instincts and a moral sense shaped by natural selection. The author is professor of political science at Northern Illinois University.

'Strongly recommended.' *Salisbury Review*

'An excellent book.' **Anthony Flew**, *Right Now!*

'Conservative critics of Darwin ignore Arnhart at their own peril.' *Review of Politics*

96 pp.,  £8.95/$17.90, 9780907845997 (pbk.), *Societas,* Vol. 18

# Doing Less With Less: Making Britain More Secure

*Paul Robinson*

Doing Less with Less
Making Britain More Secure

Paul Robinson

Notwithstanding the rhetoric of the 'war on terror', the world is now a far safer place. However, armed forces designed for the Cold War encourage global interference through pre-emption and other forms of military interventionism. We would be safer with less. The author, an ex-army officer, is assistant director of the Centre for Security Studies at Hull University.

'Robinson's criticisms need to be answered.'
**Tim Garden**, *RUSI Journal*

'The arguments in this thesis should be acknowledged by the MOD.' **Major General Patrick Cordingley DSO**

£8.95/$17.90, 9781845400422 (pbk), *Societas* V.19

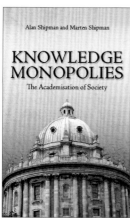
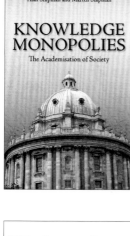

# Knowledge Monopolies
## *Alan Shipman & Marten Shipman*

Historians and sociologists chart the *consequences* of the expansion of knowledge; philosophers of science examine the *causes*. This book bridges the gap. The focus is on the paradox whereby, as the general public becomes better educated to live and work with knowledge, the 'academy' increases its intellectual distance, so that the nature of reality becomes more rather than less obscure.

'A deep and searching look at the successes and failures of higher education.' *Commonwealth Lawyer*

'A must read.' *Public* (The Guardian)

£8.95/$17.90, 9781845400286 (pbk), *Societas* V.20

# The Referendum Roundabout
## *Kieron O'Hara*

A lively and sharp critique of the role of the referendum in modern British politics. The 1975 vote on Europe is the lens to focus the subject, and the controversy over the referendum on the European constitution is also in the author's sights.

The author is a senior research fellow at the University of Southampton and author of *Plato and the Internet, Trust: From Socrates to Spin* and *After Blair: Conservatism Beyond Thatcher* (2005).

£8.95/$17.90, 9781845400408 (pbk), *Societas* V.21

# The Moral Mind
## *Henry Haslam*

The reality and validity of the moral sense took a battering in the last century. Materialist trends in philosophy, the decline in religious faith, and a loosening of traditional moral constraints added up to a shift in public attitudes, leaving many people aware of a questioning of moral claims and uneasy with a world that has no place for the morality. Haslam shows how important the moral sense is to the human personality and exposes the weakness in much current thinking that suggests otherwise.

'Marking a true advance in the discussion of evolutionary explanations of morality, this book is highly recommended for all collections.'
**David Gordon**, *Library Journal*

'An extremely sensible little book. It says things that are really rather obvious, but which have somehow got forgotten.' **Mary Midgley**

£8.95/$17.90, 9781845400163 (pbk), *Societas* V.22

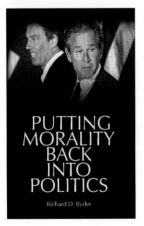

## Putting Morality Back Into Politics *Richard D. Ryder*

Ryder argues that the time has come for public policies to be seen to be based upon moral objectives. Politicians should be expected routinely to justify their policies with open moral argument. In Part I, Ryder sketches an overview of contemporary political philosophy as it relates to the moral basis for politics, and Part 2 suggests a way of putting morality back into politics, along with a clearer emphasis upon scientific evidence. Trained as a psychologist, the author has also been a political lobbyist, mostly in relation to animal welfare.

£8.95/$17.90, 9781845400477 (pbk), *Societas* V.23

## Village Democracy
### *John Papworth*

'A civilisation that genuinely reflects all that human beings long for and aspire to can only be created on the basis of each person's freely acknowledged power to decide on each of the many questions that affect his life.' In the forty years since he wrote those words in the first issue of his journal *Resurgence*, John Papworth has not wavered from that belief. This latest book passionately restates his argument for radical decentralisation.

'If we are to stand any chance of surviving we need to heed Papworth's call for decentralisation.'
**Zac Goldsmith**, *The Ecologist*

£8.95/$17.90, 9781845400644 (pbk), *Societas* V.24

## Debating Humanism
### *Dolan Cummings (ed.)*

Broadly speaking, the humanist tradition is one in which it is we as human beings who decide for ourselves what is best for us, and are responsible for shaping our own societies. For humanists, then, debate is all the more important, not least at a time when there is discussion about the unexpected return of religion as a political force. This collection of essays follows the Institute of Ideas' inaugural 2005 Battle of Ideas festival. Contributors include Josie Appleton, Simon Blackburn, Robert Brecher, Andrew Copson, Dylan Evans, Revd. Anthony Freeman, Frank Furedi, A.C. Grayling, Dennis Hayes, Elisabeth Lasch-Quinn, Kenan Malik and Daphne Patai.

£8.95/$17.90, 9781845400699 (pbk), *Societas* V.25

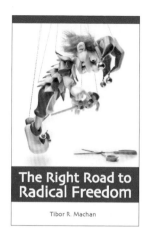

The Right Road to
Radical Freedom

Tibor R. Machan

# The Right Road to Radical Freedom *Tibor R. Machan*

This work focuses on the topic of free will – do we
as individual human beings choose our conduct, at
least partly independently, freely? He comes down
on the side of libertarians who answer Yes, and
scorns the compatibilism of philosophers like Daniel
Dennett, who try to rescue some kind of freedom
from a physically determined universe. From here
he moves on to apply his belief in radical freedom
to areas of life such as religion, politics, and
morality, tackling subjects as diverse as taxation,
private property, justice and the welfare state.

£8.95/$17.90, 9781845400187 (pbk), *Societas* V.26

# Paradoxes of Power: Reflections on the Thatcher Interlude

*Sir Alfred Sherman*

Paradoxes
of Power

Reflections on the
Thatcher Interlude

Alfred Sherman

In her memoirs Lady Thatcher herself pays tribute
to her former adviser's 'brilliance', the 'force and
clarity of his mind', his 'breadth of reading and his
skills as a ruthless polemicist'. She credits him with
a central role in her achievements. Born in 1919 in
London's East End, until 1948 Sherman was a
Communist and fought in the Spanish Civil War.
But he ended up a free-market crusader.

'These reflections by Thatcherism's inventor are
necessary reading.' **John Hoskyns**, *Salisbury Review*

£8.95/$17.90, 9781845400927 (pbk), *Societas* V.27

# Public Health & Globalisation

*Iain Brassington*

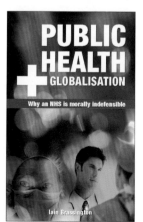

PUBLIC
HEALTH
GLOBALISATION

Why an NHS is morally indefensible

Iain Brassington

This book claims that the NHS is morally
indefensible. There is a good moral case in favour
of a *public* health service, but these arguments do
not point towards a *national* health service, but to
something that looks far more like a *transnational*
health service. Drawing on Peter Singer's famous
arguments in favour of a duty of rescue, the author
argues that the cost of the NHS is unjustifiable. If
we accept a duty to save lives when the required
sacrifice is small, then we ought also to accept
sacrifices in the NHS in favour of foreign aid. This
does not imply that the NHS is wrong; just that it is
wrong to spend large amounts on one person in
Britain when we could save more lives elsewhere.

£8.95/$17.90, 9781845400798 (pbk), *Societas* V.28

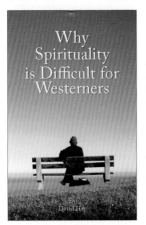

# Why Spirituality is Difficult for Westerners *David Hay*

Zoologist David Hay holds that religious or spiritual awareness is biologically natural to the human species and has been selected for in organic evolution because it has survival value. Although naturalistic, this hypothesis is not intended to be reductionist. Indeed, it implies that all people have a spiritual life. This book describes the historical and economic context of European secularism, and considers recent developments in neurophysiology of the brain as it relates to religious experience.

£8.95/$17.90, 9781845400484 (pbk), *Societas* V.29

# Earthy Realism: The Meaning of GAIA
## *Mary Midgley (ed.)*

GAIA, named after the ancient Greek mother-goddess, is the notion that the Earth and the life on it form an active, self-maintaining whole. It has a *scientific* side, as shown by the new university departments of earth science which bring biology and geology together to study the continuity of the cycle. It also has a visionary or *spiritual* aspect. What the contributors to this book believe is needed is to bring these two angles together. With global warming now an accepted fact, the lessons of GAIA have never been more relevant and urgent. Foreword by James Lovelock.

£8.95/$17.90, 9781845400804 (pbk), *Societas* V.30

# Joseph Conrad Today
## *Kieron O'Hara*

This book argues that the novelist Joseph Conrad's work speaks directly to us in a way that none of his contemporaries can. Conrad's scepticism, pessimism, emphasis on the importance and fragility of community, and the difficulties of escaping our history are important tools for understanding the political world in which we live. He is prepared to face a future where progress is not inevitable, where actions have unintended consequences, and where we cannot know the contexts in which we act. The result can hardly be called a political programme, but Conrad's work is clearly suggestive of a sceptical conservatism of the sort described by the author in his 2005 book *After Blair: Conservatism Beyond Thatcher*.

£8.95/$17.90, 9781845400668 (pbk.), *Societas* V.31